Enlisted Soldier's Guide
8th Edition

SGM Tom Gills, USA (Ret.)

T0346436

STACKPOLE BOOKS

Guilford, Connecticut

STACKPOLE BOOKS

Published by Stackpole Books
An imprint of Globe Pequot

Distributed by NATIONAL BOOK NETWORK

British Library Cataloguing in Publication Information Available

Library of Congress Cataloging-in-Publication Data

Names: Gills, Tom, 1962- editor.
Title: Enlisted soldier's guide / revised by SGM Tom Gills, USA (Ret.).
Description: 8th edition. | Guilford, Connecticut : Stackpole Books, [2017] | Includes bibliographical references and index.
Identifiers: LCCN 2016044653 (print) | LCCN 2016044929 (ebook) | ISBN 9780811736152 (pbk. : alk. paper) | ISBN 9780811765640 (ebook)
Subjects: LCSH: United States. Army—Handbooks, manuals, etc.
Classification: LCC U113 .R87 2017 (print) | LCC U113 (ebook) | DDC 355.00973—dc23

♾️™ The paper used in this publication meets the minimum requirements of American National Standard for Information Sciences—Permanence of Paper for Printed Library Materials, ANSI/NISO Z39.48-1992.

Contents

Preface

Hurdles, fences, mazes, and detours! Those were the things I perceived in front of me thirty-plus years ago when I joined the Army as a private. Until the first "true" NCO came into my life about three years in, I had no real purpose or direction despite my desire to climb, and no one to show me the ropes. The Army was a lot different back then, in many ways, but especially in the absence of dedicated mentorship and career advice. This is not an accusation about anyone. It was simply the culture back then, at least in my experience. There also was no computer, Internet, cell phone, texting, or social media (OMG!), and I actually helped install and run the first Army computer system overseas in a personnel center. Today, tons of career, regulatory, and policy information is found on the Internet. However, that too can be very confusing and daunting, because with so many sites, pages, and tabs out there, you sort of have to know what you are talking or thinking about in order to find and negotiate the mountains of information available.

So when I was given the opportunity to carry on the Herculean work of Dr. Robert Rush (CSM, Ret.) and those before him in writing this guide, I jumped on it. One of my favorite sayings is "Don't complain unless you're willing to suit up and jump in the game to help." This is my chance in the big game of giving back, and in trying to help with your career success. Because it has been roughly ten years since the last edition was written, an overhaul of the information was necessary, from tooth to tail. As the country changes in political and social norms, so do the policies and rules for a military that exists to serve the people, and the military has a history of driving social change as well. Likewise, more than a decade of war in several locations did much to change policy, culture, and procedure, as did the ending of the war in Iraq, the continued transition from Afghanistan and downsizing the Army, and some of the most uncertain international and terrorist dynamics ever seen, which continue to play out at this writing and which you will also read about in this guide. Importantly, policies will continue to change, and therefore this guide will not substitute for a detailed look at the current regulations or other doctrine. The good news, however, is that you will see what regulation or doctrine to look for in these pages, along with hundreds of updated websites and other sources.

The *Enlisted Soldier's Guide, 8th Edition* will provide you with a comprehensive reference tool, and while it is not a prescription written in detail for every situation, it will at a minimum serve as solid "directions to the drugstore" for the vast majority of topics. I begin with an explanation of the Army as an organization, with a bit of updated history, the structure, and enough detail so you can see how you and others fit into the larger scheme of things. Following this is information on the way the Army trains, service in the Army, and real-world issues you will be exposed to as a soldier. From there is where the fun starts and you begin seeing the details and advice helpful for self-development in areas like improved marksmanship. Physical fitness, considered the most important part of any soldier's day according to most leaders, myself included, is discussed in detail, along with the critical aspect of civilian education, which should be a mainstay of your path to success. Leadership competencies and career decisions (do I stay or do I go) round out this part of the guide and should provide a great overall understanding of the basics of life in Army uniform.

A quick-reference section follows and provides a litany of information, all written based on what I wish I had known as a new soldier right out of the gate, and what I also know senior NCOs would like to ensure you know today. Among those topics, you will encounter Army traditions, the assignment process for new locations, key rules and advice on promotions up the junior enlisted ranks, and the rules, requirements, and tips for joining the NCO ranks. Pay and entitlements, uniform policy, UCMJ and military justice, awards, and the all-important discussion of managing your own personal affairs cap the guide, with a handy place to write your chain of command and NCO support channel thrown in for good measure.

This edition is intended to take any perceptions of obstacles and turn them into pathways, gates, bypasses, and HOV lanes. Dr. Rush astutely noted in his preface to the seventh edition, that at some point "The Army became My Army . . ." I feel exactly the same way and would add that some may not believe in the motto "Soldier for Life," but I can assure you that even though I don't wear the uniform anymore, I still sometimes will go looking for my "headgear," much to my wife's amusement, and I use "Hooah!" at the end of virtually every e-mail sent. I love My Army, the soldiers in it, am a Soldier for Life and hope that those of you who read it, find this *Enlisted Soldier's Guide, 8th Edition* of value and help. My deepest thanks for your service and sacrifice!

SGM Thomas S. Gills,

MPA (USA, Ret.)

Acknowledgments

So many people (and a healthy pile of information gleaned from the Internet) are responsible for the publication of this book. While the specific websites and agencies credited below were critical in writing this edition, there were also more than three decades of family, mentors, superiors, peers, and, importantly, subordinates that heavily influenced the pages that follow. I had the humbling honor of working for or with the last four sergeants major of the Army (and the legendary CSM/SGM members of their board of directors), and many general officers, SES, DOD civilians and other superb senior officers and warrant officers. This list also includes senior command sergeants major, sergeants major, and senior NCOs around the Army. Each of them was inspirational and imparted vision, knowledge, and insights that helped shape who I became as a soldier and leader . . . and thus, in writing this edition. Several of them provided quotes found at the head of select chapters and deserve special thanks for their continued leadership. Likewise, some of my most important lessons in leadership and research came from bright, dedicated subordinates (the future of our Army). I am in lifelong debt to each for their example, wisdom, and counsel. As for the Internet sites I researched and for which I am grateful, they include: Department of Defense; Department of the Army; Department of Veterans Affairs; Defense Activity for Nontraditional Education Support; Army Family Advocacy Program; Army Community Services; TRICARE; Human Resources Command; Soldier for Life; Training and Doctrine Command; Forces Command; Installation Management Command; Army and Air Force Exchange Service; Association of the U.S. Army; Office of the Chief of Public Affairs; Defense Finance and Accounting Service; and Department of Education.

The following organizations also contributed: Office of the Sergeant Major of the Army, *Soldiers* magazine, *NCO Journal*, Army Continuing Education Services, Judge Advocate General's Corps, and the Center of Military History.

While I could never name all those who heavily influenced me, I am particularly thankful for the love, wisdom, and great times with my parents and two brothers growing up, the mentorship and occasional kicks in the pants from my first "True NCO," MSG Fred Hunter (USA, Ret.—the leader who told me I could quit or "become an NCO and try and make a difference"), the boundless positive energy and continued mentorship of SMA Jack Tilley and CSM Dan Elder (both USA, Ret.) for their sage advice in writing this guide. My other teammates, CSM Ruben Espinoza, SGM Johnny Myers, CSM Joe Allen, CSM Kevin Nolan (2009 Army Family of the Year), and CSM Torrey Vap (all USA, Ret.) each have contributed immeasurably, though they likely don't know it. I would be remiss if I did not sincerely thank SMA Kenneth Preston (USA, Ret.) for his wise mentorship, along with LTG Thomas Bostick for the many lessons he taught me (and for literally "changing my stars") as we served in the Army G-1. SMA Roshan Safi of the Afghanistan Army, a national treasure and friend for life, SMA Raymond Chandler (who challenged me to grow as a leader), LTG Robert (Bob) Durbin (my awesome battle buddy and leader downrange in OEF), MG (now the Honorable) Gina Farrisee (who showed me how to survive the Pentagon and so much more in leadership), Mr. Mark Davis and Ms. Cynthia Fisher, MG Dorian Anderson, MG Reuben Jones, MG Sean Byrn, MG Thomas Seamands, MG Richard (Rick) Mustion, and BG Earl Simms (who took me under his wing even though I didn't know it) and Eric (Rick) Porter; COLs Phil McNair, Phil Smith, Nick Monje, Ward Nikkish, Todd Garlick, Angela Odom (my Arctic warrior buddy and leader on staff), Patrick Rice, Lou Hinkel, Pat Gawkins, Steven Shappel, Joe Adams, Robert Manning, Jack Usrey, and Neal McIntyre. LTC Mike Palaza (my indefatigable battle buddy and leader when 1SG in Alaska, who presided over my daughter's wedding many years later) and LTC Scott Ehrmantraut, CSM John Gathers (who sadly passed all too soon after his retirement), CSMs Brunk Conley (my other battle buddy and mentor downrange), Carlos Pagan, David Nethkin, Bill Hoffer, Bruce Lee, Billy Blackmon, Wanda Blackmon, Darlene Hagood, Chris Culbertson, Todd Shirley, Wardell Jefferson, Melissa Judkins, JoAnne Cox, Keith Miller, and Jake (The Snake) Elliott (who showed along with his wife Deb, through deeds not words, what real leadership and family means). SGM Larry Strickland (killed in the 9-11 attack on the Pentagon) and his wife CSM Deborah Strickland, SGMs Mike Croom (who taught me way more than I realized at the time), Gabriel (Gabbie) Russum, John Heinrichs (who taught me to think strategically), Gerald (Jerry) Purcell (the most influential person in my life as a SGM as exemplar), Bill Palya, Chris Lyons, Mildred Lonergan, Derek Johnson, Frankie Leyro, Jose Velazquez, Caprecia Miller, John McNierny and his wife, CSM Violet McNierny. CW5 Jerry Dillard and his wife LTC Cynthia Dillard (both of S-1Net Fame), CPT Steven Barnard, CW3 Tonia McCreary (who was directly responsible for my success at Office of SMA), MSG Ria Wright (responsible for my success running HRC Promotions Branch), MSG Tamara Sorrell, MSG Pearl Houck (all USA, Ret.), and a legion of other amazing leaders, also made a significant impact on me and my writing here. SMA Dan Dailey, leading the Army from the front at this writing, was and is also a tremendous influence on what "Right Looks Like," for me and I could not be prouder or feel richer to have been in the acquaintance of superb professionals like him and the others listed above. My deepest apologies for all those I omitted, but the editors said the acknowledgments had to be shorter than any one chapter.

Of course, this project would have failed from the start were it not for professionals like Dave Reisch and Caroline McManus at Stackpole Books and all the folks there I never met but who put so much time and effort to ensuring this is the most accurate, up-to-date, effective guide it can be.

As most military families will attest, my two children, Nina and Michael, endured much, including being the "new kid" at seven schools in six years due to our frequent PCS moves, walking to school at 50 below zero in Fairbanks, Alaska, many important events and several years without Dad due to Army missions, and yet they remained stalwart supporters of all my crazy projects and missions. I love them and simply couldn't be prouder! Finally, my wife, Laurie Beth, has been my compass and guide for the last thirty-two years, and her leadership and nurturing of me and our family as well as her patience and love are squarely behind each and every success we enjoy. Nothing I do would be worthwhile without her as my life partner and my very best friend!

Code of Conduct

For Members of the Armed Forces of the United States

Serving our country as a member of the armed forces is the noblest public service a citizen of the United States can perform. Since 1955, American soldiers have memorized this Code, which defines the essence of military service and the high standards required of men and women in the military service.

I.

I am an American, fighting in the forces which guard my country and our way of life. I am prepared to give my life in their defense.

II.

I will never surrender of my own free will. If in command, I will never surrender my men while they still have the means to resist.

III.

If I am captured, I will continue to resist by all means available. I will make every effort to escape and aid others to escape. I will accept neither parole nor special favors from the enemy.

IV.

If I become a prisoner of war, I will keep faith with my fellow prisoners. I will give no information or take part in any action which might be harmful to my comrades. If I am senior, I will take command. If not, I will obey the lawful orders of those appointed over me and will back them up in every way.

V.

When questioned, should I become a prisoner of war, I am required to give name, rank, service number, and date of birth. I will evade answering further questions to the utmost of my ability. I will make no oral or written statements disloyal to my country and its allies or harmful to their cause.

VI.

I will never forget that I am an American, fighting for freedom, responsible for my actions, and dedicated to the principles which made my country free. I will trust in my God and in the United States of America.

PART I

The Army

1

The Army Today

It is a critical time in our Army now. We live in a world of uncertainty. We have to maintain readiness. Our ultimate goal is to not fight. . . . Our adversaries need to see we are an Army of preparation, and that we are trained and ready to fight in response to our nation's call. That call can happen anywhere, for any type of operation—whether it's another war, or a contingency operation in one of our partnering nations to help them. This time is just as critical as the last 12 years of war.

—SMA Daniel A. Dailey, 15th Sergeant Major of the Army

Serving in today's Army is one of the greatest forms of public service an American citizen can perform. Today's Army has 520,000 Regular Army soldiers on active duty, another 354,200 in the National Guard, and still another 205,000 in the Army Reserve. In all, about a million soldiers wear the Army uniform either full-time or part-time. The Army is reducing those numbers with the end of combat operations in Iraq and the withdrawal from Afghanistan. However, there will always be a need for a highly capable Army to answer the nation's call, and the enlisted soldier is the centerpiece of that ability. Soldiers make the Army "Go!"

Since the Spanish-American War at the end of the nineteenth century, over 41 million Americans have served in the armed forces at home and abroad. There are nearly 22 million veterans alive today. Throughout our history, twenty-six of our forty-four presidents have had military service, and of that number, seventeen served in the Army, ten of whom were generals. Within the last fifty years, only two presidents did not serve in the military.

To be a soldier is to be a member of a highly respected profession. Public opinion polls have repeatedly shown that the armed forces have the highest trust and confidence of the American people. The country knows military service is tough duty, with high risk and many hardships, and that our soldiers are dedicated to getting the job done—a job that amounts to nothing less than being the defenders of our nation's highest and most important interests.[1]

---

1   U.S. Department of Veteran Affairs (7 Nov. 2014). National Center for Veterans Analysis and Statistics. Retrieved from: www.va.gov/vetdata/Veteran_Population.asp.

ARMY HISTORY

The Army's stellar reputation is due to the professionalism of the soldiers who served in it from the days of its creation over 240 years ago. If you are in uniform, you too are a part of this long-standing and proud history. The American Army was created on 14 June 1775, when the Continental Congress first authorized the muster of troops to serve under its authority. Those soldiers came from the provincial forces of the colonies, which were at that time laying siege to Boston. From its birth, the American Army has relied on the citizen-soldier, exemplified by the militia and the Minutemen who fought the British at Lexington and Concord. Commanded by General George Washington and supported by our French allies, the Continental Army defeated the British at Yorktown and secured the freedoms so eloquently stated in the Declaration of Independence. Thus, the birth of the Army preceded and guaranteed the birth of the nation.

The Army's fundamental purpose is to fight and win the nation's wars by establishing conditions for lasting peace through land force dominance. This dominance is established through integration of the complementary capabilities of all the services. With this fundamental purpose in mind, the framers of the Constitution intended that armies be raised to "provide for the common defense!" and, together with the Navy, to "repel invasion." The Army raised for the nation's defense incorporates two uniquely American ideas: civilian control of the armed forces and reliance on the citizen-soldier. Over the years, the organization and structure of the Army have adapted to each challenge the nation has faced, but these basic ideas have remained unchanged. Throughout the formative years of the nation, the Army responded—on the frontiers, in the War of 1812, in the war with Mexico—in fulfillment of this role. During the Civil War, the Army was called upon to support another clause of the Constitution, to "suppress insurrection." As the nation became a colonial power following the Spanish-American War, the Army was called upon to secure and administer the new territories.

When the United States became a world power in the twentieth century, the Army was called upon to defend our national interests and rights on a wider scale, which drew us into alliances in regions far removed from our shores. In the combat operations of the World Wars, in Korea, Vietnam, Panama, the Persian Gulf, and Iraq and Afghanistan, the Army has responded to the call to duty and performed that duty extremely well. In the sixty years of Cold War, in many locations around the world, the Army performed a deterrent role as part of the containment strategy. In other places, at other times, the Army fulfilled the nation's expectations in operations too small to be called "wars," although no less dangerous. The Army's deployment is the surest sign of America's commitment to accomplishing any mission that occurs on land. To the soldiers on the ground, operations in Grenada (1983), Panama (1989), Kuwait and Iraq (1991), Afghanistan (2002), and Iraq (2003) are indistinguishable from the combat operations of their forefathers. Operations like those in Somalia, Haiti, Bosnia, and Kosovo, although peace operations, also proved to be dangerous. Like those who went before them, however, American soldiers responded readily in fulfilling the unlimited-liability aspect of their contract. Knowing that simply joining the Army demands a willingness to place one's life at risk, many have joined and made the ultimate sacrifice.

The Army on parade—yesterday and today.

Today, we are a nation coming off a war footing, but with soldiers still serving in far-flung corners of the globe and plenty of international uncertainty. The global al Qaeda terrorist network remains an immediate and serious threat to the United States, and the emergence of ISIL in Syria and other parts of the world in 2014 give even more proof of the continuous need for our Army to remain at the highest levels of professionalism and readiness. Since 1998, when Osama bin Laden declared all U.S. citizens legitimate targets of attack, the nature and spectrum of Army requirements have expanded. Terrorists are capable of planning multiple attacks with little or no warning. Multiple examples include the bombing of our embassies in Africa in 1998, the Millennium plots in 1999, the World Trade Center and Pentagon attacks in 2001, the Fort Hood attack in 2009, the bomb attack during the Boston Marathon in 2013, and the attacks in 2015 on Paris, France, the recruiting center in Chattanooga, Tennessee, and the social services center in San Bernardino, California.

Although terrorism is our most important challenge today, there continue to be states that are threats to the United States. The 2003 war in Iraq showed clearly that America's Army—all its armed forces—were well trained and well led. This highly skilled, agile, and flexible force, in relatively small numbers, was able to defeat a well-armed enemy in a country the size of France in a mere thirty days of combat.

There also remains uncertainty about the future of Russia and China—two major powers undergoing great change—plus other issues, such as the ongoing threat on the Korean peninsula; the question of lasting peace or continuing conflict in the Middle East; genocidal, ethnic, religious, and tribal conflict in Africa; the global impact of the proliferation of military technology; and an array of political leadership challenges in many already unstable countries.

THE ARMY MISSION

Protecting the nation's highest and most important interests is the Army's and the other services' mission. The Army's national mission is well stated in Title 10 of the Code of Laws of the United States. When it passed this law, Congress intended to provide an Army that, in conjunction with the other armed forces, would:

- Preserve the peace and security, and provide for the defense of the United States, its territories, its commonwealths and possessions, and any areas occupied by the United States.
- Support U.S. national policies.
- Implement U.S. national objectives.
- Overcome (i.e., win a war against) any nations responsible for aggressive acts that endanger the peace and security of the United States.

Today, the Army mission boils down to three major tasks:

- *Deterrence:* to be so competent and powerful that no enemy will risk attacking us, and if he does, to fight and win any resulting engagement, conflict, or war.
- *Power projection*: to be able to move combat forces anywhere in the world and support them on a sustained basis until victory is achieved or peace restored.
- *Military operations other than war (MOOTW):* to support those national and international peacekeeping, humanitarian assistance, disaster assistance, counterinsurgency, counterdrug, counterterrorist, and other related operations that the government determines are in the U.S. national interest.

This is serious business. National security, national defense, and the willingness and ability to fight for those vital interests are what the Army is all about. For the Army to accomplish these tasks, however, it needs the right strategies, tactics, techniques, and procedures; the right organizations; the right equipment; and, above all, highly trained soldiers. The Army's command structure and its organization exist to see that we have an efficient and effective Army and that it is well led and well trained.

COMMAND OF THE ARMY

Because the Army operates in response to America's most important interests, the U.S. Constitution designates the president as commander in chief. He is assisted by the secretary of defense and the chairman of the Joint Chiefs of Staff, who are in the chain of command for all military operations.

The Army chief of staff is a member of the Joint Chiefs of Staff. He and the secretary of the Army direct the Army to ensure that it is capable of performing the mission and tasks described above. They are the Army's principal advocates in the annual competition for national resources when the Army budget is negotiated within the government. They ensure that the Army is properly organized and equipped, and they make the regulations that govern all aspects of the Army from soldier recruitment through separation or retirement.

ARMY ORGANIZATION

Active Army
For combat, the active Army includes six army-level headquarters as part of all-service unified commands; three three-star corps level headquarters, ten two-star active-duty division level headquarters, and one integrated division level headquarters.

A variety of other commands, brigades, and groups provide engineer, chemical, civil affairs, intelligence, communications, medical, transportation, supply, maintenance, military police, and other support services essential to the conduct of combat operations.

Major Army Commands
In addition to the tactical organizations, there is a supporting structure of units that perform a wide range of Army activities, such as command and control, logistics, training, military education, recruiting, research and development, procurement, and engineering and base support activities.

Army National Guard
The Army National Guard has some of the oldest units in the country, whose lineage extends to the years before the United States became independent. The Guard today provides a great amount of potent combat and combat support power to the Army. It contains eight divisions and twenty-eight brigade combat teams. Eighty percent of the Army's field artillery is in the National Guard. The National Guard can be called to duty by the governor of a state for a state mission. It can also be called to active federal duty by the president to support a military operation that is beyond the capability of the active Army.

Army Reserve
The Army Reserve was first formed in 1908. It includes both units and individuals who join units when mobilized. The Army Reserve forces are essential to the accomplishment of the Army's mission. These forces provide the bulk of the Army's backup combat support and combat service support, without which many operations could not be carried out. For instance, the Army Reserve contains 100 percent of the Army's railway units, military police enemy prisoner of war brigades, and chemical brigades; 97 percent of all civil affairs units; 85 percent of the psychological operations units; 80 percent of the transportation groups; and 69 percent of the petroleum supply battalions.

Most soldiers will not complete an enlistment without working with units or individuals in the Army Reserve.

The Army in Transition
Transformation is a continual process that shapes the changing nature of military competition and cooperation through new combinations of concepts, capabilities, people, and organizations. It employs the nation's advantages and protects against asymmetric vulnerabilities. It sustains the U.S. strategic position, thus helping maintain peace and stability in the world.

Tactical Organization of the Army

The Army transformed from a division-based to a brigade-based force over the last decade, and that transformation process continues. These brigades are designed as self-sufficient and standardized brigade combat teams (BCTs), which can be more readily deployed and combined with other Army and joint forces to meet the precise needs of the combatant commanders. The number of standing brigades will fluctuate based on mission, potential threats, and budget and is currently projected to total thirty-three by the end of 2017. This modular force structure is also designed to allow active component soldiers to spend at least two years at home following each deployed year, at least four years at home following each deployed year for the Army Reserve soldiers, and five years at home following each deployed year for National Guardsmen.

Armies. Field Armies, most of which are numbered, are the Army component of a Joint Major Command and are referred to geographically. Army headquarters are capable of assuming the duties of a Joint Task Force (JTF) or a Joint Force Land Component Command (JFLCC)—with augmentation from other services—and controlling operations. Soldiers assigned to one of these commands typically wear the patch of a traditional numbered army and perpetuate its lineage and honors. Third U.S. Army/U.S. Army Central provides the Army component of Central Command; the Fifth U.S. Army, U.S. Army North, represents the Army in Northern Command; and the Sixth U.S. Army is the Army component of Southern Command. The Army component within the U.S. European Command is the Seventh Army; the U.S. Eighth Army is headquartered in Korea, and the Ninth Army is aligned with the U.S. Africa Command (AFRICOM).

Corps and Divisions. These units consist of a headquarters of about 801,000 soldiers, respectively, who are capable of functioning as a Joint Task Force and a Joint Force Land Component Command. The three-star corps perpetuates the lineages and honors of a historical corps. The two-star divisions perpetuate the lineages and honors of a historical division. There are ten active division headquarters and one integrated active-reserve division headquarters; all but one are located in the continental United States.

Brigades

The modular brigade combat team (BCT) is a stand-alone, self-sufficient, and standardized tactical force of between 3,500 and 4,000 soldiers. The total number of these units is adjusted based on the total number of brigades authorized and the current threats perceived. As a result, these units are more capable of independent action than division-based organizations, with strategic responsiveness greatly improved as well.

There are three common organizational designs for ground BCTs and five designs for support brigades. The three designs include a heavy brigade with two armor-mechanized infantry battalions and an armed reconnaissance battalion; an infantry brigade with two infantry battalions and an armed reconnaissance and surveillance battalion; and a Stryker (eight-wheel-drive armored combat vehicle) brigade with three Stryker battalions and a reconnaissance and surveillance battalion. Four of the five types of support brigades perform a single function each: aviation, fires, sustain, and battlefield surveillance. The fifth, maneuver enhancement brigade, is organized around a versatile core of supporting units that provide engineer, military police, air defense, chemical, and signal capabilities. Modularity increases each unit's capability by building in the communications, liaison, and logistics capabilities needed to permit greater operational autonomy and support the ability to conduct joint, multinational operations—capabilities that previously were at much higher organizational echelons.

Below are the active division headquarters and brigade combat teams perpetuating the honors and lineages associated with that division:

ACTIVE DIVISION AND BRIGADE COMBAT TEAM LOCATIONS[2]

Fort Benning, GA.	1 Brigade Combat Team affiliated with the lineage of the 3rd Infantry Division.
Fort Bliss, TX	1st Armored Division headquarters: 5 Brigade Combat Teams. 1 Combat Aviation Brigade.
Fort Bragg, NC	82nd Airborne Division headquarters: 4 (Airborne) Brigade Combat Teams. 1 Combat Aviation Brigade.
Fort Campbell, KY	101st Airborne Division headquarters: 4 Brigade Combat Teams. 1 Combat Aviation Brigade. 159th Combat Aviation Brigade.
Fort Carson, CO	4th Infantry Division headquarters: 5 Brigade Combat Teams. 1 Combat Aviation Brigade.
Fort Drum, NY	10th Mountain Division headquarters: 3 Brigade Combat Teams. 1 Combat Aviation Brigade.
Fort Hood, TX	1st Cavalry Division headquarters: 4 Brigade Combat Teams.
Fort Hood, TX	3rd Armored Cavalry Regiment: 1 Brigade Combat Team.
Joint Base Lewis-McChord, WA	7th Infantry Division (Integrated): Division headquarters. 3 Brigade Combat Teams affiliated with the lineage of 2nd Infantry Division.
Fort Polk, LA	1 Brigade Combat Team affiliated with the lineage of the 10th Mountain Division.
Joint Base Elmendorf-Richardson, AK	1 (Airborne) Brigade Combat Team affiliated with the lineage of the 25th Infantry Division.

---

2   Army Strong, Army Europe (2015). The Official Homepage of US Army Europe. Retrieved from: www.eur.army.mil/organization/units.htm

Fort Riley, KS	1st Infantry Division headquarters: 4 Brigade Combat Teams. 1 Combat Aviation Brigade.
Fort Wainwright, AK	1 Brigade Combat Team affiliated with the lineage of the 25th Infantry Division.
Fort Stewart, GA	3rd Infantry Division headquarters: 3 Brigade Combat Teams. 1 Combat Aviation Brigade. (Hunter Army Airfield, Ga.)
Schofield Barracks, HI	25th Infantry Division headquarters: 2 Brigade Combat Teams. 1 Combat Aviation Brigade.
Fort Irwin, CA	11th Armored Cavalry Regiment
Korea	1 Brigade Combat Team affiliated with the lineage of the 2nd Infantry Division. 1 Combat Aviation Brigade.
Germany	2nd Armored Cavalry Regiment
Italy	173rd Airborne Brigade: 1 Brigade Combat Team.

Army National Guard Divisions

Until they are federalized by order of the president, Army National Guard divisions are under the authority of their respective state governors and are available for missions within their states. State missions include disaster assistance, protection of key assets or facilities during periods of civil unrest, and similar tasks. In the past decade, units from the reserve components have been deployed overseas to support national missions at a tempo much higher than before. A by-product of those twelve years of war is a National Guard and reserve component that is highly trained and experienced in all aspects of Army missions.

National Guard divisions have the same combat function as active Army divisions when called to federal duty in time of crisis or war. These divisions are:

28th Infantry Division, Harrisburg, Pennsylvania
29th Infantry Division, Fort Belvoir, Virginia
34th Infantry Division, St. Paul, Minnesota
35th Infantry Division, Fort Leavenworth, Kansas
38th Infantry Division, Indianapolis, Indiana
40th Infantry Division, Los Alamitos, California
42nd Infantry Division, Troy, New York
49th Armored Division, Austin, Texas

Nondivisional Organizations

Soldiers assigned to combat service support and combat support organizations can serve in divisional or "nondivisional" units. Nondivisional units are also tactical formations, but their organization varies, depending on type. The most common types of nondivisional units are commands, brigades, and groups; these formations usually command battalions, which are in turn composed of companies. Nearly all soldiers are assigned to a company of one type or another. For instance, there are engineer, air defense artillery, and signal brigades; transportation commands and groups; signal commands and signal brigades; and military intelligence and Special Forces groups.

BRANCHES OF THE ARMY

The Army has twenty-two active-duty branches organized into three major categories: Maneuver, Fires and Effects (MFE), Operational Support (OS) and Force Sustainment (FS).[3]

Maneuver, Fires, and Effects

Infantry. Infantry is the oldest of the combat arms. Its mission is "to close with the enemy by fire and maneuver to destroy or capture him, and to repel his assault by fire, close combat, and counterattack." Today's infantryman can move by land, sea, or air. The modern infantryman may fight on foot or go into action by parachute, helicopter, assault boat, or Bradley fighting vehicle. The infantry can operate at night, under any climatic conditions, and it can overcome natural and man-made obstacles that would stop other forces.

Light infantry units are rapidly deployable and are especially useful in missions conducted in complex and urban terrain due to their streamlined nature and lack of dependence on masses of heavy equipment for transportation. Air assault infantry units are more heavily equipped, and although fully capable of dismounted operations, typically incorporate the large numbers of helicopters available in the air assault division's aviation groups. Airborne infantry units are uniquely qualified and equipped for arrival in combat by parachute, but are fully capable of dismounted or air assault operations as well. Mechanized infantry are the most heavily armed and protected infantry, riding into battle in Bradley infantry fighting vehicles (IFVs), which are armed with 25mm automatic cannons, antitank missiles, and machine guns. The new interim brigade is equipped with the wheeled Stryker series vehicle, which provides mobility and protection to the infantrymen riding within.

Ranger infantry are trained to go into battle by parachute, special operations helicopter, small boat, or dismounted. Although trained as infantry, ranger infantry units are increasingly being used as special operations forces.

Armor. Armor branch includes both armor and armored cavalry and is the modern successor to the horse cavalry. Armor operates in a combined arms team with infantry, artillery, and the other combat and combat support branches. Armor tactics emphasize mobility, firepower, and shock action to overcome and destroy enemy forces in rapid actions. Armored cavalry units exist in Army division and at corps level to conduct the reconnaissance and other security missions. The M1 series tank is armor's principal weapon system; it is a world-class tank. Like the Bradley IFV, the Bradley cavalry

---

3   US Army Basic. (2015). Your online US Army basic training information guide. Retrieved from: http://usarmybasic.com/army-jobs/army-branches-mos#.VScJVOG2png

fighting vehicle in the armored cavalry units furnishes great speed and mobility, as well as maximum firepower and armored protection for use on the forward edge of the battle area.

Field Artillery. A historic branch of the Army, the field artillery mission is more challenging than ever before—to destroy, neutralize, or suppress the enemy by cannons, rockets, and missile fire and to integrate all supporting fires into the combined arms operation. Howitzers, rockets, and missiles are the muscle of the field artillery. Currently, towed field artillery systems include the M102 and M119A1 105mm howitzers and the M198 155mm howitzer. Self-propelled artillery systems include the M109-series 155mm howitzer and the Multiple Launched Rocket System (MLRS). The artillery's current ground-to-ground missile system is the Army Tactical Missile System (ATACMS), which is fired from the MLRS launcher and provides long-range fires against personnel and material targets. Artillery units provide fire support teams (FISTs) that plan and coordinate artillery fire in support of infantry and armor combat teams and call for and adjust artillery fires on enemy targets. The FIST uses many tools, including the ground/vehicular laser locator designator to determine ranges to targets and the designation of targets for laser-guided munitions, such as the tank-killing Copperhead round or the Hellfire missile. When the tactical situation warrants, the FIST may employ naval gunfire and joint close air support as well.

Air Defense Artillery. The mission of the air defense artillery (ADA) is to protect the force and selected geographical assets from attack by enemy aircraft and missiles and to conduct antiaircraft surveillance. With its multi-capable, phased-array radar and long-range, high-altitude missiles, the Patriot battery is the most formidable air defense system in the world today. It has the capability to intercept incoming tactical ballistic missiles, a role it performed with success in the Gulf War. While the Patriot provides long-range protection, the Avenger missile system, mounted on a high-mobility multipurpose wheeled vehicle (HMMWV) and found in divisions and corps, is a formidable weapon against low-flying aircraft and unmanned aerial vehicles.

Aviation. Aviation branch provides combat and combat service support aviation to the combined arms Army maneuver unit from aviation brigades located at division, corps, and higher echelons. Combat missions include attack, air assault, reconnaissance, show of force, intelligence, and logistical (air delivery) support. Its principal equipment is the UH-1 and UH-60 (Black Hawk) utility and troop transport helicopter, the AH-64 (Apache) and AH-1 (Cobra) attack helicopters, the CH47D (Chinook) cargo and transport helicopter, and the OH-58D small observation helicopter.

Special Forces. Special Forces (SF) is the Army's newest separate branch. As the name indicates, SF provides the Army with special tactics and techniques to accomplish very special missions, which range from special reconnaissance, direct action, foreign internal defense, unconventional warfare, and counterterrorism. SF mobile training teams travel all over the world to assist allied armies with modern training. Soldiers destined to SF units require considerable extra training and are specially selected. In addition to their traditional roles, SF branch includes units dedicated to civil affairs and military government and psychological operations.

Operational Support

Chemical Corps. The Chemical Corps provides expertise in the area of nuclear, biological, and chemical (NBC) operations and defense. This includes use of nuclear and chemical weapons during war, training units on NBC defense, reconnaissance of the NBC battlefield, and decontamination of units and equipment contaminated by NBC hazards. The Chemical Corps is also responsible for providing large-area smoke and obscurants on the battlefield and for the use of field flame weapons and techniques against enemy forces.

Military Intelligence. Military Intelligence (MI) branch is responsible for providing a large number of critical intelligence and language support services to the battlefield commander. These include intelligence and information collection, counterintelligence support, cryptologic and signals intelligence, electronic warfare, operations security, enemy order of battle analysis, interrogation of enemy prisoners of war (EPWs), aerial surveillance, imagery (aerial and other photography) analysis, and related work.[4]

Military Police. Military police (MP) provide combat operations against opposing forces in U.S. rear areas of a battlefield. They provide traffic control to expedite movement of critical combat resources to the front. They process EPWs and evacuate them from the battle area. MPs provide security for critical facilities such as command posts and special ammunition sites, and they conduct law-enforcement operations much along the lines of the order given by General Washington in 1776 to the Army's first provost martial to "apprehend deserters, marauders, drunkards, rioters, and stragglers."

Signal Corps. As one of the Army's high-technology branches, the Signal Corps performs a broad range of communications-related tasks in support of the Army mission. These range from procuring, installing, operating, maintaining, and reconfiguring communications networks from the battlefield level to the Pentagon. It leads the Army's digitization effort for information management on the battlefield.

Combat Engineers. Today's combat engineers provide the battlefield commander with mobility, countermobility, and survivability support. Combat engineer units are located primarily in divisions and corps. They provide bridging, mine laying, mine clearing, obstacle construction and removal, electric power, topographic support (terrain analysis), and a variety of combat construction and land-clearing tasks for combat units before, during, and after an attack, defense, or retrograde operation. As a secondary mission, combat engineers are trained to fight as infantry.

Public Affairs. The Army Public Affairs branch is responsible for keeping Army members informed as well as the public at large. Ensuring that the Army point of view and information is considered when reports are published by the media is critical to public opinion. Further, Public Affairs provides advice, education, and support to Army leaders to ensure that messages are clear, transparent, and provide maximum disclosure with minimal delay. These efforts help ensure that our country has confidence in the Army and the readiness level to deal with any and all potential requirements.[5]

---

4   Human Resources Command Home Page. (2015). Enlisted Personnel Management Directorate. Retrieved from: https://www.hrc.army.mil/Enlisted/Enlisted%20Personnel%20Management%20Directorate

5   Army Home Page. (2015). Public Affairs Page. Retrieved from: www.army.mil/info/institution/publicAffairs/.

Force Sustainment Soldier Support. The Soldier Support branch encompasses a wide variety of military occupational specialties (jobs) that support the total force. These include the Adjutant General Corps (Human Resources), Finance Corps, Recruiting, Career Counselors (Retention), Army Band Personnel, Paralegal (JAG Corps), and Chaplain Corps. The majority are trained, managed, and professionally developed at Fort Jackson, South Carolina. The Paralegal Corps proponent is found in Charlottesville, Virginia, and the Recruiting and Retention proponents are located at Fort Knox, Kentucky. These critical branches provide the support that commanders and soldiers at every level need for the Army to run smoothly and for soldiers to maintain the highest level of readiness and morale.[6]

Ordnance Corps. Ordnance soldiers perform one of the Army's most important missions: repair and maintenance of equipment and materiel, supply and maintenance of ammunition, and explosive ordnance disposal (EOD). Given the extensive array of high-technology weapon systems, other sophisticated equipment, missiles, and munitions in the Army, and the need to maintain these items in the highest state of readiness, the Ordnance Corps is staffed with a variety of units at all echelons of service.

Quartermaster Corps. Along with the Ordnance and Transportation Corps, the Quartermaster (QM) Corps forms the basis of Army logistics. QM soldiers supply the Army. This includes all aspects of supply—procurement, cataloging, inventory, storage, distribution, salvage, and disposal of material. It also includes the vital commodities of food, fuel, and water and the battlefield distribution networks that get these commodities to the fighting forces. The QM Corps pioneered the technology of aerial delivery, including air-drop and parachute delivery of personnel and supplies. It provides the Army's parachute riggers. The QM Corps also provides the Army with essential field services such as laundry, bath and shower facilities, clothing exchange, and mortuary support.

Transportation Corps. As the name implies, the Transportation Corps (TC) provides motor, air, rail, and water transport in support of Army operations worldwide. It operates the Army's line-haul truck fleets, ocean ports, railroads, and watercraft and coordinates logistic air operations. It operates motor transport depots and trailer transfer points. It also provides movement control units that schedule transportation assets in and through the battle area. Transportation companies and battalions are found at all echelons in the Army.

Health Services. The Army Medical Department (AMEDD) falls under the Army Surgeon General, and the numerous skill sets and capabilities within it are organized into six corps. They include the Medical Corps, Dental Corps, Veterinary Corps, Medical Service Corps, Nurse Corps, and Medical Specialist Corps. All personnel within the medical field in the Army are trained at Fort Sam Houston, Texas, at the AMEDD Center and School. The wide scope and depth of the Army Medical Department is impressive and is also critical to the continued success of the Army. Any soldier who has needed a combat medic will attest to this, and that is only the tip of a medical field that affects every military member and their family members at some point.[7]

---

6   Human Resources Command Home Page. (2015). Enlisted Personnel Management Directorate. Retrieved from: https://www.hrc.army.mil/Enlisted/Enlisted%20Personnel%20 Management%20Directorate

7   AMEDD Center and School. (2015). AMEDD Personnel and Proponent Directorate (APPD). Retrieved from: www.cs.amedd.army.mil/appd.aspx.

TYPES OF UNITS

Enlisted soldiers are trained for and serve in each of the above branches. All enlisted soldiers progress through basic combat training (BCT) and advanced individual training (AIT) for their military specialty. Officers are commissioned through the U.S. Military Academy at West Point, the Reserve Officers' Training Corps (ROTC), or the Officer Candidate School (OCS) and attend a basic course for their branch. Once initial training is completed, all soldiers—enlisted and officer—are assigned to units within the Army, and all work together to accomplish the Army's missions.

Even though there are many different types of units, the size and designation of units is fairly standard.

DESIGNATION	SYMBOL	SIZE	USUALLY LED BY
Fire team	•(-)	About 5	Sergeant
Squad	•	9–15	Staff sergeant
Section	••	10–15	Staff sergeant
Platoon	•••	About 40	Lieutenant & platoon sergeant
Battery, company, troop	I	100–200	Captain & first sergeant
Battalion, squadron	II	400–800	Lieutenant colonel & command sergeant major
Group, regiment	III	3–5 battalions	Colonel & command sergeant major
Brigade	X	3–5 battalions	Colonel & command sergeant major
Division	XX	4–6 brigades	Major general & command sergeant major
Corps	XXX	Several divisions	Lieutenant general & command sergeant major
Army	XXXX	Several corps	General & command sergeant major

As noted above, for every officer leading an organization, there is a noncommissioned officer to advise and assist in leading with him or her. Key examples of this include:

- A sergeant first class (SFC) platoon sergeant advises and assists the platoon leader.
- A first sergeant (1SG) advises and assists the commander of a company.

- A command sergeant major (CSM) advises and assists commanders at all levels at battalion and above.

A master sergeant or sergeant major advises and assists staff officers in various large staffs from brigade level up to the Army staff and in joint positions with other services.

The Army operates extremely well in today's highly technical information age. Modernization and digitization on the battlefield—from target acquisition to logistical support—require an increased reliance on small-unit leaders and soldiers, and on a smaller yet more capable force. Operations also continue to focus on smaller, more capable, self-sustaining units digitally linked to artificial intelligence, analysis, operational support, and force sustainment nodes that provide real-time information on the battlefield, whether it is a battlefield in a traditional sense or a peacekeeping operation.

To operate all the digitized high-technology equipment, as well as fight in austere environments, the Army—as in the past—will continue to require trained, disciplined, and cohesive soldier teams. To attain this goal, the Army's enlisted training system operates for the purpose of producing the kind of soldiers needed on the modern battlefield.

2

Enlisted Training

Being a member of the Profession of Arms requires a lot from all Soldiers. A part of the profession demands that you become a master at your craft over time. That means a devotion to duty beyond the duty day. It's a lifetime commitment. That mastery includes training and education which requires a lot of self-discipline, self-study and motivation to continue to grow and get better every day.

—SMA Raymond Chandler, 14th Sergeant Major of the Army

While you are in the Army, your opportunity for military training is extensive. Training is an integral part of the Army Select, Train, Educate and Promote (STEP) system. It can be found and is described in various categories including Initial, MOS, Individual, Unit, Self-Structured, Self-Guided, Institutional, and so forth. The STEP system directly supports and enhances the Enlisted Personnel Management System (EPMS). Regardless of category or type, Army training is characterized by sequential and progressively higher levels of performance capability, experience, and rank. Six "skill levels" of training are in place to support enlisted soldier training. They are administered in three distinct but closely related phases: initial entry training (IET), Structured Self Development (SSD) (see chapter five for more on SSD), and the Noncommissioned Officer Education System (NCOES).

IET provides a foundation of professional and technical knowledge needed to perform at the first duty station; combined with subsequent individual training in the unit, the soldier qualifies at skill level one (SL-1) in one of the Army's military occupational specialties (MOSs). The next five skill levels are taught through SSD and the NCOES.

CAREER MANAGEMENT FIELDS

The military occupational specialties (MOSs) of all enlisted soldiers from private to sergeant major are grouped into career management fields (CMFs). A CMF is a grouping of related MOSs. MOSs are grouped so that soldiers in one specialty have abilities and aptitudes with potential for training and assignments in other specialties within that CMF. This flexibility means that a soldier can sometimes move laterally within a CMF as well.

Training leads to progression and promotions. Each soldier has a career path mapped out for him or her, identifying appropriate schooling, assignments, and opportunities. As soldiers climb the promotion ladder within a CMF, new recruits fill in the lower rungs of the ladder, preparing themselves for upward mobility as well. The Army has established career paths for each CMF so soldiers can be counseled on the training and education they will need.

Within each CMF, the EPMS has identified the skills necessary for successfully functioning at each rank. Soldiers seeking promotions need to constantly prepare themselves for the next higher skill level. SL-1 includes skills, proficiencies, and abilities typically needed to perform efficiently up through the rank of specialist. SL2 relates to sergeant, SL-3 to staff sergeant, SL-4 to sergeant first class, SL5 to master sergeant, and SL-6 for sergeant major and command sergeant major. Because MOSs are grouped into CMFs, the skills necessary for SL-2 in one CMF will not necessarily be the same skills required at that level in a different CMF.

Included among the CMFs for enlisted soldiers are the following:

Maneuver, Fires and Effects
11 Infantry
13 Artillery
15 Aviation
18 Special Forces
37 Psychological Operations
38 Civil Affairs

Operational Support
12 Engineer
25 Signal
31 Military Police
35 Military Intelligence
09L Language

Force Sustainment
27 Paralegal
36 Finance
42 Adjutant General
56 Chaplain Corps
79R/S Recruiter/Career Counselor
68 Health Services
88 Transportation
89/91/94 Ordnance
92 Quartermaster

The CMFs are organized into three branches: Maneuver, Fires and Effects (MFE), Operational Support (OS), and Force Sustainment (FS). The STEP system recognizes the distinction necessary among branches, but leadership training is required in all three branches.

INITIAL ENTRY TRAINING
Every soldier in the Army has gone through initial entry training (IET). The two phases of IET are basic training (BT) and advanced individual training (AIT), which is MOS training.

Generally, soldiers entering the MFE branches or the military police receive one-station unit training (OSUT); they remain in the same unit for their BT and AIT. Soldiers entering operational support or force sustainment branches generally change duty assignments for their AIT, primarily because of the technical nature of many MOSs in these branches. The primary functions of IET are to prepare recruits for military life and to provide soldiers with basic combat skills and SL-1 technical training.

Drill sergeants are key figures in preparing recruits for the rigors of Army life. It is the responsibility of a drill sergeant to teach a new soldier about the Army and to help him or her appreciate how individuals contribute to the military structure. The drill sergeant instills self-confidence, self-respect, and self-discipline in young soldiers so they can perform their duties as soldiers to the highest degree possible. Equally important, the drill sergeant must ensure that soldiers are physically fit.

It is essential that each soldier be proficient in the combat basics regardless of the branch in which they will serve. Marksmanship, field living, first aid, hand-to-hand combat (combatives), nuclear, biological, and chemical (NBC) defense, and small-unit teamwork are emphasized.

All soldiers are given additional training in basic combat skills during the advanced individual training (AIT) phase of initial entry training (IET). Field training exercises are used to combine specialized MOS training that the soldier must receive with basic soldier skills that need to be reinforced. AIT highlights the specific skills soldiers will need to perform in their MOS at SL-1 upon arrival to their first permanent party assignment as an IET graduate.

Upon completion of IET, soldiers go to their units with skills sufficient to effectively contribute to the team. Training, however, is by no means complete. Permanent party units provide continuing on-the-job training to round out the soldier's initial training and to enhance the first-termer's potential.

UNIT AND INDIVIDUAL TRAINING

Upon assignment to a unit, the new soldier practices and refines the individual soldier skills learned in BT and AIT. The individual training encountered includes battle tasks and drills and individual training that supports the unit's Mission Essential Task List (METL).

Battle tasks and drills emphasize combat skills that *all* soldiers must perform. Tasks such as weapons handling, communications, and tactical movement are reinforced through performance-oriented, hands-on training. Each year, soldiers must engage a battery of common skills tests that evaluate their ability to perform basic skills. The METL is the key document that describes the capabilities a unit must have collectively to achieve its mission. The individual tasks support the collective tasks found in that document for a given unit. Structured Self Development (SSD) is discussed in detail in chapter five.

Although the focus of each soldier's training is on developing individual soldier skills, unit leaders are responsible for ensuring that the unit can perform collective tasks. At the unit level, several types of evaluations are used to assist commanders in measuring capability against an Army or joint standard for the accomplishment of collective unit tasks. Informal assessments rely on each commander evaluating his or her unit's wartime mission to assess which tasks require emphasis in the unit's training

Quality training results in superior performance.

plans. The commander may also use formal or external assessments to measure the unit's ability and then plan, prepare, and execute future training based on the results and feedback.

During time at the unit, soldiers will also engage in Structured Self Development (SSD), another phase of training. SSD provides important training and education via distance (web-based) learning not found in IET or in the Noncommissioned Officer Education System courses. This training includes history, writing, and other topics that fill in the gap between what is taught at the unit and at the institutional schoolhouses as soldiers progress up the ladder. These SSD courses are also connected directly within the STEP system and are a requirement in order to proceed to the next level of institutional schooling and subsequent promotion.

NONCOMMISSIONED OFFICER EDUCATION SYSTEM

The third phase or aspect of enlisted training is the Noncommissioned Officer Education System (NCOES), which has a single goal: to train noncommissioned officers (NCOs) to be trainers and leaders of soldiers who work under their supervision. The NCOES prepares soldiers to perform at the next higher skill level and combines leadership study with technical training. It provides an extensive network of courses at all levels of the NCO Corps. It is conducted in service schools and NCO academies (NCOAs).

Listed below are the Army's NCO academies (listed by location) with their courses and websites, which contain welcome letters and provide packing lists, directions, phone numbers, and mailing addresses:

Enlisted Training and Progression

Rank	Structured self-development	Unit Experience	Institutional Training	Skill Level
SGM/CSM	SSD-5		USASMC	SL6
MSG/1SG	SSD-4		MLC	SL5
SFC	SSD-4		SLC	SL4
SSG	SSD-3		ALC	SL3
SGT	SSD-2		BLC	SL2
PVT-SPC	SSD-1	Initial Entry Training (IET)	OSUT BCT AIT	SL1

Fort Benning, GA; BLC/ALC/SLC
www.benning.army.mil/tenant/whinsec/ncoAcademy.html
Fort Bliss, TX; BLC/U.S. Army Sergeants Major Course (USASMC)
http://usasma.armylive.dodlive.mil
Fort Bragg, NC; BLC
www.bragg.army.mil/18abc/ncoa/Pages/default.aspx
Fort Campbell, KY; BLC
http://www.campbell.army.mil/Tenant/NCOA/Pages/default.aspx
Fort Drum, NY; BLC
www.drum.army.mil/NCOAcademy/Pages/Home.aspx
Fort Eustis, VA; ALC/SLC
http://www.jble.af.mil/Mission-Partners/Army/USAACE-NCOA
Fort Gordon, GA; ALC/SLC
www.signal.army.mil/index.php/cncoa-home-page
Fort Hood, TX; BLC
www.hood.army.mil/ncoa
Fort Huachuca, AZ; ALC/SLC
https://www.ikn.army.mil/apps/IKNWMS/Home/WebSite/NCOA
Fort Jackson, SC; ALC/SLC
www.ssi.army.mil/ncoa
Fort Lee, VA; ALC/SLC
www.alu.army.mil

Fort Leonard Wood, MO; BLC/ALC/SLC
www.wood.army.mil/newweb/mncoa
Fort Lewis, WA; BLC
https//:jbextra.lewis-mcchord.army.mil/NCOA
http://www.lewis-mcchord.army.mil/army.html
(then click on Henry H. Lind NCO Academy under Tenant Organizations, right
side of page using CAC/AKO User ID and password)
Fort Meade, MD; ALC/SLC
http://signal.army.mil/index.php?option=com_content&view=article&id=188:wel
come-guide&catid=20&Itemid=165
Fort Richardson, AK; BLC
www.usarak.army.mil/ncoa
Fort Rucker, AL; ALC/SLC
www.rucker.army.mil/usaace/ncoa/index.html
Fort Sam Houston, TX; ALC/SLC
http://www.cs.amedd.army.mil/ncoa.aspx
Fort Sill, OK; BLC/ALC/SLC
http://sill-www.army.mil/usancoa/
Fort Stewart, GA; BLC
http://www.stewart.army.mil/units/home.asp?id=212
7th Army NCO Academy; WLC
http://www.eur.army.mil/7ATC/NCOA.html
8th Army NCO Academy; WLC
http://8tharmy.korea.army.mil/NCOA
JAG Legal Center and School; ALC/SLC
https://tjaglcspublic.army.mil/ncoa
NCOA Hawaii; BLC
https://www.usarpac.army.mil/NCOA/
Updates can be found at
www.hrc.army.mil/Enlisted

The four levels of the NCOES are the Basic Leader Course (BLC), the Advanced Leader Course (ALC), the Senior Leader Course (SLC), and the U.S. Army Sergeants Major Academy (USASMA). The Army is currently developing the Master Leader Course (MLC) to prepare NCOs to assume the rank and responsibilities of master sergeant. That course is still in development at the time of this writing.

Many first-term soldiers will have the opportunity to attend the Basic Leader Course (BLC). This non-MOS-specific leadership course is conducted at fourteen non-commissioned officer academies (NCOAs) worldwide as of this writing. The course provides basic leadership training for soldiers with potential for promotion to sergeant, provides soldiers with the skills, knowledge, and behaviors needed to lead a team-size unit, and serves as the foundation for further training and development. BLC is conducted in an NCO academy live-in environment using the small-group instruction method with practical application, followed by hands-on, performance-oriented training conducted in a field environment, culminating with an extensive field training exercise (FTX). Training focuses on self-discipline; professional skills; leading, counseling, disciplining, and developing soldiers; and caring for soldiers and their families. Other areas include the planning, executing, and evaluating of individual or team training and the planning and executing of missions/tasks assigned to a team-size unit. Successful completion of BLC establishes the foundation for further training and leader development. Small-group leaders assess the students' leadership potential and evaluate their ability to apply lessons learned and effectively lead their classmates in a tactical environment.

Attendance at BLC is mandatory for promotion to sergeant, and completion of SSD-1 is required prior to attendance. This is true for each of the levels of NCOES, where completion of the online-delivered training is prerequisite to attendance at the institution for that level of rank, and completion of the course is required prior to pinning on the rank. Priority of attendance to BLC goes to sergeants who have not previously attended and were promoted under the old policies, E-4 (P), or, E-4, who have been serving in leadership positions. Soldiers may appear before promotion boards; however, they cannot be promoted until they complete BLC.

The Advance Leader Course, conducted at NCOAs, is designed to produce hard-charging squad and section leaders who can lead and train soldiers in combat. The length of the course varies according to the MOS. Graduation from ALC is required for promotion to staff sergeant and again, is preceded by completion of SSD-2.

The Senior Leader Course (SLC) is preceded by SSD-3, and attendance stresses MOS-related tasks, with emphasis on technical and common leader combat skills required to train and lead other soldiers at the platoon or comparable level. Courses are presented at NCOAs and vary in length according to MOS requirements. SLC is required for promotion to sergeant first class. The Master Leader Course (MLC) is approved and in development as of this writing. It will function in the same manner to prepare SFC prior to pin on of 1SG/MSG, with full operation expected in 2017.

The USASMA prepares master sergeants and first sergeants for troop and staff assignments throughout the Army and the Department of Defense at battalion staff and command positions and above. Graduation from the U.S. Army Sergeants Major Course at the USASMA precedes promotion to sergeant major, and attendees must have successfully completed SSD-4.

Other Military Training Opportunities
Soldiers may apply for a number of additional qualification training courses. The following courses are open to all MOSs:

Air Assault Course
Obstacle courses, physical training, aircraft safety, Pathfinder operations, combat assaults, sling-loading operations, rappelling from UH-60 Blackhawk helicopters, twelve-mile road marches with rucksack and rifle—this ten-day course is packed with challenge. To attend, soldiers must receive permission from their commander and pass the Army Physical Fitness Test (APFT) (in the seventeen- to twenty-one-year-old age group).

Airborne Course

Airborne training is available on a voluntary basis for enlisted personnel, without regard to current assignment, who will be assigned to an Airborne unit after training. This functional training conducted by the U.S. Army Infantry School is designed to qualify volunteers in the use of the parachute as a means of deployment, and through mental and physical training, to develop leadership, self-confidence, and a warrior spirit. Graduates receive an additional skill identifier (ASI) designated by a (P). Eligible personnel volunteering for Airborne training should submit applications according to the instructions contained in AR 614-200 and should be physically qualified for parachute duty in accordance with AR 40-501.

Ranger Training

This voluntary training conducted by the U.S. Army Infantry School, Fort Benning, Georgia, is designed to develop leadership skills and provide a knowledge of Ranger operations involving direct combat with the enemy. Non-Airborne-enlisted graduates receive a special qualification identifier (G) for their MOS code, while those who are Airborne qualified receive a V code. Ranger training is available on a voluntary basis for all soldiers—the first two female soldiers graduated Ranger School in August 2015. Because many of the tasks evaluated at Ranger School are outside the OS/FS arena, successful completion of a pre-Ranger program is important for OS/FS success. Submit applications according to the instructions contained in AR 614-200 for what many consider the best small-unit leadership training in the world.

Special Forces Training

Special Forces training is available for all soldiers with any MOS; however, combat arms is more prevalent. Unless enlisting into the military for Special Forces, applicants must be in the rank of specialist (SPC) (P) through sergeant first class (SFC) and meet the course criteria as outlined in AR 614-200, chapter 5, paragraph 5-5, *Special Forces Assignments* (policy and selection criteria). Soldiers who meet the prerequisites and who volunteer for Special Forces training must be Airborne qualified and must attend and successfully complete the three-week Special Forces Selection and Assessment Course, which assesses tactical skills, leadership, physical fitness, motivation, and a student's ability to cope with stress. Students are in a temporary duty (TDY) and return status during the course. Those who pass are scheduled to attend the Special Forces Qualification Course. Soldiers who attend the qualification course must complete a common phase, an MOS-specific phase, and a final phase that combines and tests what was learned in the first two phases. Depending on the MOS (weapons, engineering, communications, medical, intelligence), the qualification course can vary from twenty-six to fifty-seven weeks. Language training may also be required. The primary training site for Special Forces training is Fort Bragg, North Carolina.

DISTANCE LEARNING

The Army has fully embraced the digital age with soldiers attending classes at their post, where through digital and video teleconferencing (VTC) links they attend courses presented by schools and instructors located at far-off institutions. Soldiers attending courses, whether through a resident school, a Total Army Schools System (TASS) Training Battalion, or a digital learning facility, receive the same credit for successfully completing training, with documentation in the soldier's Enlisted/Officer Records Brief/Soldier Records (ERB/ORB/SRB) reflecting identical codes for any of the training types. All diplomas, certificates, or DA Form 1059 will be the same and not reflect nonresident, distance learning, reserve component, or other similar remarks. Promotion and evaluation boards will not discriminate against soldiers who completed their professional military training through distance learning.

The first priority for all components is mission immediate training required for mobilization, activation, deployment, or other critical, time-sensitive requirements. The second priority is to quota-managed training, as directed by Headquarters, Department of the Army (HQDA), such as MOS reclassification, NCOES, additional skill identifier (ASI) and special qualification identifier (SQI) courses, and MOS reclassification for active duty. The third priority is to reserve component ASI/SQI courses and civilian training. The remaining priorities are to functional training courses, self-development courses, and training courses provided to the civilian community.

Soldiers may split their training phases, with some at the resident school or at a TASS Battalion and the remainder conducted through distance learning while at their home station. One of the considerations for determining training location is whether the costs of TASS or distance learning exceed the costs of sending a soldier to the proponent school for the full resident course. Phase I for ALC and SLC is taught via distance learning and is a great example of reducing the backlog and saving costs.

FUNCTIONAL ACADEMIC SKILLS TRAINING

Functional Academic Skills Training (FAST), formerly called Basic Skills Education Program (BSEP), provides instruction in academic competencies necessary for job proficiency and preparation for advanced training. FAST, available at Army Education Centers (AECs) or online for self-study, this important program helps improve soldiers' job performance and helps them meet reenlistment eligibility and MOS classification requirements. Because this program is self-paced using instructional materials at those education centers or online for those who cannot attend class, FAST is available during duty and off-duty hours. FAST covers reading, writing, arithmetic, and other subjects that soldiers must comprehend to excel in service and is often also used to improve the General-Technical Score found on the Armed Services Vocational Aptitude Battery (ASVAB).

NCO EVALUATION SYSTEM

Some high-speed first-term soldiers will reach the rank of sergeant during their first enlistment and will begin receiving written NCO Evaluation Reports (NCOERs) from their immediate supervisor, along with a section of those reports completed by their supervisor's boss. The NCOER provides formal recognition of duty performance and potential, a measurement of professional values and personal traits, and is the basis for performance counseling by rating officials for noncommissioned officers. Subsequent school selection, promotion, assignment, MOS classification, and qualitative management are based largely on information found in the NCOER. The NCOER is designed to strengthen the NCO Corps's ability to meet the professional challenges of the future.

That recording of performance and potential is important for NCOs, but it is critical to you as a younger enlisted soldier as you prepare for promotion to the rank of SGT and receive periodic performance counseling. As will be discussed more in chapter 13 on promotions and reductions, the NCOER is the key document for selection at the senior NCO grades, but the performance counseling you receive periodically while in the junior enlisted ranks is the same for you. Having clear communication with your leader about what you have done and what you are planning to do to contribute to the team and unit over the next months can be a very powerful record of your commitment to your leader, your team, your unit, and the Army. As your unit looks for those soldiers to promote ahead of their peers, or to select for special training or positions in the unit, the counseling that you receive will no doubt be a great indicator of your chances at those opportunities. Make sure you bring your accomplishments and thoughts about the near future with you to a counseling session. Most bosses will remember when a soldier is late for formation. They are much less likely to remember the weekends of work as a volunteer, or the late nights when everyone else was done for the day. This is advice given to all NCOs, but you can get a head start by keeping a record of accomplishments and writing out your goals for a coming quarter, then working to have it included in your counseling records.

3

Service in Today's Army

Now more than ever, in today's uncertain and dynamic security environment, we must be prepared to meet multiple, wide-ranging requirements across the globe simultaneously while retaining the ability to react to the unknown. The velocity of instability around the world has increased, and the Army is now operating on multiple continents simultaneously in ways unforeseen a year ago. In short, our Army is busy. We are fully engaged and our operational tempo will not subside for the foreseeable future.

—Army Posture Statement (2015)

CHARACTERISTICS OF ARMY SERVICE

For over 240 years, the Army has employed its military doctrine, organization, procedures, and ideals of service to meet whatever challenge the nation has asked of it in the realm of national defense, military deterrence, security cooperation, and warfighting. Today, and for the foreseeable future, Army service will be characterized by a number of key attributes all soldiers need to understand.

Continuous Training

Training is the cornerstone of military life. The Army has an extensive program of *individual* and *unit* training that is virtually continuous. Individual training is the responsibility of the Army's NCOs. Unit training is the responsibility of the unit's leaders and commanders. Unit training is accomplished during recurring training exercises and other collective training events. Every training event, whether it lasts one day or several weeks, measures how ready individual soldiers, their teams, units, and larger collective organizations are to perform their respective missions in war. Soldiers find out how fit, tough, trained, and ready they are during a training exercise, especially when they get cold, hot, tired, wet, hungry, or thirsty and encounter other unpleasant conditions or forces, such as the simulated "enemy" opposing force found at major training centers. Training also takes place leading up to deployment to and in combat theaters so that soldiers remain familiar with tasks not accomplished daily as well as to absorb "lessons learned." With over a decade of continuous conflict and deployment in different theaters of operation, the Army is now composed of some of the most highly trained and seasoned professionals in its long history.

Professional Competence

The Army today incorporates intellectual ingenuity, critical thinking, technological innovation, and a set of corporate values that have shaped America's Army throughout its more than 240-year history. Our Army will continue to need skilled, versatile, and highly motivated soldiers capable of accomplishing their mission in ever-changing environments. Today's soldiers will become the leaders of tomorrow's soldiers. They are the young men and women who will provide to America a corps of leaders who have an unmatched work ethic, who have a strong sense of values, who treat others with dignity and respect, who are accustomed to hard work, who are courageous, who thrive on responsibility, who know how to work as a team, and who are positive role models for all around them. Today's Army is manned with professionally competent soldiers and leaders. They know their jobs, and they do them extremely well.

World-Class Missions

America's Army is the best land combat force in the world, serving the nation every day at home and abroad. It is often the commitment of our Army into trouble spots that makes the difference between success and failure of America's national security policy. When the Army puts boots on ground, the world knows the United States means business. Land forces remain decisive and provide the most visible and sustained form

Semper Paratis, "**Always Ready.**"

of U.S. commitment. Since 1989, the Army has had forty-five major deployments, including ongoing operations in Iraq, Afghanistan, the Sinai, the Philippines, Kosovo, and Bosnia. This does not include many smaller deployments of troops that have been nearly continuous during this same period. In the forty years prior to 1989, there were only ten.

Hundreds of thousands of soldiers are involved in vital roles, missions, and functions on a daily basis. In 2015, approximately 520,000 soldiers were serving on active duty, with 143,540 from all components deployed or forward stationed in more than 150 countries to support operations in Iraq, Afghanistan, and other theaters of war, and deterring aggression, while also securing the homeland. Soldiers from the Army National Guard and the Army Reserve also make a vital contribution, with thousands mobilized and performing a diverse range of missions worldwide. The Army could not achieve its national security objectives without their commitment, experience, professionalism, and sacrifice. In addition to their duties overseas, soldiers from all components of the Guard and the Reserve support civil authorities during disaster relief operations and homeland security.

An Army of Values

Soldiers learn and draw strength from other soldiers and leaders who nurture and encourage the development of values as inalienable professional attributes. Soldiers are expected to live by and exemplify those values. Internalizing these values—living by them—is what builds professionalism in America's Army and character in our nation. Values and traditions are the soul of the Army.

The Army lives by seven bedrock values to which all soldiers must adhere. Army values follow the acronym LDRSHIP:

ARMY VALUES

Loyalty	Being faithful to the country, the Army, your unit, and other soldiers in good times and bad.
Duty	Performing your military responsibilities and fulfilling your legal obligations faithfully and reliably under all conditions.
Respect	Treating all people with dignity and courtesy and as you would wish to be treated.
Selfless service	Putting the welfare of the nation, the Army, and your colleagues before your own welfare.
Honor	Having the personal integrity, courage, and honesty to know and support what is right without being forced to do so.

| Integrity | Doing what's right, legally and morally, and not allowing yourself to be corrupted by that which is not. This includes taking responsibility for your actions. |
| Personal courage | Being brave and doing your duty in the face of fear, danger, or adversity. |

These values have served the Army well both in peace and in war. Values, along with professional job competence, contribute directly to mission success. Soldiers who develop within themselves a sense of mental and moral strength—courage—will accomplish the mission directed, whether in training, a peacetime requirement, or when in combat. Understand also that commitment to the unit's mission takes priority over personal wishes, wants, pleasures, and, perhaps, needs. It means sincere involvement—doing something—to find solutions to problems and not just paying lip service to them.

Although soldierly values and character attributes are not new, there is a renewed interest in them. The Soldier's Creed best encapsulates the compact among the soldier, the leader, and the Army.

An Army of Standards

Today's Army is also an army of standards. There are two types of standards: standards of *personal behavior* and standards of *duty performance*. The standards of personal behavior apply to all ranks. The standards of duty performance apply to all soldiers according to their military occupational specialties and the levels of responsibility and authority they hold.

Standards are those principles or rules by which behaviors and tasks are measured as successfully accomplished. When members of a squad, section, or platoon share and adhere to the Army values and to the standards that flow from them, they are a more cohesive organization. Soldiers will measure other soldiers by the standard as it gradually becomes a criterion for acceptance by the whole team.

Army Doctrine Publication 1 capstones the Army's guiding beliefs, standards, and ideals succinctly in one word—trust. Trust between soldiers, between soldier and leader, between soldier and family and between soldier and nation. A key requirement of developing and maintaining trust is found by the consistent performance of duty. Duty means to fulfill your obligations. It is behavior required by moral obligation, demanded by custom, or enjoined by feelings of rightness. It requires the impartial administration of standards without regard to friendship, personality, rank, or other bias. It is one of the key Army values.

CURRENT TRENDS IN THE ARMY

Army Transformation: New Doctrines for New Missions

Assigned Army missions affect how the military is structured, trained, and employed. The Army's new regional focus, combined with major troop reductions, puts enormous emphasis on strategic mobility and small-unit capability. Airlift and sealift mobility improvements have enabled deployment of an Army light division and a heavy brigade to any crisis area in about two weeks, and two heavy divisions in about a month. The new brigade combat teams (BCTs) are able to deploy in about ninety-six hours.

New Structures
The Army transformed from a division-based to a brigade-based force during the first decade of the twenty-first century. That transformation continues based on new threats, force reductions, and as modernization requires or allows. These brigades are designed as modules, or self-sufficient and standardized brigade combat teams (described in chapter 1), that can be more readily deployed and combined with other Army and joint forces to meet the precise needs of the combatant commanders.

A CHANGING WORLD
The end of the Cold War had three key strategic events: the collapse of international communism, the demise of the Soviet Union, and an end to bipolar competition. These events, in turn, still affect power and security relationships throughout the world. One result is the relative dispersal of power away from the states of the former Soviet Union toward other regional power centers. Another is the potential struggle within regions as the dominant states vie for position within the emerging power hierarchy. A third is that in many regions the "lid has come off" long-simmering ethnic, religious, territorial, and economic disputes.

Terrorism
The United States continues to face a variety of threats from terrorist organizations such as the Islamic State of Iraq and the Levant (ISIL) and other Muslim extremist groups. The primary threat for the foreseeable future is a network of Islamic extremists hostile to the United States, and to the western hemisphere in general. The network is transnational and has a broad range of capabilities, including mass-casualty attacks.

We face a movement of like-minded groups who interact, share resources, and work to achieve shared goals. Some of the groups in the movement provide safe haven and logistical support to active members, others operate directly with fighters/terrorists, and still others fight in the targeted regions.

The Global Jihadist Movement
The global jihadist movement predates al Qaeda's founding and was reinforced and developed by successive conflicts in Afghanistan, Bosnia, Chechnya, and elsewhere during the 1990s. As a result, it spawned several groups and operating nodes and developed a resiliency that ensured that destruction of any one group or node did not destroy the larger movement. Since 2001, extremists, including members of al Qaeda and affiliated groups, have sought to exploit perceptions of the U.S.-led global war on terrorism and, in particular, the war in Iraq to attract converts to their movement. Many of these recruits come from a large and growing pool of disaffected youth who are sympathetic to radical, anti-Western militant ideology. At the same time, these extremists have branched

out to establish jihadist cells in other parts of the Middle East, South Asia, and Europe, from which they seek to prepare operations and facilitate funding and communications. Foreign fighters appear to be working to make the insurgency in Syria and Iraq what Afghanistan was to the earlier generation of jihadists: a melting pot for jihadists from around the world, a training ground, and an indoctrination center. In the months and years ahead, a significant number of fighters who have traveled to Syria have and may continue to return to their home countries, where they can strengthen existing extremist networks with their new skills and experience in the communities to which they return. Active work through the Internet has provided these extremist organizations a capability to reach many disillusioned youth worldwide, as well as conduct radical information operation-propaganda campaigns and raise funds while attracting recruits for training.

Afghanistan
Afghanistan, once the safe haven for Osama bin Laden, worked hard with U.S. and coalition partners in the development of Afghanistan National Security Forces to take aggressive action in combating terrorist activity. Despite a significant degradation of al Qaeda capability and Taliban activity, much work remains to be done in bolstering the populace's confidence in the government to provide a stable security environment. The initial announcement by President Obama to withdraw troops from Afghanistan has been extended at this writing, but the end goal is for the Afghan government to provide its own security. Updates on Afghanistan and other countries are available on the State Department's website, under "Country Reports on Terrorism."

Iraq
The American efforts in Iraq saw much movement forward in combating al Qaeda in Iraq, including the destruction of terrorist activities and strongholds, holding free elections, and structural improvements in the provinces and at the local level. This was a concerted effort by coalition partners and an engaged group of Sunni and Shiite leaders and other concerned groups. However, after the departure of U.S. and coalition partners at the end of 2011, a lack of action toward aggression by Iraq's government ultimately allowed the insurgence and rise of ISIL. That foothold remains at this writing, and there are currently designated U.S. forces in Iraq to train new or returning Iraqi security forces.

The Army is trained and ready "to be persuasive in peace and invincible in war." Despite the loss of ground gained after the withdrawal, it is evident that the Army's goals of having an army that is responsive, rapidly deployable, agile, versatile, lethal, survivable, and sustainable (as discussed earlier) is at hand.

Iran
Iran is important to the United States because of its size, location, energy resources, military strength, and hostility to U.S. interests. It actively supports terrorist groups in the region, such as Hezbollah, and could encourage increased attacks in Israel and the Palestinian territories to derail progress toward peace. Iran also aids insurgents in Iraq to drive the United States out of that country and ultimately the Middle East. In the near term, Iran's goal is a weakened, decentralized, and Shia-dominated Iraq that is incapable

of posing a threat to Iran. The country's mullah-dominated government will also continue its weapons of mass destruction and ballistic missile programs. Its drive to acquire nuclear weapons is a key test of international resolve and the nuclear nonproliferation treaty.

The government in Tehran has the only military in the region that can threaten its neighbors and Gulf stability. Its expanding ballistic missile inventory presents a potential threat to states in the region. As it fields new longer-range medium-range ballistic missiles (MRBMs), Iran will have missiles with ranges to reach many of our European allies. Although the country maintains a sizable conventional force, it has made limited progress in modernizing its conventional capabilities. Air and air defense forces rely on out-of-date U.S., Russian, and Chinese equipment. Ground forces suffer from personnel and equipment shortages. In addition, the equipment is poorly maintained. Intelligence services estimate that Iran can briefly close the Strait of Hormuz, relying on a layered strategy using predominantly naval, air, and some ground forces. In 2005 Iran purchased North Korean torpedo and missile-armed fast attack craft and midget submarines, making marginal improvements to this capability.

Iran is currently in negotiations with the United States, but will remain a threat to the national security interests of the United States for the foreseeable future.

Syria
Since 2011, Syria has escalated on the world stage as an unstable country led by a dictatorship that is hanging on to power as of this writing and in a civil war with those who wish to overthrow it. This devolving situation has allowed for the rise of ISIL there, and for the use of the country as a launch point into Iraq and other locations. Over 250,000 people have been killed since the start of the civil war in Syria, and over 1 million have been injured. While Syria does not maintain a conventional force capable of threatening the United States, the ISIL threat via its use of Syria as a launch point for training and indoctrination of terrorists and direct involvement in the operations discussed in Iraq make it a threat to our national security interests.

North Korea
After more than a decade of declining or stagnant economic growth, Kim Jong Un's military capability has significantly degraded. The North's declining capabilities are even more pronounced when viewed in light of the significant improvements over the same period of the Republic of Korea (ROK) military and the U.S.-ROK Combined Forces Command. Nevertheless, the North maintains a large conventional force of over 1 million soldiers, the majority of which may be deployed south of Pyongyang.

North Korea continues to prioritize the military at the expense of its economy. The "military first policy" has several purposes. It serves to deter U.S.-ROK aggression.

Nationwide conscription is a critical tool for the regime to socialize its citizens to maintain the Kim family in power. The large military allows the dictator to use threats and bravado in order to limit U.S.-ROK policy options. Suggestions of sanctions, or military pressure by the United States or the Republic of Korea, are countered by the North with threats that such actions are "an act of war" or that it could "turn Seoul into a sea of fire." Inertia, leadership perceptions that military power equals national power, and the inability for the regime to change without threatening its leadership also explain the continuing large military commitment.

The North Korean People's Army remains capable of attacking South Korea with artillery and missile forces with limited warning. Such a provocative act, absent an immediate threat, is highly unlikely, counter to Pyongyang's political and economic objectives, and would prompt a South Korean–U.S. Combined Forces Command (CFC) response it could not effectively oppose.

China

Beijing's military modernization and military buildup is tilting the balance of power in the Taiwan Strait. Improved Chinese capabilities have the potential to threaten U.S. forces in the region if pressed.

China remains keenly interested in coalition military operations in Afghanistan and Iraq and is using lessons from those operations to guide its People's Liberation Army's (PLA) modernization and strategy; however, it will take several years before these lessons are incorporated into the armed forces. China continues to develop or import modern weapons. Priorities include submarines, surface combatants, air defense, ballistic and anti-ship cruise missiles, and modern fighters. The PLA must overcome significant integration challenges to turn these new, advanced, and disparate weapon systems into improved capabilities. The government also faces technical and operational difficulties in numerous areas. The PLA continues with its plan to cut approximately 200,000 soldiers from its army to free resources for further modernization, an initiative begun in 2004.

China is increasingly confident and active on the international stage—trying to ensure it has a voice on major international issues, and securing access to natural resources—and countering what it sees as U.S. efforts to contain or encircle China.

Russia

Despite an improving economy, Russia continues to face endemic challenges related to its post-Soviet military decline. Seeking to restore itself as a great power, the Russian government has made some improvements to its armed forces, but has not addressed difficult domestic problems that will limit the scale and scope of military recovery.

Russian conventional forces have improved from their mid-1990s low point. Moscow has been able to boost its defense spending in line with its economy. Defense should continue to receive modest real increases in funding, unless Russia suffers an economic setback. Budget increases will help Russia create a professional military by replacing conscripts with volunteer servicemen and focusing on maintaining, modernizing, and extending the operational life of its strategic weapons systems—including its nuclear missile force. Due to Russia's illegal actions in Ukraine, the United States has authorized sanctions for those responsible for violating Ukraine's sovereignty.

The Balkans

International peacekeeping forces in Bosnia and Kosovo continue to operate in a complex environment that poses significant challenges to the establishment of a stable and enduring peace. The Bosnian factions should continue to generally comply with the military aspects of the Dayton Accords and Stabilization Force (SFOR) directives. Montenegro's potential drive for independence presents the next potential crisis.

Thirty-one countries maintain a force of over four thousand servicemembers, comprising the NATO Kosovo Force (KFOR), and this is expected to continue for the foreseeable future.

South Asia

The tense rivalry between India and Pakistan over Kashmir is our most important security concern on the subcontinent. While neither side wants war, both see their security relationship in zero-sum terms. India's larger economy and more robust military is balanced by Pakistan's threat to retaliate with nuclear weapons if the two nations go to war. With frequent low-level clashes, the potential for miscalculation and rapid escalation is constant.

Latin America

The scourge of narcotrafficking, related money laundering, weapons and contraband smuggling, insurgency, and the recent disruption in the Venezuelan oil industry all combine to provide threatening conditions for some countries and governments of the region and for U.S. interests. The potential for more serious insurgency and more widespread terrorism and crime in several areas of Central and South America and the Caribbean continues to demand our vigilance.

In summary, although the United States will not likely see a global "peer competitor" within ten years, the threats facing the United States in the next decade will be of an uncertain order of magnitude. The world remains a very dangerous and complex place, and there is every reason to expect U.S. military requirements to be at about the same level as in past years, and that use of U.S. military forces will be required along the full spectrum of operations.

THE BEST TIME TO SERVE

As crazy as it may seem, morale in heavily engaged or deployed Army units is higher than in units doing peacetime training or garrison duties. This is probably because soldiers like doing constructive and more visible Army missions. Although training is one of the Army's most important missions, actually performing the functions for which we are trained seems to be more rewarding. Understanding that higher levels of commitment and attention to detail in training and garrison activities over time leads to more success when deployed or heavily engaged can go far to make those less "glamorous" duties more tolerable to the energetic young warrior or leader.

While the Army is drawing down in size due to the end of combat operations in Iraq and the continued withdrawal of forces in Afghanistan, the opportunities for professional advancement remain great for those who really want it. Soldiers who work hard at their duties, perform to standard in training and conduct, and participate professionally in any operation are rewarded not only with decorations but also with promotion to higher ranks. The skills learned in the Army—both the technical skills and the skill of working on a team toward a cooperative goal—are treasures of a lifetime.

The Army received significant pay raises during the first years of this millennium. Army salaries, when considering all the benefits and allowances and taking into account what they would cost if they had to be purchased out of a civilian salary, are now quite competitive. Pay also increases with length of service and advancement in rank and responsibility, and so just sweetens the pot for continued service.

Above all, Army duty is exciting, interesting, and personally rewarding. How many civilians get to be part of a world event? Very few. Soldiers do all the time. As U.S. interests in the world expand, the deployment of American forces to trouble spots around the world to deter enemies, protect international friends, and keep the peace between warring factions will continue to be missions worth training for and successfully executing.

The issues that soldiers are concerned about on a daily basis would fill thick volumes, with pay and entitlements, medical care for soldiers and their families, and a stable retirement system leading the list. Daily discussions about dining facilities, guard duty, uniform costs, women in combat (or male attitudes toward them), quality of training, leadership, supervision, field training exercises, weather, separation hardships, marital discord, blisters and other ailments, orders, directives, and verbal instructions all point to the old adage that soldiers are happy when they have the opportunity to complain.

Some aspects of Army life are as follows:

- Soldiers of every race, gender, and creed are successful if treated equally and held to the same standards.
- Soldiers will get from combat training what they put into it.
- Most leaders and supervisors are competent; those who aren't fall by the wayside.
- Field training is critical to combat readiness.
- Separation from loved ones occurs in many occupational sectors of American society and must be understood and dealt with by the chain of command.

In recent years, members of the Army have had to deal with increasing deployments, attempted assaults on their benefits, and, worse yet, fellow soldiers undermining the traditional key values by bad behavior. Nevertheless, in the Army family, plenty of good people do care and go about their business because it must be done. Selfless service calls for personal sacrifice and dedication to duty, regardless of the circumstances. No one gets rich on Army pay. If some elements of the nation seem less than caring, well, that's just how it is, so don't sweat it.

Sergeant Major of the Army Kenneth O. Preston had these final words of wisdom to soldiers serving in today's Army when he retired in 2011: "You are the next 'Greatest Generation.' Be proud of your service to your nation."

4

Real-World Issues

Soldiers excel in their duty performance and have successful careers when they obey the requirements of law and Army policy and use a little common sense in other matters that can cause needless problems. Many of the issues confronting civilians also confront soldiers, but the Army has policies and rules to guide the conduct of soldiers. There is more than enough room to have serious adventure and fun and enjoy your personal life without crossing the lines that get both civilians and soldiers into trouble.

THE LAW OF WAR

The Army has received some bad press from time to time due to a few soldiers operating outside the bounds of military discipline and law over the years. Although their misdeeds have been exposed by fellow soldiers and investigated by the chain of command, their actions have brought great discredit to not only themselves, but the Army and our nation.

The United States and its military follow the laws of war. Its Army soldiers are expected to comply with both the spirit and intent of these laws in all of their actions. It is only this respect for, and obedience to, the reign of law that differentiates our Army from looters, thieves, killers, and other immoral criminals. Nevertheless, the very nature of war can lead some of the fighting forces to fall prey to violence and disorder and to participate in unlawful actions. These actions, at whatever level and for whatever reason, cannot be permitted to exist or to continue if found. Only when all members understand that every member of the Army must be absolutely opposed to any unlawful conduct, and that any of that kind of conduct will be met with immediate action, will the United States be living up to its national goals. If something looks wrong, question it. If you walk by it, you may be acquiescing to establishing a standard for patterns of abuse in the present and future.

The attack of noncombatants and protected property is illegal. You must be able to distinguish "noncombatants" from "combatants" and distinguish "protected property" from "military objectives." Combatants are defined as follows: Anyone engaging in hostilities in an armed conflict on behalf of a party to the conflict. Combatants are lawful targets unless "out of combat." Military objectives are lawful targets (Army Field Manual (FM) 27-10: *The Law of Land Warfare*, para. 40, and GP I, art. 52(2)).

RULES OF ENGAGEMENT

The *DOD* (Department of Defense) *Dictionary* defines Rules of Engagement (ROE) as "directives issued by competent military authority that delineate the circumstances and limitations under which [U.S.] forces will initiate and/or continue combat engagement with other forces encountered."

Army training about ROE envisions two general circumstances for using weapons: in self-defense and to accomplish the mission. Whether ROE are "permissive" (allowing more use of force) or "restrictive" (limited use of force) depends on the anticipated conditions in the mission—for example, presence or absence of quantities of small arms and light weapons; existing, organized opposition groups, armed and unarmed; competency of local security forces, et cetera.

Remember that in all cases and regardless of ROE, a soldier always has the inherent right of self-defense.

FRATERNIZATION

The Army has always had policies concerning senior-subordinate relationships. This is nothing new, and it is not just a problem relating to gender.

Army policy states that relationships between soldiers of different rank that involve or give the appearance of partiality, preferential treatment, or the improper use of rank or position for personal gain, and that are prejudicial to good order, discipline, and high unit morale, will be avoided.

Prohibited Relationships

Relationships between soldiers of different rank—regardless of military service—are prohibited if they:

- Compromise, or appear to compromise, supervisory integrity or the chain of command.
- Cause actual or perceived partiality or unfairness.
- Involve the improper use of rank or position for personal gain.
- Are exploitative or coercive in nature.
- Create an actual or predictable impact on discipline, authority, morale, or mission accomplishment.

Prohibited relationships between officers and enlisted people, NCOs and junior enlisted, trainers and trainees, and recruiters and recruits include:

- Any business relationships, except landlord-tenant relationships or one-time transactions.
- Borrowing or lending money, commercial solicitation, and any other type of ongoing financial or business relationship.
- Shared living accommodations other than those directed by operational requirements.
- Dating and other intimate or sexual relationships.
- Gambling.

In cases of shared living accommodations other than operationally directed and dating or other intimate or sexual relationships, there are several exceptions. For example, if two junior enlisted are living together or dating and one becomes an NCO or goes to school to become an officer or warrant officer, they would either have to terminate their relationship or become married within a year of the change or intent to change status. See your chain of command in every instance where you think you may be in a questionable status, situation, or relationship. In all cases, ignorance is not an excuse to be out of tolerance of the rules.

The reason for this policy is clear. Officers and NCOs have both punitive and reward power—and recommendation of same—over the personnel in their units. Fraternization or inappropriate association by an enlisted soldier and his or her officers or by a junior soldier and NCO will surely be interpreted as an attempt to obtain favorable treatment. Since officers are legally bound not to fraternize with enlisted soldiers, it is best for enlisted soldiers not to seek these improper associations. Normal team-building associations such as community organizations, religious activities, family gatherings, unit-based social functions, and athletic teams or events are permitted and encouraged.

These prohibitions do not negate a leader's responsibility for the professional development of soldiers. Leaders cannot stop mentoring, coaching, and teaching soldiers because they fear being accused of fraternization or worse. They must continue to encourage individual study and professional development and to mentor the continued growth of their subordinates' military careers.

EQUAL OPPORTUNITY

Equal opportunity (EO) means exactly what the words indicate: Every soldier in the Army shall have an equal opportunity to serve his or her country and obtain the benefits of military service, including training, schooling, promotion, and assignments, without regard to race, religion, ethnic background, national origin, or gender.

Army policy is to base all personnel decisions on merit and excellence of duty performance. Equal opportunity does not mean creating quotas for promotions, assignments, or apportionment of duties based on a soldier's race or other defined category, for this, too, is against the law. Rather, the purpose of EO is for all soldiers to compete on an equal basis for schooling, promotions, and assignments. Soldiers who do their jobs best, who maintain the standards and values mentioned in the previous chapter, will win in these professional competitions regardless of their race, gender, or other defined category. In the Army, these rules are well understood and enforced. Equal opportunity for minorities in the military service has been a success story. It is seen as proof that the Army's EO policies are working, notwithstanding the existence of some individual acts of prejudice that unfortunately still occur.

Gender discrimination is defined as discrimination based solely on an individual's gender in a subgroup "female" or "male." Discrimination based on gender is often linked to a set of assumptions based on sex-role stereotypes concerning the abilities, competence, status, and roles of the particular subgroup, resulting in a disparate treatment of or impact on those groups. While history holds plenty of examples of these assumptions playing out in the field, many major accomplishments in the recent past by women have gone far to dispel the notions. The awarding of the Silver Star to two female soldiers in 2005 and 2008, respectively, highlight this point well. Likewise, the graduation of the first two women from Ranger School in August 2015 made a resounding statement, both of female capability as well as the Army being serious about equal opportunity. The secretary of defense lifted the ban on females serving in all combat units, including special operations units, in December 2015, making the most deliberate statement about the importance of Equal Opportunity in the Army.

To prevent the occurrence of discrimination, the Department of the Army has placed the responsibility for EO in the hands of unit commanders and has articulated the connection between EO and unit readiness by enforcing the policy through the traditional chain of command. AR 600-20, *Army Command Policy*, states:

> The chain of command, whether military or civilian, has the primary responsibility for developing and sustaining a healthy climate. This responsibility entails, but is not limited to, promoting positive programs that enhance unit cohesion, esprit, and morale; communicating matters with EO significance to unit personnel and higher headquarters; correcting discriminatory practices by conducting rapid, objective, and impartial inquiries to resolve complaints of discrimination; encouraging the surfacing of problems and preventing reprisal for those who complain; and taking appropriate action against those who violate Army policy.

Under current regulations, commanders have the legal authority to deal with cases of unlawful discrimination or sexual harassment (see the next section). AR 600-20, paragraph 4-4, "Soldier Conduct," provides that ensuring proper conduct of soldiers is a function of command. Commanders rely on all leaders in the Army to "take action against military personnel in any case where the soldier's conduct violates good order and discipline." Although this charge is not punitive, the commander's inherent authority to impose administrative sanctions and to prosecute specific offenses under the Uniform Code of Military Justice (UCMJ) provides commanders with sufficient authority to enforce Army policy against discrimination and harassment.

SEXUAL HARASSMENT/ASSAULT RESPONSE AND PREVENTION (SHARP)

The Department of Defense defines sexual harassment as a form of gender discrimination that involves unwelcome sexual advances, requests for sexual favors, and other verbal or physical conduct of a sexual nature when:

- Submission to or rejection of such conduct is made either explicitly or implicitly a term or condition of a person's job, pay, or career; or
- Submission to or rejection of such conduct by a person is used as a basis for career or employment decisions affecting that person; or
- Such conduct has the purpose or effect of unreasonably interfering with an individual's work performance or creates an intimidating, hostile, or offensive working environment.

This definition emphasizes workplace conduct but also directly applies to off-duty time, on or off post, everywhere, at all times for all soldiers. To be actionable as an "abusive work environment," harassment need not result in concrete psychological harm to the victim but need only be so severe or pervasive that a reasonable person would perceive—and the victim does perceive—the work environment as hostile or offensive. Any person in a supervisory or command position who uses or condones any form of sexual behavior to control, influence, or affect the career, pay, or job of a military member or civilian employee is engaging in sexual harassment. Similarly, any military member or civilian employee who makes deliberate or repeated unwelcome verbal comments, gestures, or physical contact of a sexual nature in the workplace is also engaging in sexual harassment and is subject to punishment under the provisions of the UCMJ.

Sexual harassment can include verbal abuse, profanity, off-color jokes, sexual comments, threats, barking, growling, oinking, or whistling at passersby to indicate a perception of their physical appearance. It also includes nonverbal abuse such as leering, ogling (giving a person the "once over"), blowing kisses, licking lips, winking, leaving sexually suggestive notes, and displaying sexist cartoons and pictures. Unwanted physical contact such as touching, patting, hugging, pinching, grabbing, cornering, kissing, blocking a passageway, and back and neck rubs may also constitute sexual harassment.

The Army has always taken these issues seriously, but significantly intensified its efforts in recent years in eradicating sexual harassment and assault from its ranks. Beginning in 2008, the "I. A.M. (Intervene, Act, Motivate) Strong" program provides greater awareness and understanding of resources and information for all soldiers and leaders. It needs to be pointed out here, that while sexual harassment and assault are related, sexual assault, according to AR 600-20, *Army Command Policy*, is a criminal offense, punishable under the UCMJ and other local and federal laws. Both harassment and assault tear at the fabric of trust and the team and has absolutely no place in the Army, or anywhere else for that matter.

The Army provides several layers of victim support and advocates, at the unit level and at the installation level, whether in garrison or deployed. Each battalion-sized unit must have two Unit Victim Advocates (UVA), and they are key in ensuring that quick, dignified, professional assistance is available to all members of the unit in addition to the required training to prevent such need in the first place. This support is provided 24-7, on and off post.

Soldiers who are victims may report an incident in one of two ways: Restricted reporting allows a soldier to report an offense without an official investigation if desired, by reporting it to their chaplain, victim advocate, health-care professional, or installation Sexual Assault Response Coordinator (SARC). Soldiers who wish to file an unrestricted report that allows for an official investigation should contact their chain of command, law enforcement, or victim advocate. The full weight of Army leadership is committed to eliminating sexual assault and harassment, and each instance will be handled with a serious, respectful approach.

If you or someone you know believes they are the victim of sexual harassment or assault, several other ways to reach help include:

DOD Safe Helpline: Phone (877) 995-5247 (www.safehelpline.org)

Army Sexual Harassment Hotline: Phone (800) 267-9964 or DSN (312) 225-9964 (*www.PreventSexualAssault.army.mil*)

EXTREMISM

Although the Constitution guarantees freedom of speech and association, soldiers do not have the right to use these freedoms to infringe upon the rights of others.

Policy

Chapter 4-12 of AR 600-20, *Army Command Policy*, makes it clear that participation in extremist organizations or activities is inconsistent with the responsibilities of military service. It defines extremist organizations and activities as those "that advocate racial, gender, or ethnic hatred or intolerance; advocate, create, or engage in illegal discrimination based on race, color, sex, religion, or national origin; advocate the use of or use force or violence or unlawful means to deprive individuals of their rights under the [U.S.] Constitution or the laws of the United States, or any state, by unlawful means."

By regulation, soldiers are prohibited from the following actions in support of extremist organizations or activities:

1. Participating in a public demonstration or rally.
2. Attending a meeting or activity with knowledge that the meeting or activity involves an extremist cause when on duty, when in uniform, when in a foreign country (whether on or off duty or in uniform), when it constitutes a breach of law and order, when violence is likely to result, or when in violation of off-limits sanctions or a commander's order.
3. Fund-raising.
4. Recruiting or training members (including encouraging others to join).
5. Creating, organizing, or taking a visible leadership role in such an organization or activity.
6. Distributing literature on or off a military installation when the primary purpose and content of which concerns advocacy or support of extremist causes, organizations, or activities, and it appears that the literature presents a clear danger to the loyalty, discipline, or morale of military personnel or if the distribution would materially interfere with the accomplishment of a military mission.

Penalties for violations of these prohibitions include the full range of statutory and regulatory sanctions, both criminal (Uniform Code of Military Justice [UCMJ]) and administrative.

Command Authority

Commanders have the authority to prohibit military personnel from engaging or participating in any other activities that the commander determines will adversely affect good order and discipline or morale within the command. This includes, but is not limited to, the authority to order the removal of symbols, flags, posters, or other displays from barracks; to place areas or activities off-limits (see AR 190-24); or to order soldiers not to participate in those activities that are contrary to good order and discipline or morale of the unit or that pose a threat to the health, safety, and security of military personnel or a military installation.

HUMAN IMMUNODEFICIENCY VIRUS (HIV) AND AIDS

Military readiness, medical, and personnel policies associated with human immunodeficiency virus (HIV) and acquired immunodeficiency syndrome (AIDS) are an effort to protect the Army's ability both to fulfill its constitutional role and to confidentially identify, evaluate, and provide an appropriate level of care for infected members.

Policy

Active soldiers are tested biennially for the AIDS virus, reserve component soldiers every five years. Soldiers who are HIV-positive will not be deployed outside the continental United States (CONUS); Alaska, Hawaii, and Puerto Rico are considered CONUS in this definition. The fact that HIV-positive soldiers are nondeployable does not preclude their assignment to table of organization and equipment (TOE) or modified table of organization and equipment (MTOE) units, except for Ranger and Special Forces units, which are totally closed to soldiers in either of these categories. Soldiers who are HIV-positive are eligible for all military professional development schools and may also attend formal military training to qualify them for reclassification, provided the schooling does not exceed twenty weeks.

Mandatory testing and HIV prevention awareness are being emphasized Army-wide. Soldiers and their families must learn to understand how to avoid and prevent the spread of the disease. AR 600-110, "Identification, Surveillance, and Administration of Personnel Infected with Human Immunodeficiency Virus," provides greater detail as needed.

MARRIAGE OF JUNIOR ENLISTED SOLDIERS

The old saying, "If the Army wanted you to have a wife, it would have issued you one," has gone by the wayside. So has the quaint custom whereby a soldier had to get his company commander's permission to get married. Although much of this was done as a courtesy to inform the commander, it did give the company commander—the "old man"—a chance to talk to the young soldier and to discuss the pros and cons of getting married at this particular stage of life.

Marriage is a commitment to fidelity, love, mutual support, and mutual sacrifice. Junior-grade soldiers should make a serious self-assessment to determine whether they are ready to assume these responsibilities. There are several areas to consider:

Money. Can you afford to be married? The wise soldier, like the wise civilian, makes a careful evaluation of whether his or her salary, combined with their intended spouse, can support a marriage at this time.

Maturity. Sociologists tell us that the kinds of things you believe are important in a spouse when you are very young are likely to be different after about the age of twenty-five. The wise soldier thinks twice about the real meaning of marriage and whether he or she is on solid emotional ground before making the commitment to being a husband or a wife. If you are a member of a church or religious faith, you can check with your chaplain, since many denominations require multiweek prenuptial counseling before the clergyman will perform the marriage service. If your denomination requires this, it is a great way to receive professional/trained experience on what can be expected of both of you, and can strengthen your relationship at the same time.

Duty and Deployment. For more than a decade, America has experienced a large increase in the number of deployments to far-flung locations. In nearly all cases, deployments for married soldiers mean family separation. Although the Army has programs and family support groups for the spouses and families of deployed soldiers, all soldiers should consider the impact of their absence on their marital situation and the burdens this places on the spouse. For some, this will be no problem. For those who might have married too young or with too little income, it can spell unhappiness for both the soldier and the spouse.

Dual-Service Marriages. Some soldiers believe that if they marry a fellow soldier, they will not have to face the problems of separation during deployment or field exercises. This might be the situation at the moment of a marriage proposal, but it is not a guarantee that two soldiers will always share the same duty or even be in the same unit. The Army tries to assign married service couples to the same post or as close as possible within the same geographic location, depending on MOS vacancies, but you might not always end up in the same unit. Hundreds of dual-service couples have faced this situation without problems, but you should be aware of it before tying the knot. See chapter 12, "Assignments," for more details.

DIVORCE

Divorce is hard on everyone involved, and the military does tend to equal or even exceed the trend for number of divorces when compared to the general American population. The Army has available a number of family counseling services. The Family Services Center (discussed later), the post or unit chaplain, or even your sergeants and officers can help if you want to save your marriage. If your differences seem irreconcilable, then check with your local legal office to determine the legal requirements for divorce in your state.

SPOUSE AND FAMILY ABUSE

Do not ever, under any circumstances, abuse your spouse or children in any manner, physically or mentally. It is both a criminal and a moral offense. If you even suspect that you have tendencies to abuse family members, seek counseling immediately. The Army Family Advocacy Program, located at your Army Community Services Office, provides counseling and tools for both soldiers and family members. Information and counseling extends beyond victim advocacy and includes new parent support and other programs that can help reduce stressors that sometimes lead to violence or other types of abuse. The programs can also serve to take relationships in the other direction, strengthening them through education and guided, open communication. The Army is a rough-and-tumble profession, and the Army requires tough soldiers. Keep the rough-and-tumble out of your family.

SOLDIER PREGNANCY AND SINGLE PARENTHOOD

For many years, the Army has afforded pregnant soldiers options other than immediate discharge. Today, a pregnant soldier is faced with a number of choices based on Army policy, and she needs to understand these policies up front. These choices are spelled out in chapter 10, "Career Decisions."

Staying in the military as a mother of a newborn child does not afford the military mother special privileges. Although the Army is concerned for the welfare of the child, it does not adjust the assignment process to accommodate the new mother. Instead, the Army requires each soldier with family members unable to care for themselves to file an approved family care plan. Because the soldier must be ready to deploy anywhere in the world on a moment's notice, the family care plan is necessary so that the Army knows that the child will be cared for in the event the mother is deployed overseas with her unit or assigned to an area where family members are not authorized.

Married mothers usually face fewer problems, since the spouse will automatically have custody of the children and is assumed to be capable of caring for them if the mother is deployed or assigned to a no-dependents area. Unmarried military mothers have to make other guaranteed arrangements for children and document them in their family care plans, which are registered with the first sergeant.

INDEBTEDNESS

Few things will make your first sergeant or company commander more upset than receiving letters from your creditors because you have bought more than your salary can pay for. This is not just a soldier problem; it's a DOD-wide problem affecting airmen, sailors, marines, and coast guardsmen as well, predominantly those in the junior enlisted grades.

The major culprits leading to indebtedness are:

- The "gotta-have-it-now" attitude.
- Undisciplined use of credit cards.
- Buying big-ticket items that are not really needed (e.g., expensive vehicles).
- Excessive entertainment.

The reason first sergeants and company commanders are upset with soldier indebtedness is because it takes so much of their time to deal with it. One military service, for instance, had the incredible record of receiving 123,000 letters of indebtedness; furthermore, 99,000 bad checks passed through the Post Exchange and another 75,000 passed through the commissary—in one year!

To reduce the size of this problem, the DOD has issued a compact disk training program called "Financial Tips" that is available at the education center, and there are numerous financial service and budgeting programs for soldiers and their families at the local Army Community Services Office.

A good source of information for soldier financial planning is Stackpole's *Armed Forces Guide to Personal Financial Planning*, 5th edition, which was written specifically to help servicemembers manage money and is chock-full of sound advice. Likewise, Stackpole's *Servicemembers Legal Guide* is an excellent source of information on marriage, divorce, and the legal aspects of indebtedness.

ALCOHOL AND DRUG ABUSE

A drug is defined as "any substance that by its chemical nature alters structure or function in the living organism (AR 600-85)." This definition includes alcohol, glue, and aerosols, among many others. The harm and misery these substances have caused to soldiers are incalculable.

Soldiers who use drugs and those who sell drugs do not belong in the U.S. Army. A soldier who relies on alcohol to make it through the day or one who feels that he or she must turn to alcohol or some drug to get by or get high should have the personal courage to quit or to seek help from the local Army Substance Abuse Program (ASAP). Each unit at company level and above has an ASAP NCO/Officer available to help.

Alcohol Abuse

AR 600-85 states that the use of alcohol is legal, provided the consumer is of legal age. Alcohol is socially acceptable, if used in moderation. Excessive use of alcohol is not condoned or accepted in general, nor as part of any military event, as it does not fit within the values of the Army profession. As an Army athlete, maintaining optimum health and capability is a key component. Abuse of alcohol directly takes away from this ability, in addition to its other detrimental effects and potential consequences. Of course, alcohol is never permitted while on duty, unless approved in unique circumstances by a general officer. If you think or know you have a drinking problem, you can receive help through the ASAP program without reprisal, provided you refer yourself prior to any event or circumstance that causes your commander to direct it. Referrals directed by your commander will also result in your having help available, but in those cases would not protect you from reprisal for whatever caused the commander to direct it.

Drug Abuse

Any soldier who is caught trafficking, buying, selling, or using illegal drugs will be immediately processed for separation from the Army, with the exception of self-referrals. They will also face the potential to be subject to a trial by court martial or nonjudicial punishment under Article 15 of the Uniform Code of Military Justice (UCMJ), including loss of pay, reduction in grade, and the stigma of conviction attached to their official files. Soldiers caught using drugs are referred to a mandatory ASAP for rehabilitation. The Army, however, has a very strict "no-tolerance" attitude toward drug abuse, and ASAP treatment does not protect against the Army initiating separation action and punishment against the soldier. Don't do drugs.

ELECTRONIC MEDIA

The Army, like the rest of the world, has embraced electronic media, and it has provided a fantastic improvement in the speed and capability for the Army and leaders to get messages out to intended audiences. Likewise, social media has dramatically changed communication within the ranks and between leaders and their soldiers. Beyond "texting" a note to squad members about a change to formation or sending an e-mail with the week's training included, many leaders maintain Facebook or Twitter (and other) accounts to help them be more connected to their soldiers. Many senior Army leaders also maintain these pages, and there are numerous web and blog sites that cater to military audiences as well.

With all of these great opportunities and improvements comes responsibility. The issues of cyber bullying, use of sites to make unprofessional or disparaging comments, and uploading inappropriate photographs or other images is a situation that has gained the attention of top military leaders including the chairman of the Joint Chiefs of Staff, secretary of the Army, chief of staff of the Army, and sergeant major of the Army. Each has made comments concerning the need for soldiers to remain professional at all times, on and off duty, and this includes their actions and presence on social media and other sites. A great way to ensure you are not out of tolerance of Army values and expectation is to picture yourself saying or showing whatever you intend to post in front of your unit in formation. If that physical "show and tell" would be inappropriate or embarrassing, then you should seriously consider not posting the comment/image, or adjusting it so that it conveys you as a professional. Remember that you can actually be punished under the UCMJ for posting statements or images that are disrespectful to superiors or otherwise violate military law, and that once you hit the send button, you are no longer in control of what is now in the public eye.

PART II

The Soldier

5

Self-Development

As we look at training, education and professional development, Soldiers are afforded three pillars of development throughout their Army experience. The institutional Army consists of all of the professional development schools we attend throughout our Army career. The institutional pillar is the smallest pillar in what we learn during our life in the Army, but, these schools provide a critical piece of development that serves as the glue that keeps us grounded to doctrine, policy and the art and science of being a Soldier. Operational assignments are the largest pillar and have the greatest impact on who we become during our careers and throughout our lives. The leaders, the responsibilities, the people, the missions and assignments all make us who we become. The self-development pillar of learning is the key piece that sets us apart from our peers, it is the difference between being good and becoming great. Self-development provides us with the broadening perspectives that enable Soldiers throughout their careers and in positions of increased responsibility to act with maturity, subjectivity and critical thinking. Organizational programs that promote self-development should include the reading and study of operator, field and training manuals, Army regulations, unit policies and all the things that are not taught in the institution or fall low on the priority list of things to get done during the duty day. Self-development includes the academic studies in civilian institutions that enhance our occupational, leadership and management careers. Bottom line, there is no substitute for the unique and repeated experiences gained in each of these three pillars.

—SMA Kenneth O. Preston, Sergeant Major of the Army, 2004–2011

The Army's system for promotion is discussed in detail in chapter 13. This chapter offers thoughts, some supporting programs, and proven methods for developing yourself in your current profession—soldier. Individual development is one of the keys to promotion, and the first step in that process is to set goals for yourself. The quote introducing this chapter is great advice, and the more areas and tasks you can focus on each week, the more success you should enjoy. Certainly, you do not want to overdo it, but having two or three focused goals in areas that can use improvement (like new skills in your job) is sensible.

SETTING PROFESSIONAL GOALS

Everyone wants to be promoted at some point in his or her career. No one can stay forever at the same rank. The Army's retention control points force you to move up or out. Look at where you want to be five years down the road and begin working to that end today. Waiting until you are a specialist or corporal to start working toward sergeant means that it will take you longer to acquire the necessary promotion points than soldiers who started when they were privates through privates first class.

In all military occupational specialties (MOSs), some common elements are necessary for development and promotion. Four items common to all soldiers in the grades private to specialist are:

1. Develop MOS skills.

2. Qualify with your assigned weapon.

3. Maintain physical fitness.

4. Complete Structured Self Development 1 (SSD-1).

With the new changes in the promotion system, much of your fate rests in your own hands. Work hard to identify yourself to the chain of command (and later the promotion board) as the best soldier.

Soldiers seeking promotion can directly influence their qualifications by making improvements in all four key elements. First, you should be performing duties in your primary MOS at the authorized or next higher grade. Take advantage of any opportunity to serve in a leadership position at the next higher grade. Second, ensure you are spending adequate time in completing Structured Self Development 1. Waiting until you are told to do so or when promotion time comes around is folly and also indicates to your chain of command that you are not hungry for success or a self-starter. Third, attend any locally available military schools that you can at this stage in your career. The schools found at your installation can vary from air assault, combat lifesaver, nuclear, biological, and chemical (NBC) defense, or field sanitation. Finally, you should take advantage of every opportunity to attend military and civilian schools that improve your skills. Begin taking Army correspondence courses early in your career. Take college courses if you are in a position to do so. The additional military and civilian education you obtain on your own shows the chain of command that you are a self-starter seeking to improve yourself. Additionally, military and civilian schooling will improve your chances for promotion by converting educational credit into promotion points.

To keep things in perspective, however, remember that leaders look to your duty performance when recommending you for initial promotions. In an interview conducted in 1998, Sergeant Major of the Army Robert E. Hall commented that he "would like every soldier to get a master's degree—a master's degree in soldiering." While civilian education is and continues to grow in importance—and a whole chapter in this book is dedicated to it—all the schooling in the world does not replace the necessity for a highly competent soldier at work.

Seek Advice

You should actively seek information and guidance from your chain of command, mentors, and career adviser. You must play an integral part in the decision and assignment process to help attain the goals you have set. Your career branch at the Human Resources Command (HRC) is also there to assist you in determining what is right for you, both professionally and personally. You should maintain communication with your branch to inquire about your next assignment or school. For information or assistance, call (888)-ARMYHRC (888-276-9472) in the United States or Defense Switched Network (DSN) 938-9500, or e-mail *askhrc.army@us.army.mil*. More details are provided for assignment processes and management in chapter 12.

As mentioned in chapter 2, the Basic Leader Course (BLC) is the first level of the Noncommissioned Officer Education System (NCOES) and is a requirement for promotion to the rank of sergeant. This course prepares specialists and corporals (E-4) for leadership and increased levels of responsibility. Promotions (chapter 13) are governed by AR 600-8-19, *Enlisted Promotions and Reductions*. Department of the Army (DA) controls the time in service (TIS) and time in grade (TIG) requirements for promotion. Commanders have the latitude to waive both TIS and TIG to promote outstanding soldiers ahead of their peers. DA controls the rate of promotion to sergeant (E-5) and staff sergeant (E-6), but the local battalion selects the soldiers for promotion at locally conducted promotion boards. Your completion of Structured Self Development 1 will allow you to be considered for attending the promotion board should the chain of command select you.

STRUCTURED SELF DEVELOPMENT

Structured Self Development is an education program built to support and enhance the formal training received at institutional training, such as AIT and BLC. It is a key goal for you to ensure is in your self-development plan. It also supports the intent of the Army to create a lifelong learning model for all soldiers and links operational assignments to institutional education. There are five levels of this training, which are required for completion while assigned to units throughout your career. You may have already begun or completed the first level of training (SSD-1), but if not, be sure to talk with your leadership to ensure that you are not left behind. This training is mandatory for attendance at the next level of schooling and promotion, and is another great way to show your local leadership and the Army that you are serious about being a professional soldier. As you progress up the career ladder, the next levels will precede and augment your attendance at each of the NCOES levels of education and training.

ARMY CAREER TRACKER (ACT)

In addition to your chain of command and other sources discussed above, the Army Career Tracker is a powerful tool to help you manage your self-development goals.

The ACT allows and assists you in creating an Individual Development Plan (IDP) that includes your goals, education, training, and assignment information. You can select a mentor, and your own leaders can also help you with monitoring and ensuring that you are meeting the goals that are highlighted as a result of your IDP. You can also use this tool to search several education and training sites and connect with your peers as well. Access to the Army Career Tracker is found at *https://actnow.army.mil.*

MOS KNOWLEDGE
The Army rewards selfless, dedicated, confident, competent service. If you are among the best in your MOS at your skill level, NCOs and officers will view your professional potential favorably. It will help promotion, school, and training selection boards identify and select you to be among the soldiers who will lead the Army in the future. Ignoring your professional self-development can result in substandard job performance or, worse, mission failure at a critical time and place. Your knowledge in your occupational specialty, whatever it is, is important. Like all the MOSs in your unit, your technical expertise is essential to the accomplishment of your unit's mission. Be an expert in your MOS.

MILITARY EDUCATION
If you wait for the Army to send you to school to acquire military education promotion points, you will be waiting a very long time. The quickest way to achieve your 200-point goal is through the Army correspondence course program. Start earning points when you are a private or private first class, and have your military education maxed out when you are first eligible for promotion to sergeant. These same points carry over for promotion to staff sergeant.

Army Correspondence Course Program
A variety of exportable training courses specific to your career management field (CMF) and MOS are available through the Army Correspondence Course Program (ACCP). Courses and subcourses on specific topics developed by respective proponent schools are designed for your professional development. Students enrolling in individual study decide which courses to take and when to study the lessons and take the examination. Students register and enroll through the Army Institute for Professional Development (AIPD) website at *www.atsc.army.mil/tadlp/accp.*

A course consists of one or more subcourses designed to support a specific professional field, skill qualification development, or MOS-related tasks. Subcourses are issued in the sequence listed in each course. A subcourse is a basic unit of training covering one subject area, containing one or more lessons and a final examination.

The credit hour is the basic work unit for a correspondence course. The number of credit hours assigned to a subcourse is based on the estimated time required for an average student to read the material and complete all the exercises and the examination. Five hours of subcourse work equates to one military education promotion point. All subcourses for a correspondence course must be completed before any subcourse promotion points can be added to the promotion point total. This is the Army sending everyone a message that following through and completing what they start is important.

Job training is continuous.

Army E-Learning

Similar to the Army Correspondence Courses discussed above, the Army also offers about 4,800 courses under the e-Learning program. These courses further support the Individual Development Plan within the Army Career Tracker and are managed and accessed via the Army Training Requirements and Resources System (ATRRS). Subject matter including foreign languages, business, leadership, information technology, and others provide even more options for soldiers to consider as they look to increase their education and self-development. In addition to the one promotion point for every five hours as in correspondence courses, some of these programs are eligible for American Council on Education (ACE) college credit. This is a fantastic benefit in addition to your individual professional development. Check out the many choices available by logging on and registering at *https://www.atrrs.army.mil/selfdevctr.*

Soldier of the Month/Best Warrior Competition

Another important self-development program available to all soldiers is the Soldier of the Month Board/Best Warrior Competition. This program tests your ability in a variety of subjects and is a powerful way to show your local leadership that you are a dedicated professional. These boards require plenty of individual study on a range of topics and physical board appearances where you must answer military-topical questions asked by senior NCOs of the unit and are evaluated on your physical appearance (uniform/fitness), as well as ability to speak and think critically on many different topics. Boards typically start at the company level and, if successful, can take you through nearly every level of command up to the U.S. Army–level Best Warrior Competition. These boards are also a fantastic way to practice for the promotion board held at battalion level when competing for sergeant and staff sergeant. See your team or squad leader to find out how to enter this exciting professional competition.

Other Sources for Individual Development

Two books written especially for soldier development and promotion are Walter J. Jackson's *Soldier's Study Guide*, 7th edition (Mechanicsburg, PA: Stackpole Books, 2013) and Audie G. Lewis's *Career Progression Guide for Soldiers*, 4th edition (Mechanicsburg, PA: Stackpole Books, 2015). Both books should be available in Post Exchange bookstores or military clothing sales stores, or from the publisher.

IMPROVING BASIC LANGUAGE SKILLS

Reading and writing are critical skills for all soldiers. The Army depends on and must have in its ranks soldiers who read, comprehend, and communicate effectively in writing. Your ability to read, comprehend, and respond in writing to orders and directives from superiors is very important for all leaders. Your reading ability will be assessed when you attend the mandatory NCOES's Basic Leader Course (BLC), the first rung in the NCOES ladder. You must read at the tenth-grade level or face a likely consequence of nonenrollment. Chapter 6, "Continuing Civilian Education," discusses in detail programs that can help, and the tips below are good starting points in that direction.

If you have trouble reading and writing, get help at your local Army Education Center. An education counselor will assist you in identifying any literacy shortcomings. Once you know your reading and writing weaknesses, the counselor can help you enroll in courses designed to turn the weaknesses into strengths. It is better to discover and fix reading deficiencies and writing defects before some critical point in your career.

Much of Army writing is hard to understand and therefore wastes the time of the readers. When you write a military document, be sure to follow this important rule: Put the meaning of your communication in the first paragraph, in the first sentence, if possible. When you write clearly and simply, the material is easy to comprehend.

Common writing problems involve misuse of sentence structure, grammar, punctuation, mechanics, usage, tense, agreement, and "gobbledygook"—avoidable "padding" that hides meaning. Avoid gobbledygook; keep explanations of points you must make to a minimum. Use military jargon only if it is necessary. Avoid the overuse of acronyms. If you have to use acronyms, explain them before using them. One of the best sources to refine your writing skills is William A. McIntosh's *Guide to Effective Military Writing*, 3d edition (Mechanicsburg, PA: Stackpole Books, 2003).

The best way to improve your writing skills and your reading ability is to read a variety of books, magazines, and newspapers. Reading stimulates the intellect and increases your understanding of people and events. Read more than one book on a subject; challenge yourself to comprehend complex ideas and issues. Stay tuned to topics that pertain to national events, such as human rights, free enterprise, democracy, liberty, and prosperity. Read stories in daily newspapers about business, politics, and environmental issues, about how these matters relate in the global marketplace, and how they affect other nations.

Stay informed. Read to understand America's role in the world, the Army's role in America, and your role in America's Army.

PERSONAL REFERENCE LIBRARY AND RECOMMENDED READING

What follows are the works that most affected my attitudes toward my service as a soldier and that I recommend to others. Most lend a historical perspective and deal with issues we are all faced with: duty, morale, ethics, training, and leadership, especially that of the small unit in extreme circumstances. Many look at leaders who are looking at themselves.

Nonfiction

Stephen Ambrose, *Band of Brothers*
William G. Bainbridge, *Top Sergeant*
Center of Military History, U.S. Army, *American Military History*
T. R. Fehrenbach, *This Kind of War*
Ernest F. Fisher, *Guardians of the Republic: A History of the Noncommissioned Officer Corps of the U.S. Army*
David Hogan, *A Concise History of the U.S. Army: Two Hundred and Twenty-five Years of Service*
Elbert Hubbard, *A Message to Garcia*
John Keegan, *The Face of Battle*
Dandridge "Mike" Malone, *Small Unit Leadership*
Harold Moore and Joe Galloway, *We Were Soldiers Once . . . and Young*
Robert S. Rush, *GI: The US Infantryman in World War II*
Sam Watkins, *Co. Aytch*
Sergeants Major Academy, *Long Hard Road: NCO Experiences in Afghanistan and Iraq*
SMA Jack Tilley and CSM Dan Elder (USA, Retired), *Soldier for Life*

Fiction

Jean Larteguy, *The Centurions*
Anton Myrer, *Once an Eagle*
Guy Sager, *Forgotten Soldier*

Poetry

Rudyard Kipling, "The 'Eathen" and "If"
Robert W. Service, "The Quitter"

Other Works

Other recommended history and historical figure books include *The Civil War* by renowned author Shelby Foote and *1776* by David McCullough.

Though they were not intended as literary works, the U.S. Constitution and the Bill of Rights are worth your time as well, as are other historic government documents. Read about civic matters to learn more about the U.S. government and the Army's role in it.

Stackpole Books, publisher of *Enlisted Soldier's Guide*, offers more than one hundred other titles of interest to the military reader.

Soldiers, the official monthly magazine of the Army, is also a recommended source of feature information about unit activities and Army people. It is now published online as is the *Army Times* weekly newspaper and *Army* magazine, the monthly journal of the Association of the U.S. Army. These publications contain professional information and will help you keep abreast of current topics and where the Army is headed as a profession.

Official Doctrine and Guidance

You should also read material about specific subjects that become increasingly important to professional soldiers. As you read through study guides, websites, and articles that discuss relevant topics, pay attention to the doctrinal source and make a point to read the actual regulation, pamphlet, or field manual. An example you will see in this guide, reference to promotions, is made with AR 600-8-19, *Enlisted Promotions and Reductions*. While the guides and articles are great tools, nothing substitutes the actual rules and requirements found in those sources. This is true whether you are reading about physical fitness, leadership, or any other topic. The majority of topics covered in this guide list the source, and reading the actual source documents can strengthen your knowledge of the topic and often reveal new information you had not seen covered in your initial study.

EXPLORING THE INFORMATION SUPERHIGHWAY: THE ARMY ONLINE AND THE WORLD WIDE WEB

The Army has long embraced the information superhighway, with hundreds of sites currently online and more established daily. Computer literacy is vital for soldiers of all ranks, because it enables you to receive and transmit text and supporting communications across vast electronic networks. No longer do you have to thumb through old copies of the *Army Times* or look for the latest Human Resources Command (HRC) message to find information vital to your career. Just go to the HRC home page and view the most up-to-date information concerning your MOS. Entire books are online at the Center of Military History's home page. Need to prepare a class on the most current techniques to breach a minefield? Try the Center for Army Lessons Learned. It's all there—you just have to look.

The Internet

The Internet is the worldwide free-enterprise network of computers that links distant sites. It is a combination of tens of thousands of computer servers linked to computer users via telephone lines or direct circuits. Each server is a separate "site" with a unique numeric name. Another name for part of the Internet is the World Wide Web, shortened to *www* or the Web.

Web Pages

A Web page is the graphical presentation of a document on the Web. Usually each page contains one type or grouping of information with "links" to other subpages or to other Web pages at different sites. Web pages can be as simple as text pages or can be as complex as pages with pictures, animated images, video clips, and attached sound files.

U.S. Army Online

Listed below are some of the more popular websites that deal with military issues. No longer do you have to wait in the dark for the word to be passed down on Army issues. You can now go to the source.

Adjutant General Directorate
https://www.hrc.army.mil/content/The%20Adjutant%20General%20Directorate
APFT Score Converter
www.apftcalculator.com
Army and Air Force Exchange Service
www.shopmyexchange.com
Army Continuing Education System
https://www.armyeducation.army.mil/
Army Correspondence Course Program
https://www.atsc.army.mil/accp
Army Electronic Forms
http://armypubs.army.mil/
Army home page
www.army.mil
Army Housing
https://www.housing.army.mil
Army Knowledge Online access page
www.us.army.mil
Army National Guard
http://arng.ng.mil/SitePages/Home.aspx
Army Lodging
www.armymwr.com/travel/lodging/
Army Public Affairs
www.army.mil/info/institution/publicAffairs
Army Publishing Agency (USAPA)
www.apd.army.mil
Army Reserve
www.usar.army.mil
Army Retirement Services
www.soldierforlife.army.mil/retirement
Army Sergeants Major Academy
http://usasma.armylive.dodlive.mil
Army Substance Abuse Program
https://www.acsap.army.mil/

Army Training Network
  www.adtdl.army.mil
Army Training Requirements and Resources System (ATRRS)
  https://www.atrrs.army.mil/
Assignment Satisfaction Key (ASK)
  https://www.hrc.army.mil/content/Assignment%20Satisfaction%20Key
Association of the U.S. Army
  www.ausa.org/
CALL (Center for Army Lessons Learned)
  http://usacac.army.mil/organizations/mccoe/call
Center of Military History (CMH)
  www.history.army.mil
Comprehensive Soldier and Family Fitness (CSF2)
  http://www.acsim.army.mil/readyarmy/ra_csf.htm
Defense Finance and Accounting Service
  www.dfas.mil
DefenseLink
  www.defense.gov
Defense Travel System (DTS)
  http://www.defensetravel.osd.mil/
Department of Veterans' Affairs
  www.va.gov
DOD Dictionary
  www.dtic.mil/doctrine/dod_dictionary
Enlisted National Guard Association
  www.eangus.org
Enlisted Personnel Management Directorate (HRC)
  https://www.hrc.army.mil/Enlisted/Enlisted%20Personnel%20Management%20
    Directorate
GulfLink
  www.gulflink.osd.mil
Headquarters, Department of the Army
  www.hqda.army.mil
Human Resources Command
  www.hrc.army.mil
Human Resources Command, Enlisted Personnel Management Directorate (HRC EPMD)
  https://www.hrc.army.mil/Enlisted/Enlisted%20Personnel%20Management%20
    Directorate
Human Resources Command, Enlisted Promotions Branch
  https://www.hrc.army.mil/TAGD/Enlisted%20Promotions
Installations and Facilities—Installation Management Command (IMCOM)
  https://www.imcom.army.mil/
iPERMS
  https://iperms.hrc.army.mil

Medals and Ribbons/Awards
https://www.hrc.army.mil//TAGD/Awards and Decorations Branch
Military One Source
www.militaryonesource.mil
MILPER Messages
https://www.hrc.army.mil/milper/
Military Review magazine
http://usacac.army.mil/CAC2/MilitaryReview/
My Army Benefits
http://myarmybenefits.us.army.mil
My Pay
https://mypay.dfas.mil
MyRecords Portal (HRC)
https://www.hrcapps.army.mil/portal
NCO Journal
http://ncojournal.dodlive.mil
Pentagon Library
www.whs.mil/library
Per Diem
www.gsa.gov/perdiemrates
PS magazine
https://www.logsa.army.mil/psmag/pshome.cfm
Retention and Reenlistment
www.armyreenlistment.com
S1 Net
https://www.milsuite.mil
SHARP
www.sexualassault.army.mil
Soldier for Life (SFL)
www.soldierforlife.army.mil
SFL-Transition Assistance Program
https://www.SFL-TAP.army.mil
Soldiers magazine online
http://soldiers.dodlive.mil
Thrift Savings Plan
www.tsp.gov
Training and Doctrine Digital Library
www.train.army.mil/
Training Support Center, Army (ATSC)
www.atsc.army.mil/
TRICARE home page
www.tricare.mil
USAJOBS (OPM)
www.usajobs.gov

U.S. Army Reserve
www.usar.army.mil
Veterans' Affairs OEF/IF website
www.oefoif.va.gov

PROFESSIONAL ASSOCIATIONS

The Army is a profession. Like many other professions, the Army has professional organizations that serve many purposes. They are a great way to meet like-minded soldiers. You will very likely have a regimental association that is local to your duty assignment and one that is at the national level. This is true for infantry, armor, AG, and so forth. Joining associations shows your commitment to your craft and is a great way to find more senior folks who can provide valuable information and professional development in a social or learning environment. A couple of larger associations that additionally lobby Congress for the Army or otherwise are also listed here. Talk with your NCO and officer leadership; they can let you know of the organizations available to you based on your career management field (CMF) or military occupational specialty (MOS).

Association of the U.S. Army

The Association of the U.S. Army (AUSA) is a private, nonprofit organization established in 1950. It supports active and reserve component members, Army civilians, retirees, and Army families. Its goals are as follows:

- People support for those in the Army.
- Industry support of the Army.
- Public education about the Army.
- Professionalism within the Army.

AUSA's legislative affairs office stays on top of issues that affect soldiers during and after service. The association pushes for pay equity, adequate military housing, cost-of-living allowances, and standard subsistence allowances for all personnel, as well as full reimbursement of expenses for official travel and changes of station, quality medical and dental care, and an upgraded retirement system.

Regular membership costs are stepped according to grade: $21 per year for grades E-1 through E-4, $26 for E-5 through E-7, and $31 for E-8 and E-9. Among its membership benefits are opportunities to participate in chapter activities and discount product and service programs, along with subscription to *Army Magazine* and the monthly *AUSA News.*

For more information, check the AUSA website at *www.ausa.org*, or call (855) 246-6269 or e-mail *membersupport@ausa.org.*

Noncommissioned Officers Association

The Noncommissioned Officers Association (NCOA) is a federally chartered, nonprofit, fraternal association founded in 1960. The NCOA seeks to promote health, prosperity, and scholarship among its members and their families through legislative and benevolent programs to improve benefits for soldiers, veterans, and their families and survivors.

Through its office near the Pentagon, NCOA actively lobbies Congress, the White House, the Department of Veterans Affairs, the military services, and other federal agencies to fulfill its goals. It monitors state and local administrative and legislative activities affecting NCOA members, conducts a nationwide outreach program for hospitalized veterans, and operates fellowship and intern programs for undergraduate college students.

Annual membership for NCOs costs $30. The association offers many member benefits, including a certified merchants program and a buying network. Members also receive the *NCOA Journal* and may qualify for the NCOA World MasterCard.

For more information, write to Noncommissioned Officers Association, Attn: Membership Processing, 9330 Corporate Dr., Ste. 701, Selma, TX 78154; call (800) 662-2620; or check out the website at *www.ncoausa.org*.

Reserve Officers Association (ROA)

(Serving America's commissioned and noncommissioned reserve component leaders). Since its founding by General John "Black Jack" Pershing in 1922, the Reserve Officers Association has been the nation's leading advocate for all Reservists. ROA, for example, got Reservists unlimited use of the commissary. ROA's purpose is to support and promote pay and benefits, professional education, policy, and equipment for our nation's Reserve and Guard and care for our veterans. ROA is active and effective on Capitol Hill and with the military's leadership, ensuring a strong and respected reserve component.

America's newest generation of Reservists has made great contributions in uniform; they want to contribute further. ROA members in every state welcome new members to share camaraderie and support reserve component and veteran issues in their community. These citizen-warriors deserve a dedicated voice in shaping government policy: ROA provides that voice. Together ROA's members create one voice for one fight. Visit *https://www.roa.org/* to see its publications, benefits, events, congressional information, and membership information.

For more information, call (800) 809-9448 or write to ROA, 1 Constitution Ave. NE, Washington, DC 20002; or e-mail *memberservices@roa.org*.

National Guard Enlisted Association

The National Guard Enlisted Association (EANGUS) exists to promote the status, welfare, and professionalism of the enlisted members of the National Guard of the United States and promote adequate national security.

EANGUS has a home page at *www.eangus.org*. Users can access the congressional database system, the Senate, the House, EANGUS's *New Patriot* magazine and newsletter, *Congressional Quarterly*, *Legislative Updates*, and more. You can e-mail to get in touch with the various departments at the national office that can answer your questions regarding membership, events, and legislative issues.

For more information, call toll-free (800) 234-EANG (3264) or write to Enlisted Association of the National Guard of the United States, 3133 Mount Vernon Ave., Alexandria, VA 22305; or e-mail *eangus@eangus.org*.

6

Continuing Civilian Education

The Army offers each soldier $4,000 per year of tuition assistance (TA) benefit for college, and once the year has passed, they cannot go back and retrieve that money. Over a twenty-year career, that adds up to $76,000 (the first year is not authorized TA at this writing). It is a no-brainer, then, to get every dime of that well-earned entitlement. Higher education may very likely be the most valuable, lifelong asset you can take from the Army when looking for civilian employment, after one enlistment, or after an entire career.

—SGM Tom Gills, MPA (USA, Ret.), Author, *Enlisted Soldier's Guide,* 8th Edition

A critical aspect of your self-development and a key part of lifelong learning is continuing civilian education. This chapter is solely dedicated to that aspect, clearly indicating its importance. Enlisting in today's Army comes with significant monetary benefits in civilian education opportunities. Those benefits can start immediately with some programs and testing, and then continue for actual college classes after serving one year if you are on active duty and if your duty assignment and location permit it. In addition, civilian education counts for a significant number of promotion points to sergeant and staff sergeant. Each college credit hour gained through an accredited source is worth 1.5 promotion points, and an associate's degree (normally sixty semester hours or ninety quarter hours) garners you even more points. A great many soldiers enlist in the Army with civilian education benefits comprising a big part of their decision, but then do not capitalize on the opportunities. As noted repeatedly in the sections that follow, utilizing counselors at your local/closest education center are your best bet to maximize those benefits, along with GoArmyEd and other web-based resources discussed in this chapter.

ARMY CONTINUING EDUCATION SYSTEM
The Army Continuing Education System (ACES), through its many programs, promotes lifelong learning opportunities and sharpens the competitive edge of the Army overall. ACES is committed to excellence in service, innovation, and deployability. Today's soldier can take advantage of numerous educational programs. The comprehensive website for Army education is GoArmyEd at *https://www.goarmyed.com/*

Your Army Continuing Education System Record, DA Form 669, is intended to serve a very important purpose during your military career—but requires deliberate action on your part to do so. It contains information used by education counselors to document your pursuit of higher education and help you plan the next steps as you advance through your civilian education and professional development plan. Every semester throughout your career, you should (whenever the mission allows) contribute course/equivalency test completion slips to your record. Just think of it as making regular deposits to an intellectual savings account, which will grow with enormous interest—the kind of interest that Army promotion boards and civilian employers will have in you as your educational value increases. Access to your DA Form 669 is easy to obtain, either through the "My Education" tab at Army Knowledge Online (AKO) or through the GoArmyEd website. A trip to your local Army Education Center is strongly advised when accessing the form, as their counselors are highly trained to help guide you in your education development path. More will be described about that powerful benefit of expertise below.

Invest in yourself; the Army does, and benefits in the process. The Army Continuing Education System mission is, in part, to improve the combat readiness of the Army by planning, researching, and implementing educational programs and services to support the professional and personal development of quality soldiers and their adult family members

The ACES meets its mission goals by providing quality educational programs and services throughout the Army. Education and training mutually support and enhance the combat readiness of the Army and are essential elements in the NCO Development Program. ACES programs and services are designed to expand soldiers' skills, knowledge, critical thinking ability, and behavior. Programs and services discussed later in this chapter contribute to the three pillars of leader development: institutional training, operational assignments, and self-development.

Individual development, supported by ACES, is a planned, progressive, sequential program that leaders use to enhance and sustain the leadership plan discussed earlier.

Under the guidelines of AR 621-5, you should meet the following educational objectives:

- Master academic skills needed to perform duties of your primary MOS and meet prerequisites for the NCO Education System.
- Obtain a high school diploma or equivalent if lacking and start your postsecondary education efforts during your first five years of service.
- Between the fifth and fifteenth year, earn your associate's degree or complete your education goal.
- By the seventh year, develop a lifelong learning professional and personal development plan and complete your bachelor's degree by your twentieth year. I strongly recommend that you do both, as a solid plan will greatly help lead to the degree.

ARMY EDUCATION CENTER AND COUNSELORS

The Army Education Center is chock-full of fantastic programs, testing capabilities, and other benefits. But the most important of the assets found there, in my view, are the actual counselors positioned to help you establish realistic educational goals and provide a path to attain those goals. They can also help you to get the maximum benefit from limited tuition assistance and other resources. Soldiers who are new to an installation are required by AR 621-5 to receive education counseling within the first thirty days of their arrival and then receive follow-up counseling as needed.

You should not need any regulation or requirement to motivate you to get educational counseling; you should hurry to take advantage of all the valuable advice and assistance that counselors provide. Counselors help with aspects of education such as school selection, application procedures, prerequisite assessments, and financial aid.

When they cannot help you locate financial aid for formal courses of instruction, counselors can recommend free alternative methods of obtaining educational credit (see Defense Activity for Nontraditional Education Support (DANTES), College Level Examination Program (CLEP), and Graduate Record Exam (GRE) under the "Independent Study and Examination Programs for College Credit" section below). Counselors and the education centers around the Army were absolutely essential in my degree completion during my service, and I would not be writing this book were it not for their invaluable programs, counsel, and advice over the years. They can do the same for you if you will only seek and then take action on their knowledge and help.

FUNCTIONAL ACADEMIC SKILLS TRAINING (FAST)

Functional Academic Skills Training (FAST) is a powerful program that gives soldiers who need it on- and off-duty courses and test preparation to improve their basic communication skills such as reading and writing. Within FAST is the Basic Skills Education Program (BSEP). Soldiers are offered this training and education to ensure they can perform their duties as required at acceptable levels of expectation and give commanders the ability to assume that this is the case. Courses such as the General Education Development (GED) exam, General Technical (GT) Improvement exam, and others not only help ensure the ability to perform one's duties, but they are also important programs to help prepare for advanced training and continuing education goals. Talk with your squad leader or section sergeant about this program, and be sure to mention it when visiting your post/installation education center.

HIGH SCHOOL COMPLETION PROGRAM

The High School Completion Program (HSCP) is an off-duty program that provides soldiers and adult family members the opportunity to earn a high school diploma or equivalency certificate. It is open to all non–high school graduates. Tuition assistance (TA) is authorized for soldiers up to 100 percent of the tuition costs of courses. ACES will pay TA only to accredited institutions and will not pay fees covering such items as books, matriculation, graduation, and parking.

GENERAL EDUCATION DEVELOPMENT (GED)

For some soldiers without a high school diploma, earning one as discussed above may not be the best or most viable option. The General Education Development (GED) exam can take the place of a high school diploma, and for those who feel they can complete this faster or easier than obtaining a high school diploma through the HSCP, this could be a viable option. Once again, this is where the counselors at the education center can play an important role in your education pathway, providing the type of detailed counseling needed to make the best choice based on personal circumstance, unit mission, and so on (see the section on "Army Education Center and Counselors" above).

COLLEGE DEGREE PROGRAMS

When it comes to education, the buzzword today in the Army and industry in general, and for the foreseeable future, is "credential." Postsecondary education leads to credentials through programs in vocational, occupational, technical, or academic fields. Thousands of degree programs are available to soldiers—far too many to list here. But you can use dedicated resources to find out more information about obtaining an associate's, bachelor's, or master's degree in arts or science.

If you want to take college courses but are concerned about your ability to comprehend course material, the *Army Training Network (ATN)* is a great option to use in building confidence. It is filled to the brim with offerings that will teach you the basics of many subjects needed to prepare for a dedicated degree/certification program. For example, suppose you want to earn an electrical engineering degree. You could contact your local education center to request the basic electricity course. The course is open to "any student who meets the basic qualifications for correspondence study." After successfully completing seventeen sequential electricity subcourses, you should be fully prepared to enroll in a college course that deals with the subject of electricity. Apply this method to other subjects, and you will see the value of "boning up" through correspondence studies. See the detailed courses and material offered at *www.train.army.mil* or stop by your post/installation education office.

CREDENTIALING OPPORTUNITIES ON LINE (COOL)

As discussed above, credentialing is a very important concept for every soldier, both while serving and as a transition consideration for employment once time in uniform is completed. The Credentialing Opportunities On Line (COOL) website, located at *https://www.cool.army.mil*, guides interested soldiers through the certifications and licensing related to their military occupational specialty. Many of these certifications can lead to promotion points for SGT and SSG. The site identifies those opportunities with an icon of a SGT and SSG rank next to those that are eligible for points. The COOL site is a tremendous source to not only find which certifications relate to your MOS, but also how to find resources and materials to support and complete the requirements.

SERVICEMEMBERS OPPORTUNITY COLLEGES (SOC)

Under the Servicemembers Opportunity Colleges (SOC), there are degree and certification programs in which a soldier can be awarded a degree or certificate for an academic or technical course of study. The programs were developed to provide common curricula in disciplines related to Army MOSs.

The SOC is a network of schools across the country and overseas that have recognized and responded to soldiers' expectations for postsecondary education. The schools must have liberal entrance requirements, allow soldiers to complete courses through non-traditional modes, provide academic advisement, offer maximum credit for experiences obtained in service, have residence requirements that are adaptable to the special needs of soldiers, have a transfer policy that recognizes traditional and nontraditional learning obtained at other schools, promote the SOC, and provide educational support to service-members. It is important to confirm that any school you attend is an SOC member. Not only will this ensure that your military education will be given maximum consideration for credit, but it also ensures that you are joining a college or university that is not taking advantage of you. Selecting only from schools listed in GoArmyEd, described below, will go far in guaranteeing you are attending a respected institution that has been verified as following all SOC requirements.

GOARMYED

One of the most innovative and important developments in Army education in the last twenty years is the creation of the GoArmyEd website. This website provides all soldiers the ability to reach out to an Army education counselor, search hundreds of approved schools for academic and technical degrees and certificates, apply for tuition assistance, and seek scholarships for family members as well as a host of other related information. It was designed with the soldier in mind and is very user-friendly and easy to navigate. GoArmyEd is especially valuable to soldiers deployed away from home station, and to Reserve and Guard soldiers who may not have a convenient post or installation education center nearby. If you are reading about a topic in this chapter, you can be sure to find a link or tab discussing it on their website. I strongly recommend this site at or near the top of your favorites/bookmarked pages.

COLLEGE CREDIT FOR MILITARY EXPERIENCE

Army Education Center counselors can help you complete DD Form 295, *Application for the Evaluation of Learning Experiences during Military Service*. The completed form is used to inform institutions, agencies, and employers about in-service educational achievements. Schools use the form to determine how many and what kinds of college credits to award soldiers based on military education, training, and experience. Your pursuit of a degree should include completing and forwarding DD Form 295 to the college or university of your choice.

The American Council on Education (ACE) evaluates Army service school courses and recommends the number of semester hours of credit that civilian schools may award based on a soldier's military training and experience. Examples include vocational, lower-level baccalaureate and associate's degree, upper-level baccalaureate, and graduate-level credits. These recommendations are published in the *Guide to the Evaluation of Educational Experiences in the Armed Services (ACE Guide)*.

An important component of determining earned credit is found in your Joint Service Transcript. This document is easy to obtain by logging onto the Joint Service Transcript site at *https://jst.doded.mil*. All servicemembers have access, including veterans and retirees, and it is an invaluable collection of all your military training and related independent study and examination tests. Register at the site using your Common Access Card

(CAC), or register as a non-CAC holder, and you can immediately see your transcript. Simply click on the "Transcript" tab near the top of the screen and follow the onscreen instructions. Your education counselor can help you obtain this transcript if you run into difficulty, but be sure to get it in any event, as it is an important framework of support credits for any degree and helps ensure that you get the maximum credit for the training and education you have already completed.

INDEPENDENT STUDY AND EXAMINATION PROGRAMS FOR COLLEGE CREDIT

If you are working on an undergraduate (associate's or bachelor's) degree, you should know about independent ways to earn credit. These methods are perfect for those who already have a strong understanding in a given subject area or degree-related topic. They are also a great way to continue your studies and earn credit when tuition assistance (TA) is unavailable (for those in the first year of service under current policy or those who have used up their allotted TA for a given year). Credit can be earned through the following programs: Defense Activity for Nontraditional Education Support (DANTES), including the College Level Examination Program (CLEP), Defense Subject Standardized Tests (DSST), and Graduate Record Examination (GRE).

The DANTES, CLEP, DSST, and GRE offerings all require independent study. Many subject packets include texts, workbooks, and audio- or videotapes that are used in conjunction with the paper materials. Most of the for-credit tests offered by these programs and agencies are each worth three or four semester hours of credit. The GRE, which includes a general exam and subject exams, is worth much more credit. The GRE sociology examination, for example, is worth thirty semester hours of undergraduate credit—fifteen lower division (100 and 200 level) and fifteen upper division (300 and 400 level).

DANTES independent study and examination program services are available to all eligible active-duty soldiers. Two important aspects of the DANTES are the CLEP and DSST, which also enable students to earn credit by examination. The examinations measure knowledge of the basic concepts and applications involved in courses that have the same or similar titles. The CLEP examinations are divided into two types: general examinations and subject examinations.

The general examination measures college-level achievement in five basic areas of the liberal arts: English composition, social sciences and history, natural sciences, humanities, and mathematics. Test material covers the first year of college, often referred to as the general or liberal education requirement. Subject examinations, which also include many available related DSST exams, measure achievement in specific college courses/areas and are worth course credit. Examples of test titles for CLEP include Introduction to Business Management, General Psychology, Western Civilization, and American Literature.

Each civilian educational institution has its own criteria for using CLEP test scores to determine credit. You should have official transcripts forwarded to the registrar of the college or university at which you desire to receive credit (some institutions require that a minimum number of semester hours of classwork be completed before CLEP credit will be accepted). Another subject test that, like CLEP, substitutes for college classroom work is the DANTES Subject Standardized Tests. Talk to your education counselor for details on these powerful alternatives.

GI BILL

Valuable educational benefits offered under the GI Bill are available today for would-be college graduates and for those soldiers who wish to pursue certain kinds of training. Originally named the Servicemen's Readjustment Act of 1944, the GI Bill was signed into law by President Franklin D. Roosevelt on 22 June 1944. The bill, now called the Montgomery GI Bill after its latest champion, Congressman G. V. Montgomery, takes the form of the Montgomery Active Duty GI Bill and the Montgomery Selected Reserve GI Bill. The post-Vietnam Veterans Educational Assistance Program (VEAP) is also covered by the Montgomery GI Bill. A wide range of benefits valued at hundreds of dollars per month for up to thirty-six months is available. I cannot stress strongly enough that you should take full advantage of the benefits to which you are entitled.

POST 9-11 GI BILL

This bill provides monetary support for education to servicemembers who had ninety days of aggregate active-duty service after 10 September 2001. If you are a veteran who was honorably discharged or discharged with a service-connected disability after thirty days, you also could be eligible for the program. It additionally provides funding for training in many categories for those who are eligible, including national testing reimbursement, vocational/technical training, flight training, licensing and certification reimbursement, and a host of others. The college funding must be for an institute of higher learning, and in all cases, your education counselor at the education center can help guide you through the maze of options and requirements. For those who were in service on 1 August 2009, the additional option of transferring benefits to spouse or dependent children became available for eligible applicants. Thirty-six months of education funding is available in most cases, but in order to obtain the maximum benefit, you should become familiar with the "Education and Training" page at *www.va.gov*. For those who have been discharged and are attending resident schools, a housing allowance and stipends for books and supplies are available. Yellow ribbon program participant schools offer additional reimbursement to offset costs above the benefit, and once again, becoming familiar with the most current offerings at your education center and on the VA website is critical.

Montgomery Active Duty GI Bill

The Montgomery Active Duty GI Bill (Chapter 30, U.S. Code) provides up to thirty-six months of benefits. Soldiers covered by Category I of this program are those who first entered active duty after 30 June 1985, and who contributed a nonrefundable $100 a month for the first twelve months of service. Active-duty members may begin using their benefits after completing two years of service. Members of the National Guard who are in the Active Guard and Reserve Program also are covered by this contributory program, but they must have entered service after 29 November 1989, and must not have previously served on active duty. Soldiers who have money left over in their account from the

Vietnam-era GI Bill or the Veteran Educational Assistance Program (VEAP) should contact the regional Veterans Affairs office and also check out the VA website at *www.va.gov*. There are opportunities to convert those monies to the Montgomery GI Bill program for eligible soldiers and veterans.

Montgomery Selected Reserve GI Bill

The Montgomery Selected Reserve GI Bill (Chapter 106, U.S. Code) is available to members of the Army Reserve and the Army National Guard. It applies to members who entered selected reserve status after 30 June 1985. To receive up to thirty-six months of entitlements under this program, members must have made a six-year commitment that began after 30 September 1990. Members also must have completed Initial Active Duty for Training, be high school graduates or have equivalent certificates, serve in an active Reserve or National Guard unit, and remain in good standing. Soldiers entering the National Guard or Army Reserve on or after 1 October 1992 have their eligibility end fourteen years from their beginning date of eligibility, or on the day they leave the Selected Reserve. Soldiers entering service prior to 1 October 1992 have either ten years from beginning date of eligibility; their period of eligibility ends ten years from their beginning date of eligibility or on the day they leave the Selected Reserve.

Monetary Value of the GI Bill

As indicated above, the monetary value of the benefit program you qualify for will depend on various factors, including the date you entered the military, your status in the military, how long you have been or were in service, and the character of a previous discharge or separation. Also, if you are in a contributory program, the amount of money the government will contribute depends on how much you contribute, up to a maximum matching contributory amount.

In-service benefits are worth less, monetarily, than post-service benefits and normally cover only tuition and fees. But here is a kicker: Under current federal law, if you receive a college or university assistantship, fellowship, or grant that pays or offsets part or all of your tuition and fees or research expenses, you may still be entitled to receipt of military education benefits—meaning that monthly entitlements received from the Department of Veterans Affairs (DVA) are yours to keep.

Various rules and certain service- or usage-oriented restrictions cover the programs and situations described above. Visit your local DVA office, check out the VA website, or meet with an education center counselor.

OTHER FINANCIAL AID

The U.S. Department of Education (DOE), in *The Student Guide*, informs you and your family members about federal student aid programs and how to apply for them. The department also advises you contact the financial aid administrator at the school that you, your spouse, or your children are interested in and ask about the total cost of education. Ask the state higher education agencies about state aid. Check your local library for state and private financial aid information. Check with companies, foundations, religious organizations, fraternities or sororities, and civic organizations such as the American Legion.

Also ask about aid through professional associations such as the Association of the U.S. Army (AUSA) and the Enlisted Association of the National Guard (EANGUS).

The *Student Guide* is free and may be available at the local Army Education Office. Additionally, check out the GoArmyEd website. There is a scholarship tab at the bottom of the site page, which highlights both general and institution-specific scholarships for soldiers and family members.

A FINAL THOUGHT ON EDUCATION FINANCE

Buy bonds. Series EE savings bonds may be entirely tax free when used for education. If you have children and are worried about the rising cost of education, purchasing bonds on a regular basis is a smart way to invest in their future and protect your financial security. For example, assuming an annual interest rate of 6 percent, putting just $50 a month into bonds for a one-year-old child who will begin college at age eighteen will yield $17,356. Investing $100 a month will yield $34,712. If you are a soldier with a twelve-year-old who will begin college in six years, putting $50 a month into bonds will provide $4,227; $100 a month will yield $8,454—minimum.

If you are a young soldier, you may purchase bonds for yourself, hold them five years or so, then use them to augment other financial aid that you will apply toward your or your family member's bachelor's or master's degree.

Beginning with Series EE bonds purchased in 1990, the interest earned can be excluded from federal income tax if you pay tuition and fees at colleges, universities, and qualified technical schools during the same year the bonds are cashed. The exclusion applies not only to your own educational expenses but also to those of your spouse and any other dependents. You can get more information on this powerful investment option for education at *https://www.treasurydirect.gov/indiv/planning/plan_education.htm.*

7

Marksmanship

Every soldier, regardless of their job/MOS in the Army, is a warrior first. You must be a proficient marksman with your assigned weapon. Proper shooting is a physical skill enhanced by concentration, which, like riding a bicycle, can be learned. When practiced often for short periods, it becomes a skill that will be retained for some time. However, high accuracy and skill is perishable and, unlike riding a bike, must be reinforced periodically to maintain a satisfactory ability. Marksmanship is learned on the grouping, zero, and qualification ranges; in combat, it is your ultimate defense. Marksmanship fundamentals include assuming a steady position, aiming, breathing, and squeezing the trigger in a controlled manner. Knowing these fundamentals develops fixed and correct firing habits for instinctive use and will make you more effective the more you practice them.

The mechanics for zeroing your weapons, found in FM 3-22.9, *Rifle Marksmanship, M16/M4-Series Weapons*, are not described here. The basic techniques presented below apply to all positions, with or without Intercepter Body Armor (IBA). After thirty years in the Army, three years as a drill sergeant, I think it is important to note that the fundamentals have not changed, despite the amazing advancements in technology in our weapon systems. Regardless if you are firing in daylight or at night, with a scope or otherwise, mastering the fundamentals is key to success in marksmanship.

FUNDAMENTALS

Position
To assume the prone position, face the target, spread your feet a comfortable distance apart, and drop to your knees. Using the butt of the rifle as a pivot, roll onto your nonfiring side. Place the rifle butt in the pocket formed by the firing shoulder, grasp the pistol grip in your firing hand, and lower the firing elbow to the ground. Adjust your left and right elbows until your shoulders and feet are about level to provide the steadiest possible position. Your elbows provide additional support, and your feet, shoulder width apart, add stability. Rest the handguard in the V formed by the thumb and forefinger and across the heel of your nonfiring hand with the hand on the sandbag, ensuring that all the weapon's weight is on the sandbag and not on your elbows. Place the butt of the stock firmly into the pocket formed by the firing shoulder. Wrap your hand around the hand grip. The

three lower fingers come around the pistol grip and meet the thumb to form the grip. The grip should be like a good, firm handshake. If you put on a "death grip," the muscle tension will cause you to shake.

Your body must lie in a relaxed, flat position. Point your toes out so your feet lie sideways, flat against the ground. Start with your feet and think about the position of all body parts, working up to your fingers. If you are using muscles to hold your position, you will shake. Keep your forearm vertical under the rifle, straight up and down. When you angle your arms, you are using muscles to hold them still. Gravity will do this for you if you keep your forearm vertical.

Place your cheek firmly against the stock of the rifle, putting your eye close to and directly behind the rear peep sight. You can tell that you have a good position when there is absolutely no movement of the weapon as you sight on the target, exhale, hold your breath, and squeeze the trigger. This way, your head rides with the rifle as it recoils, and it will not kick you. It just pushes your shoulder, and you ride with it.

Aim

You begin the aiming process by aligning the rifle with the target when assuming a firing position. Point the rifle naturally at the desired point of aim. If you use muscles to adjust the weapon onto the point of aim, you will find that they automatically relax as the rifle fires, and the rifle will move toward its natural point of aim, which is the point at which the rifle naturally rests in relation to the aiming point. Because this movement begins just before the weapon discharges, the rifle is moving as the bullet leaves the muzzle. This causes inaccurate shots with no apparent cause (recoil disguises the movement). Since the rifle becomes an extension of your body, it is necessary to adjust your position until the rifle points naturally at the preferred aiming point on the target.

Once you are in position and aimed toward your target, the method for checking for the natural point of aim is to close your eyes, take a couple of breaths, and relax as much as possible. Upon opening your eyes, your sights should be positioned at the aiming point (target). You can change the deviation of the natural point of aim by shifting your body left or right. Elevation can be changed by leaving your elbows in place and sliding your body forward or rearward. This raises or lowers the muzzle of the weapon, respectively. By adjusting the weapon and body as a single unit, rechecking, and readjusting as needed, you can achieve a true natural point of aim.

Once your natural point of aim is established, aim your weapon at the exact point on the target.

Four aspects contribute to aiming: your shooting eye, the rear sight, the front sight, and the target. The distance between the sights does not change. The distance from your eye to the rear sight can change when you have different stock welds. The relationship between your eye and the rear sight is important. Once you find the right position for your eye, note the relationship between your nose and the stock or action of the rifle. Each time you aim, put your nose in the same place. This will help you keep your sight picture consistent. This is called a stock weld. When zeroing, it is critical to use the same aim point, regardless of the strike of the shot group, so that you do not chase the shot groups trying to hit center using "holdoff."

Aiming involves four elements: sight picture, sight alignment, aiming point, and focus.

Sight Picture

In aiming, you are concerned with correctly pointing your rifle so the bullet will hit the target when you fire. To do this, you must have the rear sight, the front sight post, and the target or aiming point in their proper relationship. This is known as sight picture. A correct sight picture is obtained when the sights are aligned and the aiming point (target) is in the correct relationship to the front sight post. The sight picture includes two basic elements: sight alignment and placement of the aiming point.

Sight Alignment

Alignment is critical. Any movement you make during firing that changes the relation-ship of the front and rear sights by one-tenth of an inch will cause a miss on a 300-meter target by five feet. When you look through the rear aperture, your mind must form an imaginary pair of crosshairs, one vertical and one horizontal. Align these crosshairs with the front sight post. Bring the top of the front sight post up even with the horizontal line and center it, ensuring that there is an equal amount of the front sight post on each side of the vertical line.

Although a small misalignment can cause problems, don't get wrapped around the axle with the thousandths of an inch—just do it correctly. Remember, it must be done the same way each and every time.

CORRECT
SIGHT PICTURE

CORRECT
SIGHT ALIGNMENT

CORRECT PLACEMENT
OF AIMING POINT

Aiming Point

When zeroing, the aiming point is the center mass of the black 250-meter scaled silhou-ette of the 25-meter target. If the aiming point is correctly positioned, an imaginary ver-tical line drawn through the center of the front sight post will appear to split the aiming point.

1. Position the front sight just to the right or left of the target, just far enough so the whole target next to the front sight post can be seen.

2. Raise or lower the front sight post so the top of the sight is halfway between the top and bottom of the target.

3. Smoothly move the front sight straight over to the target, without raising or lowering the post, and stop when the post is centered on the target.

If the sight picture gets too blurry, relax, blink your eyes, take a breath, and start over at step 1.

Focus

Remember that the human eye cannot focus on two objects at the same time. A correct sight picture has the rear sight and target blurry and the front sight in focus. The line of sight goes from the eye through the rear sight aperture (the mind forms the imaginary crosshairs). The front sight post is then brought into the line of sight and correctly aligned with the imaginary crosshairs. This is critical to good shooting and scores. Whether shooting at 25, 100, or 600 meters, you must always focus on the front sight post.

Dominant Eye

Some shooters have problems aligning the target with the sights because of their eyesight. To determine which eye is dominant, extend one arm to the front and point the index finger skyward to select an aiming point. With both eyes open, align the index finger with the aiming point, then close one eye at a time while looking at the aiming point. With one eye, the finger will appear to move off the aiming point; with the other eye, the finger will stay on the aiming point. The dominant eye is the eye that does not move the finger from the aiming point. Some individuals may have difficulty aiming because of interference from the dominant eye, if this is not the eye used in the aiming process. Such individuals must close the dominant eye while shooting.

Breathe

If you don't breathe during weapon firing, you will shake. There is a correct way to breathe when shooting. Try this exercise: Take a breath. Let it out. While exhaling, notice that there is a point at which you don't feel it necessary to continue exhaling or to start breathing in again. Now try it again. This time, when you get to that point, stop breathing for a second or two. It's easy!

This is the place in your breathing cycle where you want to take your shot. Since you can hold it for only a second or two at most, you must time the rise and fall of the rifle, the sight alignment and picture, and the trigger squeeze to coincide with that point. Notice that when you inhale, the muzzle of the rifle drops. It rises again when you exhale. When your chest expands, your shoulder rises; your forearm that supports the rifle does not move, so the muzzle drops. You must time this rise and fall so that the target is sighted at that point.

SEQUENCE FOR BREATHING AND FIRING

1. Breathe. Inhale and exhale to the natural respiratory pause. Check for consistent head placement and stock weld. Ensure that eye relief is correct. At the same time, begin aligning the front blade with the target at the desired point of aim.
2. Relax. As you exhale, relax as many muscles as possible while maintaining control of the weapon and position.
3. Aim. If you have a good, natural point of aim, the rifle points at the desired target during the respiratory pause. If the aim is off, make a slight adjustment to acquire the desired point of aim. Avoid "muscling" the weapon toward the aiming point.
4. Squeeze. As long as the sight picture is satisfactory, squeeze the trigger. The pressure applied to the trigger must be straight to the rear without disturbing the lay of the rifle or the desired point of aim.

Squeeze

Squeeze is nothing more than squeezing the trigger straight to the rear without disturbing the sight picture. You begin the trigger squeeze and continue until the rifle fires, while maintaining sight alignment. The part of the finger that should touch the trigger is the pad of flesh directly opposite the quick of the fingernail—not the fingertip, and no farther back than the first joint.

When you pull the trigger, you must apply steadily increasing pressure until the gun fires. The shot should come as a surprise every time. If you anticipate and flinch, you will never be able to shoot well. The normal reflex action of the body is such that you will miss if the trigger is not squeezed. Your concentration should be so centered on sight alignment, focus, and trigger control that you can ignore the recoil and just let it happen.

Follow-Through

You will have less tendency to jerk, flinch, and buck if you follow through after your shot. Follow-through is the act of continuing to apply all the marksmanship fundamentals as the weapon fires as well as immediately after it fires. Follow-through involves:

- Keeping the head in firm contact with the stock—stock weld.
- Keeping the finger on the trigger all the way to the rear.
- Continuing to look through the rear aperture or scope tube.
- Keeping muscles relaxed.
- Avoiding reaction to recoil and noise.
- Releasing the trigger only after the recoil has stopped.

Hearing Protection

The biggest mistake you can make is not wearing hearing protection. Not only can you damage your hearing, but the noise will be loud, and you will begin to associate the noise with the recoil. In your mind, the noise and the recoil will be one and the same.

Acting As a Coach

If you are acting as a coach, first ensure that IBA and helmet are fitted and worn correctly if used in the training. Then, watch for the following:

- Ensure that the firer assumes a good steady position.
- Make sure that the firer applies correct pressure during trigger squeeze.
- Determine whether the firer flinches, jerks, or bucks by watching the firer's head, shoulder, trigger finger, and nonfiring hand and arm.
- Make sure that the firer breathes correctly by watching his or her back occasionally.
- Make sure that the firer releases pressure on the trigger and lowers his or her rifle when the trigger is not squeezed within three to five seconds.
- Check shoulder placement of the rifle butt and pressure in the shoulder pocket. It should be snug; the top of the butt should be level with the top of the shooter's shoulder and not falling off the side of the shoulder.
- Check that the back of the nonfiring hand is fully supported by the sandbag.

References

FM 3-22.9, *Rifle Marksmanship*

8

Physical Fitness and Weight Control

Physical fitness provides Soldiers with the energy and stamina to perform at high levels during peace and war. The lifestyle of a Soldier is extremely challenging. Physical fitness will make a difference as Soldiers face arduous tasks in accomplishing their missions. The Army performs as a team. Each Soldier owes it to their teammates to maintain a level of fitness that will allow the team to operate successfully. Finally, a Soldier's family will expect them to live long and healthy lives after their service. A lifetime of fitness will help Soldiers support their families for many years after they take off the uniform.

—LTG Thomas P. Bostick, 53d Chief of Engineers, Army Corps of Engineers

The real value of being physically fit is as clear today as it has been on battlefields throughout history. Soldiers not physically fit put themselves and their comrades at risk during wartime, and they are not as effective in duty performance overall. It is difficult to survive in 130-degree heat or at altitudes above 5,000 feet in body armor when you are not in top shape. Soldiers who fought and won battles can attest to the value of strength, endurance, and mobility. All soldiers must be fit to fight. Infantrymen, engineers, medics, cooks, mechanics, tankers, AG/finance, MPs, supply, artillerymen, air defenders, and every other type serve on the same team, and every one of them is a warrior first.

According to Army policy, all soldiers must train to accomplish their wartime Mission Essential Task List (METL). A unit METL includes all its critical wartime tasks. So, soldiers should engage in physical training programs that include events that fully prepare them to accomplish METL, or wartime, tasks.

This chapter focuses on two of the three areas of a complete fitness program: physical readiness training (PRT) and weight control. The third piece of a complete fitness program is sleep, and it's important to mention here. The Army continues to study this aspect of fitness, and suffice it to say a good night's rest is imperative if you are going

Physical fitness training prepares you for "the real deal."

to ask your body to continually improve and adapt to tougher and more rigorous activity and then also to perform with limited rest or sleep when the mission demands it. The bottom line is that you deserve the opportunity to participate in a fitness regimen daily, and if you are in a unit or staff that does not allow the time, then you must find the time and make it a personal responsibility. Of all the things you do each day as a soldier, physical readiness training will set the best tone and set you up for the most success. It is the core asset for better performance in literally every other thing you will do. It provides increased energy and reduces stress. It promotes resistance to injury, improved physical and mental toughness, and can provide higher promotion points for rank advancement. I always thought of a daily PRT session as an hour to ninety minutes of my life I would never get back and so wanted to not waste a single minute of it by slacking. Consider this as you attend to your own fitness program, then check out FM 7-22, Army Physical Readiness Training, to get all the details for increasing your performance.

PRINCIPLES OF PHYSICAL READINESS TRAINING (PRT)
To ensure that soldiers engaged in a PRT program get the maximum benefit and remove risk of injury to the greatest degree possible, three principles are incorporated: precision, progression, and integration. Precision means that you should execute each exercise, drill, or activity with strict form and consider form just as important as the number of repetitions completed, speed achieved, or pounds lifted. This will go far in mitigating risk of injury as well as providing the maximum training effect for improved performance.

Progression is also critically important, in both risk management and performance. If you tried to go from pushing your own body weight in a push-up to a bench press of 400 pounds with no training progression, the results would be obviously disastrous in both risk and performance. Incremental increases in stress, such as number of repetitions and so forth, is a key aspect of any fitness improvement program. Finally, integration is critical in a variety of ways when it comes to a fitness program. By integrating various activities, you are able to work out more often and concentrate on specific areas or components of fitness, while allowing recovering muscles or fitness systems, like the cardiovascular, to rest. This principle also supports a balanced program that ensures that key aspects of fitness required for Warrior Task Battle Drills (WTBDs) are practiced and executed to support the Mission Essential Task List.

Components of PRT

The three components of PRT are also important to understand: strength, endurance, and mobility. Strength comes in two forms: muscular strength and muscular endurance. Muscular strength is the ability to exert power against external resistance in a one-time, maximum amount, like lifting a heavy object. Muscular endurance is the ability to repeatedly perform a strength movement, such as a foot march under full combat load. Muscular endurance also includes the ability to hold a muscular contraction for an extended period of time.

Endurance is the ability to maintain a physical activity over time. It also has two forms, anaerobic and aerobic. Anaerobic is the execution of high-intensity activity for a short period of time (like sprints), and aerobic endurance involves lower-intensity activity over a longer period of time (as in a long-distance run).

Mobility is the combination of strength and endurance to perform an exercise or task with efficiency and proficiency. By improving both strength and endurance through mobility movement drills, you increase your performance of fitness activities and WTBDs, while also controlling injury risk. The aspects that affect or enhance mobility are agility, balance, coordination, flexibility, posture, stability, speed, and power. The mobility movement drills detailed below help develop skill in each of those areas.

Sustainment PRT

Soldiers who have completed their initial military training and are in the advanced stages of AIT move from the toughening phase of PRT to the sustainment phase, which will carry them to their operational units and beyond. The sustainment phase is punctuated with a consistent method of preparation and then plenty of variety in the activity segment of PRT, before once again entering into a consistent recovery period. The preparation and recovery are both critical in warming up the body for the higher levels of physical activity.

Preparation Phase

Before engaging in high levels of physical activity, it is very important to warm up both the muscles and joints of the body, along with the cardiovascular system. Going from a relaxed (sedentary) state to one of very high physical stress is both dangerous and also ensures that less than optimal activity goals are reached. The following are the exercises conducted in the preparation drill to get you ready:

1. Bend and reach, 5–10 repetitions, done at a slow cadence
2. Rear lunge, 5–10 repetitions, done at a slow cadence
3. High jumper, 5–10 repetitions, done at a moderate cadence
4. Rower, 5–10 repetitions, done at a slow cadence
5. Squat bender, 5–10 repetitions, done at a slow cadence
6. Windmill, 5–10 repetitions, done at a slow cadence
7. Forward lunge, 5–10 repetitions, done at a slow cadence
8. Prone row, 5–10 repetitions, done at a slow cadence
9. Bent-leg body twist, 5–10 repetitions, done at a slow cadence
10. Push-up, 5–10 repetitions, done at a moderate cadence

Activity Phase

While the preparation drill is very constant in the number and type of movements, the activity phase of PRT is characterized by a wide diversity of rigorous options. These choices allow for much-needed variety in an ongoing fitness program. There are some general themes, such as alternating days between muscular strength/endurance and mobility endurance. These types of requirements ensure that appropriate rest and recovery are achieved or have other important reasons underpinning them. Within those general needs, the menu of different PRT options in the sustainment phase is impressive. It includes training such as conditioning drills, climbing drills, guerrilla drills, movement mobility drills, ability group runs, release runs, terrain runs, foot marches, confidence obstacle courses, and a host of others. To check out the full list of twenty-three options, see paragraph 5-26 in FM 7-22.

Drill Examples

The following are just a sampling of the drills that you can expect to encounter in the sustainment phase. The drills are always conducted in sequence and for the number of repetitions prescribed. If more repetitions are desired (and allowed in a specific drill), it's important to repeat the entire sequence and not just one exercise in that drill. Again, for a full list of the different drills, see Table 9.1 of FM 7-22.

Conditioning Drill 1 (CD1). This drill is composed of basic through intermediate calisthenics, done at a moderate cadence. It is focused on foundational fitness that helps improve strength, endurance, and mobility and includes five exercises, executed for 5 to 10 repetitions: power jump, V-up, mountain climber, leg tuck and twist, and single-leg push-up.

Conditioning Drill 2 (CD2). Like CD1, this drill of advanced exercises is executed for 5 to 10 repetitions each. It also challenges your strength, endurance, and mobility capability, but adds more complex plyometric and bilateral movement requirements as well. The five exercises in this drill are the turn and lunge (slow cadence), supine bicycle (slow cadence), half jacks (moderate cadence), swimmer (slow cadence) and 8-count push-up (moderate cadence).

Conditioning Drill 3 (CD3). This is an advanced set of drills and is not allowed for use in basic training or early stages of advanced individual training (red, white, and blue phases). When used in the sustainment phase of the PRT (black and gold phase and operational/permanent party units), you should progress from 5 to 10 repetitions and do a repeat set of the entire drill if you desire more repetitions. This set of exercises introduces much more complex coordination movements and jumping and landing activity that produces increased requirements on the legs and feet. The CD3 is designed to better prepare you for the Warrior Task Battle Drills.

The ten exercises and cadence for each are as follows:

1. Y squat, slow cadence
2. Single-leg dead lift, slow cadence
3. Side to side knee lifts, moderate cadence
4. Front kick with alternate toe touch, moderate cadence
5. Tuck jump, slow cadence
6. Straddle run forward and backward, moderate cadence
7. Half-squat laterals, moderate cadence
8. Frog jumps forward and backward, moderate cadence
9. Alternate one-quarter turn jump, moderate cadence
10. Alternate staggered squat jump, slow cadence

Push-up and Sit-up Drill: This drill is exactly how it reads and is simply a platoon- or other sized team that conducts 30 to 60 seconds of push-ups and sit-ups until the desired number of sets is achieved. In a platoon formation, the first and third rank would do their push-ups, followed by the members of the second and fourth rank. The same procedure would be followed for the sit-ups, with the rank members switching out. It is important to switch between exercises (push-up and sit-up) to ensure enough rest is received before engaging in the next set that taxes the same muscles. It should also be noted that the intent of this drill is to increase the muscular endurance of the upper body, but also directly helps in the preparation for the Army Physical Fitness Test. Since the APFT counts for promotion points and is a staple method of recording each soldier's fitness level, you should make this a key feature of your own fitness program, regardless of whether it is key in your unit's program.

Climbing Drills 1 & 2. There are two climbing drills in FM 7-22. Both have most things in common, including increased arm and thorax (trunk) strength. Climbing requires using the hands and feet as grounding points and then the arms and legs to pull or push the body along. When climbing drills are combined with the other drills in the PRT program, more balance and variety is achieved, while also ensuring that a key aspect of Warrior Task Battle Drills is practiced. There is no other drill that will prepare you more for the challenges of negotiating obstacles, crossing obstacles via a rope, climbing up on ledges and through windows, and so on. Both CL1 and 2 have five exercises and differ primarily in that in CL2, the added weight of load-bearing equipment in the sustainment phase is added to further condition you for negotiating challenges while in full gear. As with the other drills, the goal is to increase from 5 to 10 repetitions and do several sets mainly unassisted.

Mobility Movement Drills (MMD) 1 & 2. These two drills improve/enhance running form and focus on agility, balance, and coordination while preparing the body for the more rigorous portion of the PRT session to come. They are conducted after the preparation drill (see FM 7-22). Each of the two drills consists of three exercises. Each of the exercises is completed on a twenty-five-yard-wide piece of level ground. MMD 1 includes verticals, laterals, and the shuttle sprint. MMD 2 consists of the power skip, crossovers, and the crouch run. If both MMD 1 and 2 are conducted in a single PRT session, MMD 1 should always be completed first, and the exercises within each drill must not be switched around or mixed with the other MMD.

Recovery Phase
Once the preparation and activity phases of your PRT session have been conducted, whether speed or distance running, strength circuit training, a foot march, or other main event, after your warm-up exercises described above, it is critical to complete the recovery drill of your PRT session. Recovery not only helps return the heart rate and blood pressure to normal along with the breathing rate, it does wonders for increasing flexibility and reducing post-exercise soreness. The recovery drill consists of five stretches that you hold for 20 to 30 seconds: overhead Army pull, rear lunge, extend and flex, thigh stretch, and single-leg over. Note that for all but the extend and flex, you must hold for 20 to 30 seconds on each side (arm or leg as indicated).

ARMY PHYSICAL FITNESS TEST
Soldiers taking the APFT are encouraged to make a maximum effort to pass and excel. The test is administered at least twice a year, with four months minimum between events for active duty and yearly for reserve component soldiers. Described in detail in appendix A of FM 7-22, the APFT includes timed push-ups, sit-ups, and a two-mile run (or alternative aerobic event in certain circumstances). The event is completed on the same day with a minimum of ten minutes and a maximum of twenty minutes between events. This is important to note, because the closer you can get to twenty minutes between events, the better. This is often impractical with unit-level testing, as it would take the whole day to grade a company-sized element. However, if conditions do exist and you can make use of it, every extra minute between events is short-term recovery time with blood-carrying oxygen going to muscles needing it. Hopefully you are on your way to easily achieving the maximum score for each event and for the total score, but understanding that you need a minimum of ten minutes between events is critical to peak performance.

Push-up Event

The push-up measures the endurance of the chest, shoulder, and triceps muscles. This first event is a two-minute push-up test. The push-ups must be properly completed to be counted as valid repetitions. The starting position is as follows:

- Hands are placed a comfortable distance apart.
- The body must remain in a generally straight line.
- Arms are straight and fully extended.
- Feet may be separated up to twelve inches apart.

To execute a repetition, bend your elbows, evenly lowering your body until your upper arms are parallel with the ground. Then straighten your arms until they are fully extended. Throughout the repetition, your body should remain generally straight, and your hands and feet must not break contact with the ground. Only your hands and feet may touch the ground during this exercise. You may change the position of your hands and feet, provided they remain in contact with the ground at all times. If you fail to maintain proper form for the entire repetition, it will not be counted.

Sit-up Event

The second event is a two-minute sit-up test that measures the endurance of the abdominal and hip-flexor muscles. To assume the starting position for this exercise, do the following:

- Lie flat on your back.
- Bend your knees so that your feet are flat on the ground and a ninety-degree angle is formed by the upper and lower portions of your legs.
- Place your feet together or up to twelve inches apart.
- Clasp your hands behind your head with your fingers interlocked.

To execute a correct repetition, raise your body to the vertical position with the base of your neck above the base of the spine. Lower your body so your back touches the ground. The repetition will not be counted if you fail to reach the vertical position, arch your back, raise your buttocks off the ground, fail to keep your fingers interlocked and behind your head, or allow your knees to exceed a ninety-degree angle. Another person will assist you during this exercise by holding your feet firmly on the ground. They may only hold your ankles with their hands, and no other form of bracing or assistance is allowed.

PUSH-UPS

Age Group	Male Min.	Male Max.	Female Min.	Female Max.
17–21	42	71	19	42
22–26	40	75	17	46
27–31	39	77	17	50
32–36	36	75	15	45
37–41	34	73	13	40
42–46	30	66	12	37
47–51	25	59	10	34
52–56	20	56	9	31
57–61	18	53	8	28
62+	16	50	7	25

SIT-UPS

Age Group	Male/Female Min.	Male/Female Max.
17–21	53	78
22–26	50	80
27–31	45	82
32–36	42	76
37–41	38	76
42–46	32	72
47–51	30	66
52–56	28	66
57–61	27	64
62+	26	63

Two-Mile Run

The two-mile run or alternative aerobic event measures cardiorespiratory and leg muscle endurance. Instructions for each APFT event in FM 21-20 must be read verbatim before each event is administered.

The current APFT standards are shown on the following chart.

TWO-MILE RUN

Age Group	Male Min.	Male Max.	Female Min.	Female Max.
17–21	15:54	13:00	18:54	15:36
22–26	16:36	13:00	19:36	15:36
27–31	17:00	13:18	20:30	15:48
32–36	17:42	13:18	21:42	15:54
37–41	18:18	13:36	22:42	17:00
42–46	18:42	14:06	23:42	17:24
47–51	19:30	14:24	24:00	17:36
52–56	19:48	14:42	24:24	19:00
57–61	19:54	15:18	24:48	19:42
62+	20:00	15:42	25:00	20:00

ARMY FITNESS REGULATIONS

Army Physical Fitness Badge

The Army Physical Fitness Badge is awarded to soldiers attaining a score of 90 points in each event, for a total of 270 points. Under the current standards, soldiers must score 270 points annually to continue to wear the badge. Doing well on the APFT also assists soldiers in obtaining promotion points up to the rank of staff sergeant, ranging from 50 points to 10 points, and achieving excellence in the appropriate category on the NCOER for all NCOs. Fit soldiers also receive verbal commendations and other accolades, are more likely to be retained in service and selected for advanced military schooling, and can be promoted if they meet other selection criteria, including presenting a sharp military appearance.

Medical Profiles

Soldiers on permanent profile may be unable to take some or all of the APFT events for medical or other authorized or unavoidable reasons. In order to get credit for the APFT, however, the two-mile run or an alternative aerobic event must be taken and passed. Alternative aerobic events include the 800-yard swim, 6.2-mile bicycle ride (in one gear), and 2.5-mile walk. Like the run, the alternative events must be completed unassisted in a prescribed amount of time relative to age and gender. Unlike the run, the other events are not scored; test takers either pass or fail the event. Soldiers who fail any or all of the events must retake the entire test. In case of test failure, commanders may allow soldiers to retake the test as soon as they are ready. Soldiers without a medical profile will be retested no later than three months following the initial APFT failure.

Failure to Pass

In compliance with Army retention policy, soldiers who have six months or more time in service who fail two consecutive record APFTs must be processed for separation for unsatisfactory performance under chapter 13 of AR 635-200, *Enlisted Personnel.* Receipt of a "chapter 13" for fitness failure indicates that the soldier is unqualified for service because he or she will not develop sufficiently to participate in further training or become a satisfactory soldier. It also means that failures would be likely to recur, and the soldier is unlikely to be able to perform duties effectively in the future, as well as lacks the potential for advancement or leadership. Entry-level soldiers (those with less than six months' time in service) who repeatedly fail diagnostic and record APFTs may be separated under chapter 11 of the *Enlisted Personnel* regulation. A "chapter 11" covers inability, lack of reasonable effort, or failure to adapt to the military environment.

With your commitment to serve in uniform comes the requirement to be physically fit, among other attributes of duty performance. Another is the critically important and related requirement to control your weight and maintain it within established standards.

WEIGHT CONTROL

AR 600-9, *The Army Body Composition Program*, states that each soldier (commissioned, warrant, or enlisted) is responsible for meeting service weight-control standards. To help soldiers meet their responsibility, height and weight screening tables are published in the weight-control regulation. The regulation also recommends that soldiers strive to remain at least 5 percent below their individual screening table weight maximum. The Department of Defense recommends 20 percent body fat for males and 26 percent for females as maximum percentages of fat. Soldiers should individually attain and maintain an acceptable weight and body composition through self-motivation or involvement in an official weight-control program. For some, the weight-control guidance is easy to follow. For others, weight can be a real problem.

Dealing with Body Fat

If a soldier consistently exceeds their personal weight goal, he or she should seek the assistance of master fitness trainers for advice in proper exercise and fitness and healthcare personnel for a proper dietary program. Soldiers exceeding the screening table weight or identified by the commander or supervisor for a special evaluation will have their body fat measured using the tape test method. When men are tape tested, they have the abdomen and neck measured; women have the hips, forearm, neck, and wrist measured. All measurements are taken three times and must be within one-quarter of an inch to be considered valid.

Body Composition Program

To help soldiers fight fat, the Army provides educational and other motivational programs to encourage personnel to attain and maintain proper weight and body fat standards. Programs include nutrition education sessions conducted by qualified health-care personnel, as well as exercise programs. Commanders will enforce body fat standards and monitor, measure, and, if necessary, place individuals into the Army Body Composition Program and continue to monitor them, in compliance with AR 600-9. Soldiers entered into the program are not allowed to reenlist or extend their enlistment, are considered nonpromotable, and are not assigned to command positions (e.g., squad leader, platoon sergeant, first sergeant, or command sergeant major).

Further, overweight soldiers are flagged. This means that their personnel record is coded such that they are ineligible for favorable personnel actions. Among those actions, affected soldiers are denied attendance at professional military or civilian schooling. AR 351-1, *Individual Military Education and Training*, states that personnel who do not meet body composition standards are not authorized to attend professional military schooling. All soldiers scheduled for attendance at schooling will be screened prior to departing the home station or losing command. Their height and weight will be recorded on their temporary duty orders, DD Form 1610, or on their permanent-change-of-station orders. Soldiers exceeding established screening weights will not be allowed to depart their commands until the commander has determined that they meet the standards.

School commandants will take the following action upon determining that a student has arrived exceeding established body fat composition standards. Soldiers arriving at any Department of the Army (DA) board select school or professional military school as a permanent change of station (PCS) who do not meet body fat standards will be processed for disenrollment and removed from the DA board select list if they are on it. Personnel arriving at professional military schools (other than DA board select or PCS schools) who do not meet body fat composition standards will be denied enrollment and reassigned in accordance with AR 600-9.

Actions to initiate mandatory bars to reenlistment or initiation of separation proceedings for soldiers who are eliminated for cause from NCOES courses, will be in accordance with AR 601-280, *Army Reenlistment Program*, and AR 635-200, *Enlisted Personnel*. Additionally, soldiers who by the definition in AR 600-9 are considered weight-control failures will be processed for separation from the Army.

Soldiers who are entered into the weight-control program and then successfully meet their body fat reduction goal will be removed from the program and monitored for a year. Failure to meet the standards at any time during the monitoring period will result in initiation of separation action.

WEIGHT FOR HEIGHT TABLE
(SCREENING TABLE WEIGHT)

Height (in inches)	Male Age				Female Age			
	17–20	21–27	28–39	40+	17–20	21–27	28–39	40+
58	—	—	—	—	119	121	122	124
59	—	—	—	—	124	125	126	128
60	132	136	139	141	128	129	131	133
61	136	140	144	146	132	134	135	137
62	141	144	148	150	136	138	140	142
63	145	149	153	155	141	143	144	146
64	150	154	158	160	145	147	149	151
65	155	159	163	165	150	152	154	156
66	160	163	168	170	155	156	158	161
67	165	169	174	176	159	161	163	166
68	170	174	179	181	164	166	168	171
69	175	179	184	186	169	171	173	176
70	180	185	189	192	174	176	178	181
71	185	189	194	197	179	181	183	186
72	190	195	200	203	184	186	188	191
73	195	200	205	208	189	191	194	197
74	201	206	211	214	194	197	199	202
75	206	212	217	220	200	202	204	208
76	212	217	223	226	205	207	210	213
77	218	223	229	232	210	213	215	219
78	223	229	235	238	216	218	221	225
79	229	235	241	244	221	224	227	230
80	234	240	247	250	227	230	233	236

Note: For screening purposes, body fat composition is to be determined in accordance with appendix B, AR 600-9. Males add 6 pounds per inch and females add 5 pounds per inch if over 80 inches.

Soldiers who consider themselves too fat—or who come close to qualifying for the Army Body Composition Program—should look at modifying their lifestyles and eating habits for life. Soldiers interested in an improved diet may seek guidance in appendix C of AR 600-9, "Weight Loss."

ALLOWABLE BODY FAT

Age Group:	17–20	Age Group:	21–27
Male (% body fat):	20	Male (% body fat):	22
Female (% body fat):	30	Female (% body fat):	32
Age Group:	28–39	Age Group:	40 & older
Male (% body fat):	24	Male (% body fat):	26
Female (% body fat):	34	Female (% body fat):	36

According to appendix C of AR 600-9, proper nutrition and regular exercise are necessary to help you lose weight and improve your state of fitness. It says, "Invest in yourself." Here are some examples of how this can be done:

- Make a decision to lose weight and shape up.
- Get motivated.
- Develop a strategy (diet, exercise routine, lifestyle changes).
- Carry out this strategy and enjoy the payoff—a healthy appearance, an improved self-image, a sense of accomplishment, and a feeling of pride.

Studies show that the average American man eats 2,360 to 2,640 calories per day. The average woman eats between 1,640 and 1,800. Reducing calories taken in leaves fewer calories for the body to have to burn to lose weight.

According to AR 600-9, appendix C: "A healthful diet contains sensible portions of fruits, vegetables, grains, lean protein, and skim and/or low-fat dairy products. In addition, it is recommended that foods and beverages consumed contain little or no added sugar, sodium, and solid fats. Eating four to six small meals per day and not skipping meals, especially breakfast, is helpful for weight loss."

With the right combination of diet, exercise, and sleep, you can be sure that you are engaged in a fitness program that will allow you to enjoy a long, healthy life and a successful time in the military as well.

9

Leadership Development

. . . As compared to managers, leaders are expected to inspire and influence. In my view, you do that in how you go about creating relationships with your people. You build their faith in your ability to lead, and in your actions that show that you really care for them. To me that is just another way of saying that you work to gain their respect and trust. Army leaders often have to be firm and unwavering in the challenges of the profession—some might call it tough love. But you can do that and still create an environment of give-and-take, and you do that by fostering an open channel of communication that builds a positive environment in which soldiers can grow and mature.

—SMA Jack L. Tilley, 12th Sergeant Major of the Army From his book with
CSM Dan Elder (USA, Ret.): *Soldier for Life,* Historical Society of Texas

It is absolutely reasonable and certainly possible for you or any first-term soldier to aspire and be promoted to the rank of corporal or sergeant during your first term of enlistment. Such a promotion, however, requires that you develop and possess certain leadership competencies—that is, be competent to lead.

The Army defines leadership as "the process of influencing people by providing purpose, direction, and motivation while operating to accomplish the mission and improve the organization." Leadership, despite the great strides in technology, remains the same—influencing and motivating people to get a job done. ADP 6-22, *Army Leadership*, and FM 6-22, *Leader Development*, provide the details on various aspects and levels of leadership and leadership development. The regulation and manual discuss character-based leadership, clarify values, establish attributes as part of character, and, most importantly, focus on improving people and organizations for the long term. Rather than provide a one-size-fits-all leadership model, Army leadership doctrine now outlines three levels of leadership—*direct*, *organizational*, and *strategic*, and the field manual focus is on the operational and tactical levels where most enlisted soldiers will find themselves at work. Leadership doctrine can be best examined in an overview fashion from the Leadership Requirements Model found in ADP 6-22. The model explains the three key leader attributes of character, presence, and intellect and then the three categories of competence:

SOLDIER'S CREED

I am an American Soldier.

I am a Warrior and a member of a team.

I serve the people of the United States and live the Army Values.

*I will always place the mission first.

*I will never accept defeat.

*I will never quit.

*I will never leave a fallen comrade.

I am disciplined, physically and mentally tough,

trained and proficient in my warrior tasks and drills.

I always maintain my arms, my equipment and myself.

I am an expert and I am a professional.

I stand ready to deploy, engage, and destroy the enemies

of the United States of America in close combat.

I am a guardian of freedom and the American way of life.

I am an American Soldier.

leads, develops, and achieves, which are explained in detail below. *Leaders of character and competence act to achieve excellence by providing purpose, direction, and motivation.* Above all, Army leadership doctrine anchors leaders of character and competence in moral bedrock—the Army values and warrior ethos.

LEADERSHIP AND CHARACTER

Character describes who a person is inside, and at the core of Army leaders are Army values. Those values—*loyalty, duty, respect, selfless service, honor, integrity*, and *personal courage* (LDRSHIP)—capture the professional military ethos and describe the nature of our soldiers. Our common values help us understand the purpose of our missions and devise appropriate methods to accomplish them. Values are the foundation of all that we are and do. Within those values, integrity is punctuated, in that the willingness to follow and stick to the other values, policies, rules and laws, and lawful expectations will ensure that you are respected as a soldier and leader who desires to set an example for others by living it yourself. By learning, practicing, and living the Army values, you are well on your way to becoming a leader of character who lives the warrior ethos.

Just as vital and a key companion to the seven Army values is the warrior ethos. This is an important concept that professional soldiers and leaders see as their bond and guide. It can be described as your dedication to your fellow soldiers, your leaders, the Army, and our country and national interests. The Soldier's Creed carries the warrior ethos as its centerpiece, indicated by the four asterisks. The Soldier's Creed, if adhered to closely, provides a pathway for every soldier to honorable service and success.

Leadership and Presence

Being present as a leader is important, but it is not enough. A professional leader is present but also has presence. If you think back to your drill sergeant or some other leader that had "it," that intangible aura about them that inspired you, that is presence. It includes the physical (fitness), bearing (uniform appearance, body posture, confidence, strength of voice, etc.), and actions seen on the outside of a person. It also includes the intellect and character a person maintains on the inside, which combine with the outward attributes to make the whole leader impression on those around him or her. The same can be said about you and how you are perceived by those around you. Do you maintain a fitness level and bearing, and conduct yourself in words and action such that leaders and other soldiers could see you leading? It's an important thought to consider.

Leadership and Intellect

Intellect is the same—how smart we are—regardless of the conditions or a person's role in life. However, while the teacher or professor at a high school or respected university has clear intellect, it is of a unique nature, used and imparted in a way that is important for that role. Military intellect differs in that it relates to how one will lead, critically think, and adapt to situations. It involves making decisions that can mean success or could put soldiers or innocent civilians in harm's way if lacking or made poorly. It includes mental agility, sound judgment, innovation, interpersonal tact, and expertise. Leadership intellect is developed through personal (self) development, deliberate training, and exercises involving critical thinking, both in operational units and in institutional schoolhouses as well. The first step on this path is to become an expert in your craft of soldiering (WTBDs) as well as in the technical skills required in your MOS. The more competent you are in your job and battle drills, the more confidence you will exude, which will allow you to start growing to leadership situations.

Placing yourself in opportunities to lead whenever possible, such as volunteering to lead a detail, volunteering to lead PRT for your squad or team, or volunteering as an assistant squad leader if time permits, can provide valuable practice in taking charge, with critical thinking opportunities to help you grow and develop. Reading professional journals in your field of work, taking college classes and military correspondence courses, and advancing in your Structured Self Development courses are all ways to also work on your military intellect for leadership. One other great opportunity to practice here is to compete in your local Soldier of the Month (or quarter) boards. In addition to the benefits discussed in previous chapters, you will gain invaluable experience in look-ing leaders in the eyes and speaking confidently, both about yourself and your goals. You will also be improving all the attributes discussed above and developing yourself as you practice and demonstrate expertise, mental agility, interpersonal tact, bearing, presence, and critical thinking skills in answering questions, both specific and situational or general discussion types too.

Leads Competency

The Army expects all leaders to lead effectively and to do so while following all laws, regulations, and policy as they apply to a given situation. There are five components that make up the Leads Competency. The first is *leading others*. This is the ability to compe-tently influence those soldiers and Department of the Army civilians who are assigned in the same unit or staff. *Extending influence beyond the chain of command* is the ability to influence those not assigned or under a leader's span of control. This component is well illustrated at the local level by the old saying, "Good leaders never walk by a mistake." If you see someone at the Post Exchange or downtown who is out of uniform or otherwise acting inappropriately, it takes much more interpersonal tact and diplomacy to correct that situation than if the soldier is within your chain of command and you have legitimate authority over them. General military authority allows for a correction and it should be made, but leaders must approach it with a bit more discretion. At the more senior levels, extending influence can involve joint and other assignments working with coalition or other partners.

The third component of the Leads Competency is *builds trust*. Building trust is a key element in the fabric of any leader, and it is a two-way street for the follower as well. You will and should expect your leaders to gain and keep your trust, but you must also gain theirs. This aspect of leadership never changes, regardless of how high in rank and leadership positions you go. If there is not mutual trust, the organization will suffer greatly. Of course, leaders are responsible for everything a unit does or fails to do, so this building of trust begins with them. *Leading by example* is another component that is crit-ical to the success of a leader. Children do as parents do, not as they say, in many cases. The same holds true in the military. If a leader is giving direction, guidance, or setting standards but failing to maintain them, that message to the team erodes their trust, as well as signals what the "real" standard must be. It is hard to lead a unit run from the back of the formation.

The final component is *communication*. While actions speak louder than words, words do matter. In previous Army leadership doctrine, communication was extremely important to the success of any leader or their organization. That has not changed. It is critical that leaders communicate clear and effective directives. They should be asking you to state that information back to ensure the message was received in the way it was intended. As you work on leader development, practicing to speak with clear, concise messages will be important to your success.

Develops Competency

Leaders are indeed responsible for the success or failure of their unit and for serving as long-term stewards of the Army profession. By ensuring that they are focused on the first three components of the Develops Competency—*prepared themselves, developing others, and create a positive environment*—they are continuing to perpetuate that fourth, longer-term component of *stewardship of the profession*. It is hard to develop others if you are not prepared yourself. Reading this guide is a great example of how you are preparing yourself as a professional and leader. The preparation never ends, since new rank, larger responsibilities, and diverse assignments will always require you to keep preparing. Developing others is at the foundation of Army success, since the development of the next generation of leaders is the only way for the Army to continue to meet the obligations of our national interests. Development is achieved in a variety of ways, and it is up to the leader to determine what methods are used for a given individual or situation. Creating a positive environment is leader business, and is one area you can personally help with and affect each day. As a leader or a follower, having a positive outlook and looking at every task and exercise as an opportunity to learn and develop can go far in helping grow and maintain a healthy unit climate. Avoiding rumors, never saying anything about someone that you would not say directly to them, keeping a highly motivated persona at all times, and volunteering for the tough jobs are also things that indicate a healthy unit climate. There is not a leader at any level in the Army who does not appreciate a follower who is positive, and the same is true for leaders at every level and how they are perceived by subordinates.

Achieves Competency

This category has but one component: *Gets Results*. When all is said and done, the desired end state is to accomplish tasks and missions on time and to standard. However, that can be dangerous to the long-term success of an organization if it is not balanced with the other competencies and attributes of leadership defined above. When leaders become so focused on mission accomplishment that they lose focus of the opportunities to further develop subordinates (the next generation), they miss fantastic opportunities and once again fail to develop the positive environment and other attributes to their fullest.

The irony of leaders or units that focus solely on mission accomplishment and leave out the all-important balance of welfare of soldiers is that their chances of long-term success are hindered in important ways. Right from the start, they are failing the ideal of a long-term steward of the Army profession. Beyond that and the critical competency of developing others being diminished, building trust becomes more difficult over time, as members of the team recognize quickly where the focus is and that there is not genuine concern for them or the team as a whole. Leadership is a skill that is learned over time and with much practice. Keeping the important aspect of getting results as a priority, while ensuring that all the other aspects of an ethical leader who has leadership character are included, will go far in ensuring that you develop as the best leader you can be.

Discipline
A military guide for success would be woefully lacking if it did not have a discussion of discipline. While being the recipient of discipline will be covered in chapter 17 on UCMJ, having self-discipline as an individual and as a disciplined unit is important in your approach to leadership development. From the start, your personal conduct on and off duty will say much about you as a professional (or not). The old catchphrase of "Spotlight Ranger" described a soldier who performed and gave it his all when the leadership was around and then completely slacked off (a slacker) when leaders were not present. Self-discipline is all about the actions you take or avoid when nobody is watching. Likewise, conduct including alcohol abuse, drug use, spouse abuse, sexual assault, and the like will not only quickly show the Army that you are undisciplined and probably unfit to serve, but also tears at the fabric of our country and its faith in the uniformed services.

That faith and high regard for the military has existed for years, where uniformed services are repeatedly found at the top of the polls as a respected institution. So when a few bad soldiers do bad things, it reflects even more poorly on the military, because the country does and should hold you to a higher standard than the average citizen. It comes with the territory of being so highly regarded in the first place. When units are undisciplined, it affects unit morale and effectiveness too. Each member of the team can positively affect that unit discipline by following the ideals of the leadership attributes and competencies and letting their chain of command know when they see a violation or a standard not being met. By having that self-discipline and courage to be a positive part of the unit, the conditions are set for your transition to a leader.

Soldiers learn leadership every day. Simply by watching other leaders and performing their duties, they will learn leadership. Those who deliberately apply the process—study examples of leadership, reflect on their own experiences, apply lessons learned, and seek comments—become better leaders now and for the future.

Leadership skills are one of the lifelong benefits of military service. The skills are worth learning well. They are indispensable while on active duty and invaluable when you return to civilian life.

Additional information on leadership is found in FM 6-22 *Leadership Development*.

10

Career Decisions

Just as one day you enlisted, someday you will face separation. So what you do in the meantime is vital to your future (and, if you are married, your family's future). Have you remained qualified to reenlist? Will you "make the cut" if your MOS is targeted for reduction during drawdown policy initiatives? What are your "re-up" options? Do you want to reenlist? What if you choose not to re-up? Whatever you do, begin considering your options at least a year out—two years is more prudent—even though you may change your mind at the last minute.

If you separate, you will most certainly need to go to work unless a lottery jackpot or some other bonanza drops in your lap. If you choose not to re-up but have a remaining service obligation, you still have military career decisions to make about joining the Army Reserve or the Army National Guard. If you choose to remain in service to the nation full-time, do you have what it takes to become a senior NCO, warrant, or commissioned officer?

If you enlisted when you were eighteen or nineteen years old, and you continue your Army career, you will be only thirty-eight or thirty-nine when you become eligible for retirement. Would you like to draw an Army retirement check before age forty, knowing that that check will arrive monthly for the rest of your life?

Soldiers must be in the grade of staff sergeant or higher to be eligible to serve twenty years. Soldiers not promoted beyond the grade of sergeant may serve only fourteen years. Corporals and specialists—those who do not get promoted before their separation dates—may serve no more than eight years, and privates to privates first class may serve no more than five years. Talking to your unit's career counselor is critical in this process, as they are trained to provide you with all the options and help you make the most informed decision. Included in this chapter are some things to also consider.

REENLISTMENT DECISION
If you decide that the Army is right for you and you want to continue to serve, you should consider all options when reenlisting. Begin early. Visit your unit's career counselor. Discuss your decision with your fellow soldiers. Seek counseling from your immediate supervisor and others in your chain of command. Talk to your family. Consider at least the following:

Soldiers reenlisting at the World Trade Center.

- Why you are reenlisting.
- What options are available should you decide to separate.
- How reenlisting can enhance your career.
- Whether you will receive a regular or selective reenlistment bonus.
- MOS training and schooling, or MOS reclassification options.
- Travel and assignment options.
- Your promotion potential.
- The needs of the Army and the nation.

Reenlistment Bonuses

The Army offers reenlistment bonuses as a means of encouraging soldiers in certain critical MOSs to reenlist or extend their current enlistments. Critical MOSs are determined by the needs of the Army. The Army updates the list of critical MOSs regularly and publishes it through MILPER messages. Your unit's career counselor should be able to provide you with the list.

The Selective Reenlistment Bonus (SRB) Program is available to all soldiers, regardless of rank, who hold a primary MOS designated as critical. Soldiers reenlisting through the SRB Program are eligible for reenlistment bonuses up to $45,000 if they reenlist or extend for a minimum of three years. They may receive a maximum of three such SRBs during their military careers, and only one in each established time zone. The zones, based on time of active military service, are zone A, extending from twenty-one months to six years; zone B, from six to ten years; and zone C, from ten to fourteen years of active military service.

The actual amount of the SRB is determined by a formula based on the soldier's monthly basic pay. The bonus cannot exceed six times the monthly pay, multiplied by the number of years of additional obligated service, nor can the bonus exceed $45,000. The SRB is based on the current needs of the Army and on current reenlistment trends in specific MOSs. The more critical the Army's need, the higher the SRB. Consequently, sometimes no MOS qualifies for the maximum rate.

The following examples illustrate how the program operates: A soldier receiving basic pay of $800 a month reenlists under the SRB Program for four years; the bonus amount for his MOS is the maximum, six times the monthly basic pay. The SRB bonus would be ($800 x 6) x 4 = $19,200. If, however, the soldier was receiving a basic pay of $1,000 a month, the SRB would not be ($1,000 x 6) x 4 = $24,000; instead, this soldier would receive the maximum allowable bonus—$20,000. Since qualifying MOSs and their SRB rates fluctuate based on the needs of the Army, interested soldiers should contact their career counselor in the unit retention office to obtain current information. The SRB is paid in addition to any other pay and allowance to which the soldier is already entitled.

Training and Duty Station Options

If you decide to remain on active duty, you have a number of options. Upon reenlistment, you can elect additional training, a particular duty station elsewhere, or current duty station stabilization.

Options for the first-termer include reenlisting for the needs of the Army, current assignment stabilization for twelve months, assignment to an available choice in the continental United States (CONUS), assignment to an available specific overseas country, or training in a PMOS, SQI, or ASI, including Airborne training. PMOSs and SQI and ASI training that have openings for soldiers have prerequisites, and all of these options change from time to time. So it is very wise to get to your unit's career counselor early and examine all the options that are available at the time you are considering reenlistment.

Soldiers willing to reenlist or extend their enlistment can also apply for a number of interesting career development programs that become available as new soldiers are needed: explosive ordnance disposal (EOD), presidential support activities (working at the White House), technical escort (for chemical, ammunition, and EOD specialists), Army bands, instructors at service schools, drill sergeants, and recruiters. Selection of a new duty station may also be an option for your reenlistment as discussed above. You may be eligible for the overseas area option, the CONUS-to-CONUS station option, or, if overseas, the CONUS station of choice option.

Information and requirements for each career program are contained in AR 601-280; and career counselors are essential to the soldier who wishes to explore some of the more unusual career options in the Army.

OTHER MILITARY OPPORTUNITIES

Your career choices at the end of your first term are not limited to reenlisting in the Army or returning to civilian life. You may elect to serve in the Army Reserve or Army National Guard while pursuing a civilian career. Or you may decide to seek a commission as an officer or a warrant officer through Officer Candidate School, Warrant Officer Entry Courses, the U.S. Military Academy, or an ROTC program. All Army installations have reenlistment NCOs and in-service recruiters who can provide more detailed information about these options.

Army Reserve

The Army Reserve is a federal military force composed of the Ready Reserve and the Standby Reserve. The Ready Reserve is made up of combat support and combat service support units available for quick mobilization in times of national emergency or war. The Standby Reserve is a pool of soldiers who have a remaining military obligation and are eligible for recall to active duty.

Through the Ready Reserve, a former soldier can supplement his or her civilian income while taking full advantage of the technical and leadership training he or she received while on active duty. Reservists receive four days' pay for each weekend of reserve training, which is usually held monthly. An additional requirement is a two-week annual training session. Salary ranges depend on time in service and pay grade.

Each soldier leaving active duty who enlists in the Ready Reserve within sixty days of discharge from the Army retains his or her active rank, pay grade, and time-in-grade status. Additional benefits include $400,000 Servicemen's Group Life Insurance (SGLI), low-cost health and dental care, and commissary and Post Exchange privileges.

Army National Guard

The Army National Guard is a federal-state military force. Its primary mission is to maintain combat divisions and support units available for active duty in time of national emergency or war. Under its state mission, the Guard protects life and property and pre-serves state internal security.

Pay and benefits are essentially the same for the Guard as for the Army Reserve. One unique feature of the Guard is its Officer Candidate School (OCS) program. This sixteen- to eighteen-month program provides training on weekends through the state OCS. Guard members can also attend the active Army OCS and earn a commission in twelve weeks.

Officer Candidate School

Enlisted personnel who elect to remain on active duty may be eligible to apply for OCS training. Applicants must meet the following basic criteria:

- Be less than thirty-three years of age upon enrollment.
- Be a college graduate with at least a four-year degree.
- Have not more than six years of active federal service at the time of arrival to OCS, and be eligible for a secret security clearance.

During their assignment at OCS, candidates are paid at the E-5 level unless they previously held higher rank.

The fourteen-week program is rigorous and requires a high level of physical fitness, mental fortitude, and dedication to succeed. Upon completion of the course, graduates are commissioned as second lieutenants. See Human Resources Command website at *http://www.hrc.army.mil* and search the popular HRC "Resources" link for more details.

Warrant Officer Entry Course

Warrant officers are highly specialized experts and trainers who operate, maintain, administer, and manage the Army's equipment, support activities, and technical and tactical systems for their entire careers. The career progression of warrant officers is designed to encourage them to seek in-depth knowledge of particular systems and activities and maintain proficiency in their particular skills.

The Warrant Officer Entry Course, located at Fort Rucker, Alabama, trains selected enlisted personnel in the fundamentals of leadership, ethics, personnel management, and tactics. Following completion of the rigorous six-week course, warrant officers go on to additional specialized training in their particular MOSs.

To qualify for entry to the Warrant Officer Entry Course, a soldier must fit the following basic criteria, as well as other career field/MOS specific criteria as needed:

- US citizen and possess a Final Secret or Top Secret security clearance (interim clearances will not satisfy the requirement).
- Pass the standard APFT and meet Army height/weight standards within prior six months of packet being boarded.
- Pass the flight physical for aviators or the commissioning physical for technical MOS.
- Have a minimum of twelve months remaining on enlistment contract.
- Be thirty-three years of age or less if seeking 143A (aviator) and forty-six years of age or less if seeking a technical MOS (waivers accepted).
- Have earned a high school diploma or general education development (GED) equivalency.
- Have served less than twelve years' active enlisted service.

Warrant officers may serve in a variety of MOSs, but there is an emphasis on administration, maintenance, and aviation specialties. The requirements may periodically change; check the Warrant Officer Recruiting team website at *www.usarec.army.mil/hq/warrant/WOEligibility.shtml*.

U.S. Military Academy

Soldiers wishing to attend the U.S. Military Academy at West Point may seek direct nomination under the provisions of AR 351-12 if they meet the entrance requirements without further study. The easiest way is to complete the candidate questionnaire online at *https://candidate.usma.edu/guest/cq/dad_pcq_part1.cfm?field1=BW* to get you started. You also can find questions answered at *www.usma.edu/admissions/SitePages/FAQ_Soldiers.aspx*, which will provide a link to the application process as well as answer frequently asked questions.

Basic prerequisites are to be:

- A U.S. citizen.
- Unmarried, not pregnant, with no legal obligation to support dependents.

- Under twenty-three years of age prior to July 1 of the year entering USMA (under twenty-two prior to July 1 of the year entering the Prep School).
- A high school graduate or have a GED.
- Of high moral character.

All applications are made directly to West Point. Soldiers not directly admitted to West Point will be automatically considered for admission to the Prep School. Soldiers who meet the basic eligibility requirements, have achieved SAT scores greater than 1,000 or an ACT composite score of 20 or higher, and achieved average grades or better in their high school curriculum are especially encouraged to apply. Soldiers must obtain an endorsement from their company or lowest-level unit commander. While this endorsement constitutes a nomination, soldiers are also strongly encouraged to obtain additional nominations from their congressional nomination sources.

ROTC

One other great option for the soldier to consider is to separate from the service under a special ROTC scholarship program. In this program, the soldier may earn a degree, be commissioned a second lieutenant, and return to active duty. Through the "Green to Gold" program, these soldiers become civilians specifically to enter the ROTC program, complete a baccalaureate program, and then be commissioned as officers in the Regular Army or the Army Reserve. Once discharged, the soldier forfeits the pay and benefits of active duty, but he or she may still use any veterans' educational benefits earned while on active duty.

The ROTC cadet is not a soldier in civilian clothes. The former soldier leads the life of a normal college student with few additional responsibilities. Cadets must complete prescribed military science courses, a minimum of one semester of foreign language, Leader Development and Assessment Course (LDAC—a paid six-week training program between the junior and senior years), and any other training identified by the secretary of the Army as a requirement for commissioning.

Returning to active duty as a Regular Army second lieutenant is not a guarantee. Based on the needs of the Army, some cadets are commissioned as second lieutenants in the U.S. Army Reserve instead. Cadets select the branch of service in which they would prefer to serve, but branch selection is also not guaranteed; again, the needs of the Army must take precedence. Active-duty service can sometimes be delayed up to two years at the request of the individual in order to complete postgraduate studies; educational delays are also based on the needs of the Army at the time of commissioning.

Basic Requirements

The Green to Gold Scholarship basic eligibility requirements are to:

- Be a U.S. citizen (nonwaiverable).
- Be under thirty-one years of age on December 31 of the year you complete all requirements for a commission and a college baccalaureate degree. (This is a statutory requirement and there are no waivers authorized.)
- Have no criminal convictions.

- Have a minimum of two years active duty. Additionally, must have three months of active duty for every one month of specialized training (waivers are considered).
- Have a general technical (GT) score of 110 or greater.
- Pass the APFT within the last six months.
- Be a high school graduate or equivalent.
- Have a cumulative high school or college GPA of 2.5.
- Have a letter of acceptance to school of choice offering Army ROTC.
- Have a letter of acceptance from the PMS of that Army ROTC battalion.
- Have a favorable National Agency Check.
- DODMERB Medical Qualification.
- Four-year applicants must have a minimum of 19 scored on the ACT or 920 minimum on the SAT (waiverable).
- Have no more than three dependents including spouse (waiverable).

Green to Gold Scholarship Option Program
The Green to Gold Scholarship provides scholarship funding for up to four years depending on degree requirements. The scholarship will provide tuition or room and board support; additional money for books, supplies, and equipment; a stipend for up to ten months per school year, increased annually depending on the Military Science Class, and pay for attending the Leader Development and Assessment Course (LDAC) between the junior and senior years of college. Soldiers will be discharged in accordance with (IAW) AR 635-200, chapter 16. Soldiers will be able to use the Montgomery GI Bill/Army College Fund (MGIB/ACF) benefits in addition to the scholarship. Many colleges offer additional incentives, and the PMS of your desired school can provide these details.

Green to Gold Active-Duty Option Program
This is different than above; this two-year program provides eligible, active-duty enlisted soldiers an opportunity to complete a baccalaureate degree or graduate degree and be commissioned as an Army officer upon receiving the appropriate degree. Soldiers selected to participate in this program will continue to receive their current pay and allowances while in the program (up to a maximum of twenty-four consecutive months), as well as permanent change of station (PCS) entitlements and, if qualified, Montgomery GI Bill/Army College Fund (MGIB/ACF) benefits.

Green to Gold Nonscholarship Option Program
The Green to Gold Two-Year Nonscholarship Option Program is available to soldiers who have completed two years of college, and who can complete their college degree requirements in two years. Upon graduation, participants receive commissions as second lieutenant. While undergoing ROTC instruction, students receive a monthly stipend for up to ten months each school year that increases each year based on their Military Science Class, pay for attending the Leader Development and Assessment Course (LDAC) between the junior and senior years of college, and, if qualified, Montgomery GI Bill/Army College Fund (MGIB/ACF) benefits. Green to Gold Nonscholarship Option members can also participate in the Simultaneous Membership Program (SMP). As SMPs,

soldiers are members of either a drilling Reserve or Guard unit and ROTC. SMPs are entitled to reserve component pay of E-5 under this program. Also, many states offer tuition assistance to Reserve and National Guard soldiers.

You can get more details on this option at *www.goarmy.com/careers-and-jobs/current-and-prior-service/advance-your-career/green-to-gold/green-to-gold-nonscholarship.html.*

For the soldier interested in a possible career as an Army officer, or for the soldier who simply wants to make the road toward the baccalaureate degree shorter by attending college full-time, the ROTC Scholarship Program offers a viable alternative.

THE SEPARATION DECISION

Whether you decide on an Army career or separation after your first enlistment, sooner or later you must quit the service. In this section, we examine the various types of discharges, the operation of the U.S. Army Transfer facilities, and veterans' rights.

Separations

How and why a soldier is separated from the Army depends on many factors, according to AR 635-200, *Enlisted Personnel.* Separation policies in AR 635-200 promote readiness of the Army by providing an orderly means to accomplish the following:

- Ensure that the Army is served by individuals capable of meeting required standards of duty performance and discipline.
- Maintain standards of performance and conduct through characterization of service in a system that emphasizes the importance of honorable service.
- Achieve authorized force levels and grade distribution.
- Provide for the orderly administrative separation of soldiers in a variety of circumstances.

AR 635-200 provides the authority for separation of soldiers upon expiration of term of service (ETS); the authority and general provisions governing the separation of soldiers before ETS to meet the needs of the Army and its soldiers; the procedures to implement laws and policies governing voluntary retirement of soldiers for length of service; and the criteria governing uncharacterized separations and the issuance of honorable, general, and other than honorable conditions discharges.

The following are the authorized types of separation under the provisions of AR 635-200:

Chapter 4—Separation for Expiration of Service Obligation. A soldier will be separated upon expiration of enlistment or fulfillment of service obligation.

Chapter 5—Separation for Convenience of the Government. A chapter 5 separation covers the following: involuntary separation due to parenthood; lack of jurisdiction as ordered by a U.S. court or judge thereof; aliens not lawfully admitted to the United States; personnel who did not meet procurement medical fitness standards; failure to qualify medically for flight training; personality disorders; concealment of arrest record; early release of reserve component personnel serving AGR tours under Title 10; early separation to further education and address other designated physical or mental conditions.

Chapter 6—Separation Because of Dependency or Hardship. Soldiers of the active Army and the reserve components serving on active duty or active duty for training may be discharged or released because of genuine dependency or hardship. Dependency exists when death or disability of a member of a soldier's (or spouse's) immediate family causes the family or one of its members to rely on the soldier for principal care or support. Hardship exists when in circumstances not involving death or disability of a member of the soldier's (or spouse's) immediate family, separation from the service will materially affect the care or support of the family by alleviating undue and genuine hardship.

Chapter 7—Defective Enlistments, Reenlistments, and Extensions. This chapter provides the authority, criteria, and procedures for the separation of soldiers because of minority (discovery of age under seventeen), erroneous enlistment or extension of enlistment, defective enlistment agreement, and fraudulent entry.

Chapter 8—Separation of Enlisted Women for Pregnancy. Chapter 8 provides authority for voluntary separation of enlisted women because of pregnancy. A pregnant soldier is faced with a number of choices, the most basic of which is whether to separate from the Army. This decision can be very difficult because of its far-reaching ramifications. Once the soldier has decided to be retained on active duty, she will be expected to complete her full enlistment before she is again given the choice of continuing in the military or returning to civilian life.

Being the mother of a newborn child does not afford the soldier special privileges, but normally she will not receive PCS orders for an overseas assignment during the pregnancy. Such orders can often be deferred or deleted (for up to one year) if they should be issued. After the child is born and the mother is released from normal postnatal care, however, the military mother is given no unique consideration for assignments. She is expected to fulfill the needs of the Army just like any other soldier. This means that she could receive orders for worldwide assignments, including to dependent-restricted overseas areas.

The Army is concerned for the welfare of the child, but it does not adjust the assignment process to accommodate the new mother. Instead, the Army requires each soldier with dependents who are unable to care for themselves to file an approved family care plan. Failure to complete an adequate plan will result in a bar to reenlistment. The plan specifies what actions the soldier has taken to ensure care for her dependents in the event she is assigned to an area where dependents are not authorized. In addition, she is expected to make provisions for the care of her dependents while she is away or on military duty (both on a daily basis and in the event of a necessary temporary duty).

One other consequence of the pregnant soldier's decision to continue in the military is the possibility of involuntary separation. If the soldier cannot handle her normal duties during the pregnancy or once she is a new mother, she may be separated from the service involuntarily. Such decisions are made on the grounds of unsatisfactory performance of duty or misconduct, whichever is appropriate. Involuntary separation is covered by AR 635-200, paragraphs 5-8 and 13-2, in addition to chapter 14. If a soldier in an entry-level status becomes pregnant, she will be evaluated by a medical officer to determine whether she can fully participate in the training required for the MOS. If it is determined that she cannot participate in the training, she will be involuntarily discharged. Otherwise, the soldier will be retained unless she specifically requests discharge under AR 635-200, chapter 8.

The soldier will be provided medical care during and after the pregnancy. Again, she has a choice. She may remain at her present duty assignment and receive care through a military facility within thirty miles of that location; if such care is not available, she will be treated through a civilian doctor and civilian facilities. Or she may choose to take ordinary leave, advance leave, and excess leave so that she may return to her home or other appropriate and desired location for her maternity care and the birth of her child. Once labor begins, her leave status changes to convalescent leave for the period of labor, hospitalization, and postpartum care. Convalescent leave for postpartum care is limited to the amount of time the doctor specifies as essential for the medical needs of the mother. Generally, postpartum convalescent leave does not exceed forty-two days. Leave status and the pregnant soldier are covered in AR 630-5, chapter 9, section II.

If the soldier decides to return home to deliver the baby, it is her responsibility to first ascertain if military facilities near her home have obstetrical care available. Many military facilities do not provide such care. The soldier cannot choose to return home for maternity care and have the government pay for that care at a civilian facility. This is prohibited in AR 40-3, except for bona fide medical emergencies that justify the use of a civilian facility. Using civilian facilities away from the duty location means that the soldier, not the government, is normally responsible for the medical bills. The health benefits adviser at the nearest military medical facility is the best source for further information on this matter.

If the pregnant soldier chooses to separate from the Army, she receives an honorable discharge and any benefits applicable to soldiers with the amount of time in service she has at the time of separation. Separation due to pregnancy is authorized under chapter 8 of AR 600-200.

Unit commanders must counsel women who are eligible for pregnancy separation. Army chaplains and the American Red Cross also offer counseling, and the judge advocate general's (JAG) office can instruct the soldier in legal matters regarding the birth and care of her child. The soldier will have at least a week to consider her options but must indicate her choice of either separating or remaining on active duty in writing.

Whether the soldier is allowed to reconsider her choice depends on the choice she initially made. If she originally chose to stay on active duty but then decides to separate, the Army must separate her. If she originally elected to separate and then decides she wants to remain in the Army, the case will be reviewed, and a decision whether to retain her will be made based on the best interests of the Army.

An abnormal pregnancy places a difficult burden on the woman involved. The Army allows a woman the option of seeking a discharge in the event of a miscarriage, abortion, or premature delivery if she had been pregnant for at least sixteen weeks at the time the pregnancy terminates.

Medical treatment for obstetrical and postpartum care is provided at government expense through a military medical facility. The separating soldier may not use TRI-CARE or civilian medical facilities at government expense. In fact, the pregnant soldier is required to sign a statement before she decides to separate from the military, clearly stating that she understands that under no circumstance can TRICARE, any military department, or the DVA reimburse her civilian maternity care expenses; the statement further clarifies that she understands that any costs for civilian care will be her personal financial responsibility. Therefore, careful planning must be made to ensure that she settles in an area where military medical facilities provide maternity care. The separating pregnant soldier will be authorized postpartum care for up to six weeks after the birth of the child.

Chapter 9—Alcohol or Other Drug Abuse Rehabilitation Failure. A soldier who is enrolled in the Alcohol and Drug Abuse Prevention and Control Program (ADAPCP) for substance abuse may be separated because of inability or refusal to participate in, cooperate in, or successfully complete such a program.

Chapter 10—Discharge for the Good of the Service. A soldier who has committed an offense or offenses punishable by a bad conduct discharge or dishonorable discharge under the provisions of the UCMJ and the *Manual for Courts-Martial* may submit a request for discharge for the good of the service. The request does not prevent or suspend disciplinary proceedings. (See AR 635-200, pages 81–85 for details.)

Chapter 11—Entry-Level Status Performance and Conduct. This chapter provides guidance for the separation of personnel because of unsatisfactory performance or conduct (or both) while in entry-level status. It covers inability, lack of reasonable effort, or failure to adapt to the military environment.

Chapter 12—Retirement for Length of Service. A soldier who has completed twenty years' active federal service and who has completed all required service obligations is eligible to retire. Upon retirement, the soldier is transferred to the U.S. Army Reserve Control Group (Retired) and remains in that status until active service time plus control group time equals thirty years, and then is placed on the retired list. A Regular Army soldier who has completed at least thirty years of active federal service will, upon request, be placed on the retired list.

Chapter 13—Separation for Unsatisfactory Performance. A soldier may be separated per this chapter when unqualified for further military service because of unsatisfactory performance, under the following circumstances: (1) the soldier will not develop sufficiently; (2) the seriousness of the circumstance is such that retention would have an adverse impact on military discipline, good order, and morale; (3) it is likely that the soldier will be a disruptive influence; (4) it is likely that the circumstances will continue to recur; (5) the ability of the soldier to perform duties effectively is unlikely; (6) potential for advancement or leadership is unlikely.

Chapter 14—Separation for Misconduct. This chapter establishes procedures for separating personnel for misconduct because of minor disciplinary infractions, a pattern of misconduct, commission of a serious offense, conviction by civil authorities, desertion, and absence without leave. A discharge under other than honorable conditions is normally appropriate for a soldier discharged under this chapter.

Chapter 16—Selected Changes in Service Obligations. A soldier may be separated for a variety of reasons/purposes under this chapter. They include: (1) order to active duty as a commissioned or warrant officer; (2) discharge to enroll in a program that leads to officer or warrant officer appointment; (3) discharge for purpose of immediate enlistment or reenlistment; (4) non-retention on active duty; (5) oversees returnees; (6) early separation due to MOS disqualification; (7) early separation due to force reduction or strength limitations; (8) separation of soldiers in Warrior Transition Units; (9) separation of soldiers assigned to installations or units scheduled for inactivation or permanent change of station; and (10) holiday transition program. There is a wide variety of categories as can be seen in this listing. See AR 635-200, pages 104–107 for details and character of service for each.

Chapter 18—Failure to Meet Weight Control Standards. This chapter applies to those soldiers entered in the Army Body Composition Program (weight-control program) who fail to make satisfactory progress after a reasonable amount of time, as shown in counseling and personnel records. They may only be separated using this chapter if it is the sole reason for separation. This means that if they were also eligible for a separation due to misconduct under Chapter 14, that chapter would take precedence. Soldiers will also not be separated under this chapter if qualified medical personnel determine there is a legitimate underlying medical condition that precludes their participation in the Army Body Composition Program.

Chapter 19—Qualitative Management Program. This chapter contains policies and procedures for voluntary and involuntary separation, for the convenience of the government, of Regular Army (RA) NCOs and U.S. Army Reserve (USAR) NCOs serving in Active Guard and Reserve (AGR) status, under the Qualitative Management Program (QMP). Soldiers separating under this chapter have their discharges characterized as honorable. This chapter does not apply to soldiers in the rank of SGT and below.

Types of Discharge

Honorable Discharge

An honorable discharge is given when an individual is separated from the military service with honor. An honorable discharge cannot be denied to a person solely on the basis of convictions by courts-martial or actions under Article 15 of the UCMJ. Denial must be based on patterns of misbehavior and not isolated instances. An honorable discharge may be awarded when disqualifying entries in an individual's service record are outweighed by subsequent honorable and faithful service over a greater period of time during the current period of service. Unless otherwise ineligible, a member may receive an honorable discharge if he or she has, during the current enlistment or extensions thereof, received a personal decoration or is separated by reason of disability incurred in the line of duty.

General Discharge

A general discharge is issued to an individual whose character of service has been satisfactory but not sufficiently meritorious to warrant an honorable discharge. Such persons would have, for example, frequent punishments under Article 15 of the UCMJ or be classified as general troublemakers.

Other Than Honorable Discharge
Discharges that fall within this category are given for reasons of misconduct, security, or the good of the service and are covered by AR 635-200. No person shall receive a discharge under other than honorable conditions unless afforded the right to present his or her case before an administrative discharge board with the advice of legal counsel.

Uncharacterized Separations
There are two types of uncharacterized separations: those given when a soldier is in entry-level status and those given because of void enlistments or inductions.

Bad Conduct or Dishonorable Discharge
A soldier will be given a bad conduct discharge pursuant only to an approved sentence of a general or special court-martial. A soldier will be given a dishonorable discharge pursuant only to an approved sentence of a general court-martial. The appellate reviews must be completed and the affirmed sentence duly executed. Dishonorable and bad conduct discharges result in expulsion from the Army.

TRANSITION ACTIVITIES
U.S. Army transfer facilities provide an informal but professional atmosphere, centrally located at a post where personnel being separated may be processed within acceptable time limits. AR 635-10 prescribes that overseas returnees, except retirees, be separated on the first workday after their arrival at the separation transfer point, when possible. Personnel being released from active duty who are discharged before expiration, term of service (ETS), or the period for which ordered to active duty are separated by the third workday after approved separation. All others are separated on their scheduled separation dates, except for those individuals who elect to be separated on the last workday before a weekend or a holiday.

Medical Examination
There is no statutory requirement for soldiers to undergo a medical exam incidental to separation. It is Army policy, however, to accomplish a medical examination if a soldier is active Army and retiring after twenty or more years of active duty. An examination is also required if a soldier is being discharged or released and requests a medical examination, if review of the soldier's health record by a physician or physician's assistant warrants an exam, or if an examination is required by AR 40-501.

Each soldier undergoing separation processing will have his or her medical records screened by a physician, regardless of whether a separation physical has been requested. *A separation physical may be one of the most important medical examinations of your life.* If you believe you are eligible for VA disability benefits due to conditions incurred on active duty, you can request to receive the VA Compensation Physical Exam at the same time as your separation physical. You have to start the exam process no later than six months before ETS, and no less than four months before transition leave starts. Separation physicals end in a personal interview with a doctor. That interview is the proper time to bring up every single medical fact incident to military service. This interview substantiates service connection should a soldier, after discharge, request disability compensation from the DVA based on military service. Above all, each soldier being separated from the service should make a copy of his or her medical and dental records and keep them after discharge.

Soldier for Life Program

The Soldier for Life (SFL) Program replaced the Army Career and Alumni Program (ACAP) that your NCOs may mention from the past. It is an umbrella program designed to initiate and maintain programs intended to improve and provide meaningful assistance and benefits to soldiers and their families during their service, in transition, and beyond separation. It is your link to the Army and a valuable addition to your separation package of benefits and information.

Soldier for Life—Transition Assistance Program. The Soldier for Life—Transition Assistance Program (SFL-TAP) is one of the most valuable benefits you and your family (if married) will be provided. Regardless of how long you stay in the Army, you will move back to the civilian sector at some point. Having state-of-the-art resources and people to help you make that transition is a huge help in what is certainly a stressful time for most. All soldiers, their families, and DA civilians undergoing a reduction in force or base realignment and closure may use this program. Understanding what benefits you have and how to go about obtaining them is an important part of being a soldier or leader, for yourself, your family, and your assigned soldiers and their families as you move up in rank. Fortunately, the law (VOW Act) requires that you engage in the SFL-TAP no later than 180 days before separation, and it includes counseling and a mandatory five-day program. The more energetic and focused you are in taking advantage of the various training, programs, and workshops offered, the smoother you can expect your transition to be. What you can expect when you begin to negotiate the SFL-TAP:

Pre-Separation Counseling. While this is a mandatory first step for all soldiers who served more than 180 days of active duty, which must be started not later than 90 days before separation, it should be viewed as the start of what can be an exciting and proactive time of preparation instead of just some boring requirement. The counselor at your session will go over each area on the pre-separation checklist. There is a ton of information related to each area, and you will want to annotate the areas where you desire more information. This is a great way to ensure that you don't forget to investigate a key piece of information as you go through the various programs and workshops.

Training. There are a multitude of classes that will significantly help you in your transition once you are permanently in civilian clothes. Some of the classes offered, which you can take online and present a certificate of completion to your SFL-TAP trainer, include Dress for Success, Family Concerns, (job) Interview Techniques, Individual Training Plan (ITP) Review, Salary Negotiations, Skills Development, Special Issues, and Value of a Mentor. See those links at *https://www.sfl-tap.army.mil/pages/transition/VOWTraining.aspx.*

Department of Labor Employment Workshop. This three-day workshop is designed to help you set an objective of a next occupation or career and then take the steps to reach that objective. It includes two briefings by the Veterans Administration on all benefits entitled to armed service members, including those who were disabled during service. The counselors at SFL-TAP are all qualified and should be sought for their wealth of knowledge. Online resources are also abundant and should be kept as favorites on your personal computer if you have one.

Job Assistance. The SFL-TAP was initially created to ensure that you are most prepared to seek and secure employment upon separation. It provides each soldier with job search training, individual assistance and counseling, and referral service. It conducts individual, small-, and large-group workshops to help soldiers prepare for interviews, evaluate job offers, track job leads, develop their résumés, and so forth. The training available, job search engines, job fairs announced (both physical and virtual), and other valuable capabilities are located on the SFL-TAP website at: *https://www.sfl-tap.army .mil/default.aspx.*

Individual Transition Plan (ITP). Like any mission you undertake in the military, planning is the key to success, and your ITP is your personal plan for success in transition. It will include the key elements of your transition, and since you write it yourself, you can easily adjust it as you go through the process. Elements of the ITP include personal transition needs, employment, education, vocational/technical, entrepreneur, and milestones. The first and last elements are mandatory, and you place your focus on the other four based on your personal needs and then establish the milestones to achieve them before separation. While the requirement is to start by 180 days from separation, SFL-TAP recommends that you start no earlier than twelve to eighteen months before separation. This helps ensure you are not over-rushed, especially if mission requirements come up that interrupt this critically important mission of transition success.

Terminal Leave

Deciding whether to take terminal leave may not be an easy decision; it depends on how much leave a soldier has accrued at the time of separation, how much leave he or she may have previously cashed in for pay, and what plans the servicemember has for job-hunting activities, travel, or vacation.

Soldiers taking terminal leave will be allowed to finish processing at the local transfer activity before departure on leave. The separation transfer point will send you your DD Form 214 at the time of actual separation.

Discharge Certificates

Your DD Form 214, *Certificate of Release or Discharge from Active Duty*, is the most important document you will receive during your outprocessing, and is one of the most important documents you will ever receive during your military career. At the time of your separation, you will receive copies one (original) and four of DD Form 214. Be sure to make copies of these forms and protect the originals. Do not let the originals out of your possession. Having notarized copies and storing them in a separate location is also advisable, just in case of fire or theft. This document is often used for employment verification, especially if the company has experience with the military; it also can be requested by other agencies including the VA when claiming disability. It cannot be overemphasized how critical safeguarding this document is to your future ability to validate your service.

Travel and Transportation Allowances

Soldiers are authorized travel allowances from their last duty station to their home. Shipment and storage of household goods incident to retirement is authorized on a one-time basis, subject to weight limitations and other controls. Specific information relative to shipment and storage of household goods is contained in DA Pam 55-2, *Personal Property Shipping Information.*

Wearing the Uniform

Wearing of the uniform by separated soldiers is a privilege granted in recognition of faithful service to the country. Former members of the Army who served honorably during a declared or undeclared war and whose most recent service was terminated under honorable conditions may wear the Army uniform in the highest grade held during such war service. The uniform may be worn only for the following ceremonies and when traveling to and from such ceremonies:

- Military funerals, memorial services, weddings, inaugurals, and other occasions of ceremony.
- Parades on national or state holidays, or other parades or ceremonies of a patriotic nature in which any active or reserve U.S. military unit is taking part.

If worn during the above authorized occasions, only service and dress uniforms are allowed for wear. Wearing of the combat or physical fitness uniform is not allowed. Wearing of the Army uniform at any other time or for any other purpose is prohibited.

VETERANS' RIGHTS AND BENEFITS

The benefits discussed in this section are available to all veterans regardless of status. All Veterans Administration (VA) benefits (with the exception of insurance and certain medical benefits) payable to veterans or their dependents require that the particular period of service on which the entitlement is based be terminated under certain conditions. Honorable and general discharges qualify the veteran as eligible for benefits; however, dishonorable discharges and bad conduct discharges issued by general courts-martial are a bar to VA benefits. Other bad conduct discharges and discharges characterized as other than honorable may or may not qualify. Qualification depends on a special determination made by the VA and is based on the facts of each case.

In order to prove your eligibility for VA benefits, you must have the following:

- A complete copy of your medical records.
- DD Form 214, *Certificate of Release or Discharge from Active Duty.*

Conversion of SGLI to VGLI

A servicemember has 240 days after separation to apply for Veterans Group Life Insurance (VGLI), with no medical examination requirements. Beyond the 240 days, a soldier has one year to apply, with exam requirements. During the 120 days after separation, the SGLI coverage continues without premiums.

You can keep your VGLI coverage for your lifetime, as long as you continue paying premiums. At any time, however, you may convert your VGLI coverage to an individual policy of life insurance with a commercial company that participates in the program at the company's standard premium rate regardless of your health. No disability or other supplemental benefits will be provided on converted policies. You may convert up to the amount of VGLI coverage you hold. The link at *http://benefits.va.gov/insurance/vgli.asp* provides information on how to convert to an individual policy, with a list of participating companies. Additional benefits for service-disabled veterans are available, including a two-year extension at no cost as well as other programs to explore.

Employment

Priority referral for job openings and training opportunities is given to eligible veterans, with preferential treatment for disabled veterans. In cooperation with VA regional offices and Veterans Outreach Centers, the job service assists veterans who are seeking employment by providing information about such opportunities as hiring fairs/job fairs, on-the-job training, and apprenticeship training.

Veterans seeking employment with the federal government may receive special opportunities, such as the following:

- A five-point preference is given to those who served during any war, in any campaign, in an expedition for which a campaign medal has been authorized, or for 180 consecutive days between 31 January 1955, and 15 October 1976.
- A ten-point preference is given to those who were awarded the Purple Heart, have a current service-connected disability, or are receiving compensation, disability retirement benefits, or pension from the VA.
- A veteran with a 30 percent or more disability may receive appointment without a competitive examination—with a right to be converted to a career appointment and with retention rights during reductions in force.
- Many other programs are available for you in terms of employment, including opportunities to fill permanent positions in the federal government (Veterans Employment Opportunity Act), and the Veterans Recruitment Appointment, where you may be appointed to a federal position without having to compete for it in a job announcement. Once again, your SFL-TAP counselor should be able to provide you all the details or link you to the best sources of information.

Educational Benefits

See your Army Education Center counselor for details on the GI Bill (also covered in chapter 6) and other educational benefits programs. You can also access more information by visiting the GI Bill web page at *www.va.gov/*.

VA Loans

The purpose of VA loans is to buy a home; to buy a residential unit in certain condominium projects; to build a home; to repair, alter, or improve a home; to refinance an existing home loan; to buy a manufactured home (with or without a lot); to buy a lot for a manufactured home that you already own; to improve a home through installation of solar heating and/or cooling systemss or other weatherization improvements; to purchase and simultaneously improve a home with energy-conserving measures; to refinance an existing VA loan to reduce the interest rate; to refinance a manufactured home loan in order to acquire a lot; and to simultaneously purchase and improve a home. Eligibility requirements vary, based on period of service, with the exception that all eligible veterans must have been discharged under conditions other than dishonorable.

The loan terms are subject to negotiation between the veteran and the lender. The repayment period or maturity of VA home loans may be as long as thirty years. Newly discharged veterans are mailed certificates of eligibility shortly after discharge. Other veterans may secure their certificates by sending VA Form 26-1880, *Request for a Certificate of Eligibility*, along with the required supporting documents, to the VA regional office nearest them. Certificates of eligibility are also available online at *www.ebenefits.va.gov*. Active-duty personnel may also take advantage of these loans.

Unemployment Compensation

The purpose of unemployment compensation for veterans (called Unemployment for Ex-Servicemembers, or UCX) is to provide income for a limited time to help meet basic needs while employment is sought for those discharged under honorable conditions. The amount and duration of payments vary because they are governed by state laws, although benefits are paid from federal funds. Interested veterans should apply at the nearest state employment service, not at the VA. A copy of DD Form 214 is needed to establish the type of separation from the service.

One-Time Dental Treatment

In addition to dental conditions that qualify for treatment because of service connection, veterans are entitled to a one-time dental treatment without review of service records to establish service connection. This treatment must be applied for within ninety days of separation. Do not fail to take advantage of this important benefit. You can apply by contacting the local VA office, or apply online at *https://www.1010ez.med.va.gov/sec/vha/1010ez/*.

Department of Veterans Affairs (Disability) Compensation

If you believe that you have a condition that may entitle you to VA compensation, file your claim at the time of separation. If the VA, upon reviewing your medical records, finds that you do have grounds for seeking compensation, an appointment for a physical exam will be made for you at the Department of Veterans Affairs hospital closest to your retirement home. Your claim will be processed based upon the examination results. Note that if you plan before separation, you can already have this important benefit taken care of before out of service (see the section on "Medical Examinations" above).

Medical Benefits

The Department of Veterans Affairs provides a Medical Benefits Package, a standard enhanced health benefits plan available to all enrolled veterans. Through it the VA offers the whole spectrum of medical benefits to qualified veterans: aids and services for the blind, alcohol treatment, domiciliary care, drug treatment, hospitalization care for dependents or survivors, nursing home care, outpatient dental treatment, outpatient medical treatment, and prosthetic appliances.

The VA maintains an annual enrollment system to manage the provision of quality hospital and outpatient medical care and treatment to all enrolled veterans. A priority system ensures that veterans with service-connected disabilities and those below the low-income threshold are able to be enrolled in the VA's health-care system. Veterans who are receiving compensation or who would be eligible to receive compensation (except for retirement pay) and who need treatment for an ailment connected with their service are admitted as beds are available. Under certain circumstances, veterans who were not discharged or retired for disability or who are not receiving compensation and who apply for treatment of a non-service-connected disability may be admitted to a VA hospital. Any veteran with a service-connected disability may receive VA outpatient medical treatment.

Vocational Rehabilitation

Generally, a veteran is eligible for vocational rehabilitation for twelve years following discharge or release from active service. A four-year extension is possible under certain circumstances, and further extensions may be granted for veterans who are seriously disabled, as determined by the VA. Eligible disabled veterans may receive training up to a total of four years or the equivalent in part-time or a combination of part-time and full-time training. Eligibility for this training is determined by the VA.

Correspondence and Records

Keep a file of every paper the VA sends you. Your dealings with the VA will require patience and persistence; the required degree of each will depend to a large extent on how busy your local VA office is. Invariably, VA personnel are courteous, and they try to be helpful, but processing your claim may take some time.

Burial

Burial is available to any deceased veteran of wartime or peacetime service (other than training) at all national cemeteries having available grave space, except Arlington Cemetery. The veteran must have been discharged under conditions other than dishonorable.

Eligible veterans' dependents may receive a headstone or grave marker without charge, shipped to a designated consignee. The cost of placing the marker in a private ceremony must be borne by the applicant. The VA may partially reimburse (up to the average actual cost of a government headstone or marker) costs incurred by an applicant acquiring a nongovernment headstone or marker for placement in a cemetery other than a national cemetery.

References

AR 635-8 *Separation Processing and Documents*

AR 614-30, *Overseas Service*

AR 635-200, *Active Duty Enlisted Administrative Separations*

AR 670-1, *Wear and Appearance of Army Uniform and Insignia*

Soldier for Life Resources website: *https://soldierforlife.army.mil/resources*

Veterans Administration website: *https://www.va.gov*

PART III

Quick Reference

11

Army Traditions, Customs, and Courtesies

As a soldier serving in today's Army, you have earned the honor to be a member of a proud profession that is long in history and rich in tradition and heritage. These traditions date back to the founding of our country, and some customs stem from those of the British Empire before we became a nation. Warriors today continue Army traditions by respecting long-held customs and courtesies, by being model citizens, by respecting one another, and by respecting symbols of national unity such as the U.S. flag. These traditions are an important part of why our country respects and trusts our military to the highest degree. Learning and adhering to traditions, customs, and courtesies is important to you as a soldier in order to understand how vital you are, personally, in continuing this foundation of respected uniformed service. It is also important to be recognized as a dedicated professional within your unit and, in a larger view, to ensure that the Army is viewed as an organization that is rightfully held to the highest standards of conduct by the American people and around the world.

MILITARY COURTESY

Military courtesy is the respect shown to superiors by subordinates and the mutual respect demonstrated by senior to subordinate personnel, as well as to peers in uniform at every level. It is basic to military discipline and founded on respect for and loyalty to authority, dedicated service, and mission accomplishment. Military courtesy has an effect on every aspect of military life.

The Salute

One of the oldest and most common military courtesies is the salute. Although many forms of salutes are authorized, depending on the arms you may be carrying and the situation involved, the most common salute is the hand salute. It is initiated by the subordinate and will be returned by the officer. A sharp, crisp salute exchanged between you and the officer saluted shows pride in recognizing a comrade in arms; conversely, a sloppy or halfhearted salute shows a lack of pride and is a poor reflection on the individual rendering it.

When the overseas cap, cold weather cap, or beret is worn, the hand salute is to the forehead—except when wearing glasses, when the tip of the fingers should touch the corner of the frame. When the utility cap, camouflage cap, or helmet is worn, the salute is to the visor.

Exceptions to saluting are made when the situation requires—in public transportation (such as buses and planes) or in public places (such as theaters), or when the salute would be impractical (at work, when driving a vehicle, or when actively engaged in athletics). Even though saluting is not required by military regulation when both soldier and officer are in civilian clothes, the soldiers who exchange this courtesy are following long-standing military tradition. If you know that an individual is an officer when you see him or her, it is important that you initiate the salute exchange to show your dedication to service and professionalism.

Every soldier should learn the following guidelines:

- If running, slow to a walk before saluting.
- Always hold your salute until it is returned by the officer.
- Never salute while holding an object in your right hand.
- Render the greeting of the day in a firm, crisp voice. A confident "Good morning, sir/ma'am" demonstrates pride in yourself. The response by the leader seals the bond. Some units have specific salute exchange phrases like "Rangers lead the way," "Airborne, all the way," or "Air Assault," and these unit-unique exchanges add pride and esprit de corps for those who exchange them (see "Unit Customs," page 129).
- In formation, salute only on the command "Present arms." Keep in mind that if you are in charge of a detail or formation, you are responsible for rendering the courtesies for the group.

The salute itself should be made in one movement, raising the right arm so that the upper arm is parallel to the ground and bending the elbow so that the tip of the forefinger touches the forehead slightly to the right of the right eyebrow. The fingers and thumb should be extended and "joined," or touching one another. Neither the palm nor the back of the hand should be visible from a front view.

If you wear eyeglasses, the forefinger fingertip of your right hand should touch the point on the glasses where the front frame joins the temple or earpiece. When you are wearing a utility cap or a helmet, your fingertip should touch the visor of that headgear.

On some occasions, you should exchange salutes with the officer twice. Specifically, if you salute an officer and the officer stays in your general vicinity but does not converse directly with you, all military courtesies have been fulfilled. When the officer spends a few moments talking with you, however, you should salute a second time at the end of the conversation. This custom is considered a preliminary greeting followed by a farewell.

When a vehicle passes carrying an officer that you recognize, you should render a salute. Likewise, if an official vehicle passes displaying vehicle plates or flags that depict the rank of the passenger, you should salute.

The salute is also used to show respect to the American flag, when the flag passes or during the retreat ceremony.

The best advice on saluting is to render the salute whenever any doubt exists as to whether the salute is actually required. Again, rendering the salute is a matter of pride. It is one of the most basic customs and should never be considered a task or requirement

ENLISTED INSIGNIA OF GRADE

AIR FORCE	ARMY	MARINES	NAVY
Chief Master Sergeant of the Air Force (CMSAF)	Sergeant Major of the Army (SMA)	Sergeant Major of the Marine Corps (SgtMajMC)	Master Chief Petty Officer of the Navy (MCPON)
Chief Master Sergeant (CMSgt) — Command Chief Master Sergeant	Command Sergeant Major (CSM) — Sergeant Major (SGM)	Sergeant Major (SgtMaj) — Master Gunnery Sergeant (MGySgt)	Fleet/Command Master Chief Petty Officer — Master Chief Petty Officer (MCPO)
Senior Master Sergeant (SMSgt) — First Sergeant (E-8)	First Sergeant (1SG) — Master Sergeant (MSG)	First Sergeant (1stSgt) — Master Sergeant (MSgt)	Senior Chief Petty Officer (SCPO)
Master Sergeant (MSgt) — First Sergeant (E-7)	Platoon Sergeant (PSG) or Sergeant First Class (SFC)	Gunnery Sergeant (GySgt)	Chief Petty Officer (CPO)
Technical Sergeant (TSgt)	Staff Sergeant (SSG)	Staff Sergeant (SSgt)	Petty Officer First Class (PO1)
Staff Sergeant (SSgt)	Sergeant (SGT)	Sergeant (Sgt)	Petty Officer Second Class (PO2)
Senior Airman (SrA)	Corporal (CPL) — Specialist (SPC)	Corporal (Cpl)	Petty Officer Third Class (PO3)
Airman First Class (A1C)	Private First Class (PFC)	Lance Corporal (LCpl)	Seaman (Seaman)
Airman (Amn)	Private E-2 (PV2)	Private First Class (PFC)	Seaman Apprentice (SA)
Airman Basic (AB) (no insignia)	Private E-1 (PV1) (no insignia)	Private (Pvt) (no insignia)	Seaman Recruit (SR)

OFFICER INSIGNIA OF GRADE

AIR FORCE	ARMY	MARINES	NAVY
General of the Air Force	General of the Army	(None)	Fleet Admiral
General	General	General	Admiral
Lieutenant General	Lieutenant General	Lieutenant General	Vice Admiral
Major General	Major General	Major General	Rear Admiral (Upper Half)
Brigadier General	Brigadier General	Brigadier General	Rear Admiral (Lower Half)
Colonel	Colonel	Colonel	Captain
Lieutenant Colonel	Lieutenant Colonel	Lieutenant Colonel	Commander
Major	Major	Major	Lieutenant Commander

OFFICER INSIGNIA OF GRADE

AIR FORCE	ARMY	MARINES	NAVY
Captain	Captain	Captain	Lieutenant
First Lieutenant	First Lieutenant	First Lieutenant	Lieutenant Junior Grade
Second Lieutenant	Second Lieutenant	Second Lieutenant	Ensign

	SILVER AND BLACK	SCARLET AND SILVER	
(None)	W-5 W-4 W-3	W-5 W-4 W-3	W-4 W-3
	Chief Warrant Officer / Chief Warrant Officer / Chief Warrant Officer	Chief Warrant Officer / Chief Warrant Officer / Chief Warrant Officer	Chief Warrant Officer / Chief Warrant Officer

	SILVER AND BLACK	SCARLET AND GOLD	
	W-2 W-1	W-2 W-1	W-2 W-1
	Chief Warrant Officer / Warrant Officer	Chief Warrant Officer / Warrant Officer	Chief Warrant Officer / Warrant Officer

COAST GUARD

Coast Guard officers use the same rank insignia as Navy officers. Coast Guard enlisted rating badges are the same as the Navy's for grades E-1 through E-9, but they have silver specialty marks, eagles and stars, and gold chevrons. The badge of the Master Chief Petty Officer of the Coast Guard has a gold chevron and specialty mark, a silver eagle, and gold stars. For all ranks, the gold Coast Guard shield on the uniform sleeve replaces the Navy star.

but a unique bond and display of respect and professionalism between the initiator and recipient in conducting America's most important business, our national security.

Correct Use of Titles

Each member of the armed forces has a military rank: private to general in the Army and Marine Corps, airman to general in the Air Force, and seaman to admiral in the Navy. The Coast Guard closely follows the Navy rank system with minor differences (e.g., Master Chief Petty Officer of the Navy has the rank of MCPON, while his equivalent in the Coast Guard is the MCPOCG). The accompanying chart shows the ranks used in the U.S. armed forces.

Rank becomes a soldier's military title by force of regulation and custom. In official documents, a member's rank or title always accompanies his or her name, and it is also used in conversation. By custom, military titles are used between civilians and the military, just as the custom has been established to use the title "doctor," "professor," or "governor." A person who has earned a military title carries it permanently and, if desired, into retirement.

When addressing another soldier, preface the soldier's last name with his or her rank. "Sergeant Jones," "Sergeant Major Smith," "Private Henderson," and "Major Brown" are examples of appropriate means of addressing soldiers conversationally.

When referring to persons not present, always use ranks and names. Use of last names only is disrespectful; use of pay grades (e.g., "I was talking to an O-4" or "It was an E-7") is unmilitary and degrading. All soldiers, like you, have earned their ranks, from the newest private first class to the most senior general; you should use them accordingly.

Titles of Commissioned Officers

Lieutenants are addressed officially as "Lieutenant." This applies to both first lieutenants and second lieutenants. The same applies to colonels and lieutenant colonels, both of which are addressed officially as "Colonel." Likewise, all generals are addressed as "General," regardless of whether they are brigadier, major, lieutenant general, or general.

When not using the rank title, "Sir" is used for all officers. "Ma'am" is used to address female officers when "Sir" would be used with male officers. All chaplains are officially addressed as "Chaplain," regardless of their military rank or professional title. Likewise, doctors are addressed as "Doctor."

Titles of Warrant Officers

The warrant officer (all five grades) officially ranks below second lieutenant and above cadet. He or she is a commissioned officer and differs only in that there are certain regulated restrictions on command functions. The warrant officer is the Army's top-grade specialist and is addressed as " Mr./Mrs./Miss/Ms.," as appropriate. Under informal conditions, a chief warrant officer may be addressed as "Chief."

Titles of Cadets

Cadets of the U.S. Military Academy and the ROTC often serve summer internships with regular units where they experience military life during their training. In written communications and in conversations when they are not present, cadets are addressed as "Cadet." In direct conversation, they are addressed as "Mr./Mrs./Miss/Ms./Cadet."

Titles of Noncommissioned Officers

The Sergeant Major of the Army is typically addressed by that full title or as "SMA." Command sergeants major and sergeants major are addressed as "Sergeant Major." A first sergeant is addressed as "First Sergeant." Other sergeants, regardless of rank, are addressed as "Sergeant." While this is the guidance prescribed in AR 600-20, *Army Command Policy*, some drill sergeants may also *politely request* that they be addressed as "Drill Sergeant." It would likely be in a trainee's best interest to comply with that request as an additional informal custom. Corporals and specialists are addressed with those titles. Privates first class are addressed with the abbreviation of their rank: PFC. Privates E-1 and E-2 are called "Private." The full titles of all enlisted members are used in official communications.

The Place of Honor

The place of honor is on the right. When a junior walks, rides, or sits with a senior, the junior takes position abreast and to the left of the senior. The junior should walk in step with the senior, step back and allow the senior to be the first to enter a door, and render similar acts of courtesy to the senior. The same applies when riding in a van or sedan. The junior enters the right door first and sits on the left seat; the senior enters second and sits to the right of the junior. These customs may seem ancient or archaic, but remember, the more senior you become, the more courtesy and accommodation will be made for your hard-earned work, and so it is an ongoing cycle of respect.

Courtesies to Officers and Noncommissioned Officers (NCO)

A number of customs and courtesies for showing respect to officers and NCOs have evolved over the years. For instance, an officer entering a room is shown courtesy. The first soldier to recognize the officer calls the other personnel in the room to attention, but the soldier does not salute. A salute is rendered indoors only when the soldier is reporting. Soldiers should remain at attention until the officer gives an "at ease" command. Do not call the room to attention if the entering officer is junior in grade to an officer already in the room. Coming to attention in the work environment is required at the start of the day when the commander or senior person first enters the building. It is not required thereafter. If at all practical, however, when an officer not commonly working directly with a soldier is in the work environment and addresses the soldier directly, the soldier should stand.

Outside of the work environment, standing at attention is always expected of the soldier when he or she is talking with an officer. Frequently, the officer will instruct the soldier to stand at ease. When the conversation is completed, the soldier should return to attention, salute, and voice an appropriate acknowledgment of the conversation, such as, "Yes, ma'am," or "Good afternoon, sir."

One final recommendation on rendering courtesies to officers: You should regard "requests," "desires," or "wishes" expressed by a commanding officer as orders.

Frequently, the wording is softened as a courtesy to the subordinate, but the intent is the same as an order.

For NCOs entering a room, it is typical that an announcement is made if they are the senior individual and no officers are present. First sergeants and above are normally announced upon arrival by their rank if they are within the organization, such as "the Brigade Sergeant Major." If they are outside of the organization, then it will normally be by rank and name: "the Alaska Sergeant Major, Sergeant Major Smith."

When talking with an NCO superior, it is customary to stand at parade rest/at ease and only talk when asked a question or when otherwise appropriate in the conversation. The NCO will normally set the tone and whether or not an informal discussion is to occur. Once the NCO has entered the work area, then the unit-section-squad norms will drive the operational tempo and customs from there.

Appointments with Commanding Officers

Soldiers are authorized under the Army's "open-door policy" to speak with each commander in their chain of command. It is usually under the most serious conditions that this is done, when a soldier believes that he or she has been wronged or has some important information that the commander may need to know.

Soldiers are usually able to get help with difficulties from offices on post or from their NCO support channel, which is the squad or section leader, the platoon sergeant, or the first sergeant. It is essential, however, that each soldier knows that he or she has the right to appeal directly to the commander for redress of wrongs.

When a soldier believes that a matter requires a commander's attention, he or she should make an appointment to see the commander. The first sergeant can make appointments to see the company commander and can coordinate appointments with the battalion commander by going through the battalion command sergeant major. Just inquire, "May I see the commanding officer?" Often it is appropriate to state the reason, unless the matter is extremely private. Once an appointment is made with the commander, be sure to arrive promptly for the meeting and render all military courtesies.

TABOOS

Do Not Defame the Uniform. When you wear your uniform, you are acting in a capacity as a member of the government of your country. Do not defame yourself, your uniform, your unit, or your country by behaving badly while wearing the uniform or by wearing the uniform in any manner other than as prescribed. Be especially strict with yourself when in foreign countries. You should wear your uniform every day, as if people you want proud of you (family or friends back home) are watching you.

Never Slink Undercover to Avoid Retreat. Now and then, thoughtless people are observed ducking inside a building or undercover just to avoid a retreat ceremony and the moment of respect it includes. Never slink away from an opportunity to pay respect to our flag and our national anthem. The flag and anthem are the symbols of what soldiers and, indeed, the whole Army exist to protect and pay tribute to, including all those who have served in the past.

Proffer No Excuses. Never make excuses or explain a shortcoming unless an explanation is demanded. The Army demands results. Soldiers of all grades make mistakes, and when that happens, admit the mistake, correct the error if possible, and find out how to do it right the next time. Admitting and bearing the consequences of a mistake will earn you the respect of subordinates, peers, and superiors alike.

Never Lie to a Superior. The fourth "rule" of the 1759 Standing Orders for Rogers Rangers says: "Tell the truth about what you see and do. There is an army depending on us for correct information. You can lie all you please when you tell other folks about the Rangers, but don't never lie to a Ranger or officer." This applies to noncommissioned, warrant, and commissioned officers, and you as well.

Avoid Going over a Superior's Head. It is both a customary and a legal right for soldiers to discuss grievances with their chain of command. Except for the most exceptional cases, it is bad form for a soldier to take a problem or grievance to the battalion commander without first having sought relief with the platoon leader and platoon sergeant or the first sergeant and company commander.

Do Not Associate Inappropriately. It is a long-standing Army tradition that enlisted soldiers do not associate socially with officers. Enlisted soldiers do not gamble, borrow, or lend money, or drink intoxicants with officers. See chapter 4 for more details on this matter.

Never Lean on a Superior's Desk. When called before a senior commissioned or noncommissioned officer, avoid leaning or resting against the senior's desk. Stand tall until offered a seat.

Never Keep Anyone Waiting. Report at once when notified to do so. Never keep anyone waiting unnecessarily. This is certainly an old Army tradition. The failure of a soldier to appear at his or her place of duty is a punishable offense.

COURTESY TO THE FLAG

Four common sizes exist for the national flag: The garrison flag, flown on special occasions and holidays, measures twenty by thirty-eight feet. The post flag, flown for general use, is ten by nineteen feet. The storm flag, used in inclement weather, is five by nine and one-half feet. The last size is that of the grave-decorating flag, which measures seven by eleven inches.

In addition to the national flag, we can speak of the national color, the national standard, and the national ensign. The national color, carried by dismounted units, is a three-by four-foot flag trimmed on three sides by a golden yellow fringe measuring two and one-half inches in width. The national standard is identical to the national color, except that it is carried by a mechanized, motorized, or mounted unit. The national ensign is a naval term designating a flag of any size used to indicate the nationality of ship personnel. The term *flag* does not technically refer to colors, standards, or ensigns. Other terms associated with flags are also a part of military tradition. The hoist is the width, the fly is the length, and the truck is the ball at the top of the flagstaff.

Honor the Flag; Honor Yourself

Honoring the nation's flag is an integral part of military customs and courtesies. The hand salute is rendered to show respect when the flag passes in front of a soldier in uniform. You should initiate the salute when the flag is approaching and is within six paces, and then you should hold the salute until the flag has passed six paces. If you are walking past a stationary flag, the same six-pace rule applies. In addition, you should turn your head in the direction of the flag. Soldiers marching in formation render salute only on command. If you are indoors when the flag passes, do not render the hand salute; however, you should stand at attention.

A soldier in civilian clothes still honors the flag with a salute, but it is modified to a "civilian salute," with the right hand placed over the heart. If headgear is worn with civilian clothing by a male soldier, the headgear is removed with the right hand and held over the heart; a female soldier in civilian clothing wearing headgear does not remove the headgear but still places her right hand over her heart.

The national flag should never be dipped low as a means of salute or greeting. The only exception is made for military vessels under specific international courtesies. Organizational flags, including the U.S. Army flag, are dipped lower than the national flag during the playing of the national anthem, "To the Color," or a foreign national anthem.

Out of respect for the flag, you should never use it as part of a costume, on a float, or on a vehicle, unless it is displayed on a staff. No lettering of any kind should ever be added to the flag. When a flag is damaged, soiled, or weathered, it should be burned or disposed of in a dignified manner. No portion of the flag should ever be allowed to touch the ground; if it does, the flag is considered soiled. The proper way of folding the flag should be followed exactly (see illustration).

Another means of showing respect to the flag is the Pledge of Allegiance, first adopted by Congress in 1942. The tradition surrounding the pledge specifies that it should be said while standing at attention, with the right hand over the heart. The Pledge of Allegiance is normally not recited in military formations or in military ceremonies.

Raising and Lowering the Flag

Military customs and traditions govern the raising and lowering of the flag as well. Reveille is the daily military ceremony honoring the flag at the beginning of the day. Retreat is the counterpart when the flag is lowered at the end of the day. Reveille is a bugle call, often recorded and played over a public-address system on military installations today. The flag is hoisted quickly to the top of the flagpole, beginning on the first note of reveille. Retreat ceremonies, full of traditions, are discussed in the following section.

The flag is sometimes flown at half-staff as a salute to the honored dead. Memorial Day, the last Monday in May, is one occasion when the flag is flown at half-staff from reveille to 1200 hours. A twenty-one-gun salute is then fired before the flag is raised to the top of the staff until retreat. Whenever the flag is to be flown at half-staff, it should first be hoisted to the top of the staff and then lowered to the midpoint. Likewise, before lowering the flag, it should be hoisted the full height of the staff and then lowered and properly folded.

Full details on flag courtesies can be found in AR 840-10.

OPEN EDGE

FOLDED EDGE

FOLD THE LOWER STRIPED SECTION OF THE FLAG OVER THE BLUE FIELD.

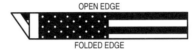

OPEN EDGE

FOLDED EDGE

FOLD THE FOLDED EDGE OVER TO MEET THE OPEN EDGE.

OPEN EDGE

FOLDED EDGE

START A TRIANGULAR FOLD BY BRINGING THE STRIPED CORNER
OF THE FOLDED EDGE TO THE OPEN EDGE.

FOLD THE OUTER POINT INWARD PARALLEL WITH THE
OPEN EDGE TO FORM A SECOND TRIANGLE.

CONTINUE FOLDING UNTIL THE ENTIRE LENGTH OF THE FLAG IS FOLDED
INTO A TRIANGLE WITH ONLY THE BLUE FIELD AND MARGIN SHOWING.

TUCK THE REMAINING MARGIN INTO THE POCKET FORMED BY THE
FOLDS AT THE BLUE FIELD EDGE OF THE FLAG.

THE PROPERLY FOLDED FLAG SHOULD RESEMBLE A COCKED HAT.

Folding the American flag

CUSTOMS
The customs of the service make up the unwritten "common law" of the Army. These customs are rich in tradition, and every soldier should know and observe them.

Retreat Ceremony
The purpose of the retreat ceremony is to honor the national flag at the end of the day. Often the evening gun is fired at the time of retreat so that soldiers throughout the installation will be aware of the ceremony even if they are outside the range of the bugle. The evening gun is also used to mark the end of the workday.

Retreat is not necessarily observed at the same time at each installation. The post commander sets the time of the sounding of both reveille and retreat.

During the retreat ceremony, the evening gun is fired at the last note of retreat. At that time a band, a bugler, or recorded music plays the national anthem or sounds "To the Color." Soldiers begin lowering the flag on the first note of the national anthem or "To the Color" at a rate that ensures that the lowering is completed with the last note of music. Then, following strict custom, the flag is folded and stored until reveille the next morning.

Special respect is rendered to the flag and to the national anthem during retreat by soldiers all across the installation, not merely by those participating directly in the ceremony. Under no circumstances should a soldier run into a building or elsewhere to avoid rendering this courtesy to the flag.

During the playing of the national anthem, soldiers in uniform should stand at attention, facing the flag if visible or the music if the flag is not visible. A salute should be rendered on the first note and held until the final note. The same courtesy applies to "To the Color." When indoors, the salute is omitted. Soldiers in civilian clothing render the "civilian salute" in the same manner as to the flag. Female soldiers never remove headgear.

All vehicular traffic should stop during the retreat ceremony. For cars and motorcycles, the driver and passengers should get out of the vehicle and show proper respect. For other vehicles, such as buses or armored vehicles, the ranking soldier should get out and render the appropriate salute. All other passengers should sit quietly at attention inside the vehicle. Commanding officers of tanks or armored cars can salute from the vehicle.

The same respect should be rendered to the national anthems of friendly nations when they are played during official occasions.

Bugle Calls
In addition to reveille and retreat, several other bugle calls play important roles in military tradition. In general, bugle calls can be divided into four categories: alarm, formation, service (which includes reveille and retreat), and warning.

First call is the first bugle of the day. Considered a warning call, it alerts you that reveille is about to take place and that you will be late if you're not ready within the next few minutes.

The last bugle call of the day is taps, a service call dating back to Civil War days. Taps is traditionally used at military funerals as well, giving the final bugle call for the fallen soldier.

"To the Color" is the alternative music used during the retreat ceremony. It signals that the flag is being lowered. You should render the salute during "To the Color" as you would during the national anthem. Both are meant to honor the flag.

Tattoo is usually played near 2100 hours and has traditionally been the call for lights-out in fifteen minutes.

Unit Customs

Individual units foster pride and esprit de corps by observing a variety of customs that set them apart from the rest of the Army. Since it is a matter of personal honor for a soldier to know in which battles his or her unit took part, soldiers joining a new unit should learn its history. A quick check of the Internet for the unit or the post library is often the best way to start. Many units have study guides for soldiers and NCO boards that include the history of the post and unit as well, and your sponsor should be able to provide you information before you arrive at your new assignment.

Units perpetuate their history through their organizational properties, mottoes, and insignia. A unit's organizational properties include flags and standards (including battle honors and campaign streamers) and other physical representations of its heritage. Many units claim regimental silver with a unique history as part of their organizational property. For example, the 23rd Infantry's silver bowl was made from the metal of 5,610 combat infantrymen's badges earned by the 23rd's infantrymen during the first eighteen months of combat in Korea. Perhaps the most famous regimental silver property is the 31st Infantry's "Shanghai Bowl," which was presented to the regiment by the citizens of Shanghai after the Boxer Rebellion.

Unit mottoes provide another link with the past. The 19th Infantry's motto, "The Rock of Chickamauga," recalls the regiment's service at the battle of Chickamauga. The 7th Cavalry's motto and song, "Garry Owen," was brought to the regiment in the 1860s by Irish immigrants. The 22nd Infantry's motto, "Deeds, Not Words," speaks for itself.

Many units have acquired infantry's nicknames as a result of past service. The 31st Infantry is known as the "Polar Bears" as a result of duty in northern Russia after the end of World War I. The 28th Infantry's "Lions of Cantigny" recalls the regiment's service at the first American offensive battle in World War I.

Unit insignia also embody unit traditions. For example, shoulder-sleeve insignia, first authorized during World War I, were originally conceived to foster esprit de corps and heighten the individual soldier's identification with his unit. The 81st Infantry Division was the first division to develop a sleeve insignia, that of a black wildcat on a circular path. The idea was so well received by the headquarters of the American Expeditionary Force that General John J. Pershing directed the other divisions to develop their own distinctive cloth patches.

The Army Song

Another tradition that literally brings soldiers to their feet is the Army song. When you hear it being sung or being played, the appropriate action is to stand at attention. The melody is that of the "Caisson Song," composed in the early 1900s by then Lieutenant Edmund L. Gruber, who later was promoted to brigadier general. But the words for "The Army Goes Rolling Along" were selected much later. The eight-year process began in 1948 with a nationwide contest to create an official Army song. Within four years, the Army had also enlisted the aid of several music composers, publishers, and recording studios. Their joint efforts produced the new lyrics, set to the music of the old "Caisson Song." "The Army Goes Rolling Along" became the official Army song when it was dedicated on Veterans Day, 11 November 1956, at Army installations throughout the world. You should memorize the first verse, chorus, and refrain below, as it is sung out loud by all participants at the end of ceremonies such as changes of command, retirements, and many others.

The Army Goes Rolling Along

Verse:

March along, sing our song
with the army of the free.
Count the brave, count the true
Who have fought to victory.
We're the Army and proud of our name!
We're the Army and proudly proclaim:

1st Chorus:

First to fight for the right
And to build the nation's might,
and THE ARMY GOES ROLLING ALONG.
Proud of all we have done,
Fighting till the battle's won,
and THE ARMY GOES ROLLING ALONG.

Refrain:

Then it's hi! hi! hey!
The Army's on its way,
Count off the cadence loud and strong: (two! three!)
For where'er we go, you will always know
That THE ARMY GOES ROLLING ALONG.

2nd Chorus:

Valley Forge, Custer's ranks,
San Juan Hill and Patton's tanks,
And the Army went rolling along.
Minutemen from the start,
Always fighting from the heart,
And the Army keeps rolling along.

Refrain: Then it's hi! hi! hey!
The Army's on its way,
Count off the cadence loud and strong: (two! three!)
For where'er we go, you will always know
That THE ARMY GOES ROLLING ALONG.

3rd Chorus: Men in rags, men who froze,
Still that Army met its foes,
And the Army went rolling along.
Faith in God, then we're right
And we'll fight with all our might
As the Army keeps rolling along.

Refrain: Then it's hi! hi! hey!
The Army's on its way,
Count off the cadence loud and strong:
(two! three!)
For where'er we go, you will always know
That THE ARMY GOES ROLLING ALONG.
(Keep it rolling!)
And THE ARMY GOES ROLLING ALONG.

12

Assignments

Moving from one post to another, or making a permanent change of station (PCS), can be one of the most exciting times for a soldier and his or her family if married. It also can be highly stressful if not prepared for properly. When the move is to an overseas location, the excitement or stress is magnified given the challenges of a new culture, language, laws, and so forth. The further in advance you take action to put in your desires and then prepare for a move once instructions are received, the more likely you will be to see it as an adventure rather than a pain. Moving around the Army during your career is vital to gain different operational and growth experiences to put in your professional toolbox. This chapter discusses some of the more important aspects of assignments to consider and provides a variety of ways to inform the Army in terms of your desires and, in some cases, specific needs. Filling valid vacancies is the top priority for the Army, so if you wait until the last minute or, worse, do nothing, the Army will make the decision without your input. It is strongly recommended that you take proactive measures and have a vote in your next assignment. Read on.

COMMUNICATING WITH HUMAN RESOURCES COMMAND

The U.S. Army Human Resources Command (HRC) continues to evolve, with a series of initiatives designed to increase enlisted soldiers' participation in managing their careers. What was once paper-intensive and not very responsive is now, with automation, highly responsive to those soldiers who care about their assignments.

To help soldiers communicate better with their career managers, the Enlisted Personnel Management Directorate (EPMD) provides a variety of methods to help you manage your career. These initiatives include their website, *https://www.hrc.army.mil/content/Enlisted%20Personnel%20Management%20Directorate*. They also provide the Assignment Satisfaction Key—Soldier Assignment Module (ASK SAM), which will be covered in detail in this chapter, expanded e-mail capabilities, Interactive Personnel Electronic Records Management System (iPERMS), high-speed fax machines, mailgrams, and a pocket reference information card that lists telephone numbers, e-mail addresses, and other valuable information to soldiers wanting to help manage their careers.

EPMD also encourages you to use e-mail to contact your branch. Inquiries concerning the status of personnel actions, future schooling, or assignments are examples of typical information exchanges that can be conducted twenty-four hours a day. Soldiers can also correspond with their career managers by calling on the phone. The EPMD telephone, email, and mail addresses are shown below.

Points of Contact
You can contact the Enlisted Personnel Management Directorate in the following ways:

Telephone
(888) 276-9472 (888-ArmyHRC)
DSN 983-9500

Mail
Human Resource Service Center
U.S. Army Human Resources Command
Attention: Your branch office symbol (Column 3 in below table)
1600 Spearhead Division Ave., Dept. 420
Fort Knox, KY 40122-5402

e-mail
https://www.hrc.army.mil/content/Enlisted%20Personnel%20Management%20Directorate

---

ENLISTED ASSIGNMENT BRANCH CONTACT INFORMATION

1 Directorate	2 Abbreviation	3 Office Symbol	4 Phone
Maneuver & Fires Division	MFD	AHRC-EPA	5726
Operations Support Division	OSD	AHRC-EPB	5910
Force Sustainment Division	FSD	AHRC-EPC	5217
Sergeants Major Branch		AHRC-EPS	5874
Command Management Branch		AHRC-EPZ-D	5455
Force Alignment Division	FAD	AHRC-EPF	5923
Readiness Division	RD	AHRC-EPD	5869
Operations Management Division	OMD	AHRC-EPO	5499

ASSIGNMENT SATISFACTION KEY (ASK)—SOLDIER ASSIGNMENT MODULE (SAM)
The Army will determine assignments based on valid requirements to fill vacancies, and when qualified individuals are identified, other factors such as career progression, individual preferences, and so forth, are factored in the selection. ASK—SAM provides a virtually instant capability for your assignment manager and professional development NCO to identify all open requirements you may be eligible for, provides the capabilities to hone in on the most eligible soldiers, and also identifies all

volunteers for a specific assignment location or specialty position (like drill sergeant, for example).

ASK is accessible from the HRC Website or by going directly to the page at *https:// www.hrc.army.mil/content/Assignment%20Satisfaction%20Key*. This innovation provides the soldier with an automated tool to quickly update his or her preferences and contact information. In the past, soldiers had many assignment locations to choose from but little chance of actually being assigned to where they asked, unless they were able to correspond with their assignment manager and a vacancy happened to be available at that location at the time of the PCS move. Today the majority of assignment locations are available to you to request, and those who decline to submit a preference will be assigned according to the needs of the Army. Bottom line, ASK provides soldiers the capability to post assignment preferences directly onto the Total Army Personnel Database. If you don't use ASK, however, SAM will select for you based solely on the needs of the Army first, and then based only on things the assignment manager can see in your file. So it is critical that you get your preferences submitted early and keep it up to date with your desires for Army consideration.

THE ENLISTED PERSONNEL ASSIGNMENT SYSTEM

The primary goal of the enlisted personnel assignment system is to satisfy the personnel requirements of the Army.

Secondary goals are to:

- Professionally develop soldiers in positions that require skills, knowledge, and abilities related to their primary military occupational specialty. This is an effort to strengthen and broaden MOS qualifications and prepare soldiers for career progression, greater responsibility, and diversity of assignments.
- To maximize dwell time between deployments and permanent changes of station.
- To meet soldiers' personal desires.

First-term soldiers with initial enlistments of three years or less will receive only one assignment before expiration term of service (ETS) following basic and skill training. If required to serve in an unaccompanied hardship tour area outside the continental United States (OCONUS), they will then be given no more than two assignments in different locations. Those with enlistments of more than three but less than four years will receive, following basic and skill training, no more than one CONUS assignment or two OCO-NUS assignments. Soldiers with enlistments of four or more years, following basic and skill training, will serve no more than two assignments in different locations, regardless of the tour length. Exceptions such as those made for members in the Exceptional Family Member Program and others can be found in chapter 3, Army Regulation 614-200, *Enlisted Assignments and Utilization Management*.

Consistent with Army needs, soldiers will remain as long as possible at their continental U.S. (CONUS) duty stations. The Army's time on station (TOS) requirement for CONUS is forty-eight months; for OCONUS it is the length of the prescribed tour. Soldiers complete the forty-eight-month TOS/tour requirement unless operational or training

Some reenlist for the "highest" assignments.

necessities are so overriding that they must be reassigned earlier. There is no statutory limitation on the amount of time soldiers may remain overseas, just as there is no statutory limit as to how long a soldier must remain at a post. Except for CONUS requirements that are filled from OCONUS returnees who are immediately available, qualified volunteers are considered first for all assignments.

Soldiers may submit a request for reassignment before completion of TOS requirements, but they must complete minimum TOS requirements at their present duty station before movement. When possible, soldiers will remain on station for the maximum number of years possible consistent with Army requirements.

MANNING STRATEGY

For more than a decade, the Army conducted combat operations while transitioning to a unit-focused manning strategy. This unit-focused strategy, in support of the Army Force Generation (ARFORGEN) model continues and is key to the Army as an expeditionary force with combat readiness and unit cohesion in deploying forces as the primary objectives. At the same time, the Army is undergoing a drawdown of forces expected to continue until at least 2018. With the assumption that deployments of units will continue for the near future at a minimum, the ARFORGEN model can also be expected to continue. ARFORGEN is made up of three phases, constituting a unit's life cycle: train/ready, available, and reset. Each phase allows the Army and unit leadership to do those things needed to prepare a unit for deployment, conduct that deployment, and then reset once the requirement/deployment is completed. The personnel system supports this model by providing units with soldiers to directed levels of fill or strength (number of people assigned) based on the unit category and the phase they are executing.

Not all units are ARFORGEN units. Your basic training and advanced individual training units are a good example of this. The categories of units, from a manning perspective include Directed Fill Forces, ARFORGEN Forces, Urgent Forces, Essential Forces, and Important Forces. Each has a percentage of fill required as stated in the published *Army Manning Guidance*, and those percentages help ensure that each type of unit is manned with the right soldiers at the right time to conduct operational requirements and the unit's METL. Your S-1/G-1 can get a copy of this for more details, or you can find it on the HRC and Army G-1 websites.

Stabilization

It is in the Army's best interest to stabilize soldiers for as long as possible in units, except where higher demand is required elsewhere or developmental assignments are needed for fill and for the growth of the soldier or leader. The intent during the reset period of a life cycle–manned unit is to bring in new soldiers to replace soldiers scheduled to ETS, retire, or PCS; minimize HQDA-directed departures; and retain as many soldiers already assigned to the unit as possible. Some soldiers with recent combat troop experience, however, will be transferred to fill other high-priority assignments. Stabilizing and retaining soldiers in their recently redeployed units is the optimal solution.

Stop Loss Program

The Stop Loss Program is authorized by statute and allows the military services to retain trained, experienced, and skilled manpower by suspending certain laws, regulations, and policies that allow separations from active duty, including retirement. Those affected by the order generally cannot voluntarily retire or leave the service as long as Reserves are called to active duty or until relieved by proper authority. There are two types of stop loss that apply to soldiers in the reserve components: unit stop loss and skill-based stop loss. Army intent is to man units and manage losses in such a way as to minimize the use of the Stop Loss Program. It is important to know that this statute is available to the Army, however, in the event that it is invoked due to world events/national interest.

Normally, the local military personnel office (MILPO), in coordination with the unit, compares authorized and projected positions with current assigned strength and known or projected gains and losses to determine the requirements for assignments. Requisitions are then prepared for these requirements and submitted to the commanding general, Army Human Resources Command (HRC), in Fort Knox, Kentucky. Upon receipt, HRC edits and validates the requisitions. It is the responsibility of the requisitioning unit not to over- or under-requisition and to resolve any discrepancy before submitting the validated requisition for processing. Soldiers become available to be assigned against these requisitions for a variety of reasons. Soldiers who enlist in the Army are available for assignment upon completion of training and award of an MOS. Others are available when they have done one of the following:

- Volunteered for reassignment.
- Completed an overseas tour of duty.
- Completed schooling or training.
- Completed a stabilized tour of duty.
- Completed normal time on station in the continental United States (CONUS) for a given MOS ("turnaround time" varies by MOS).

Homebase and Advance Assignment Program

The Homebase and Advance Assignment Program (HAAP) is governed by chapter 9, AR 600-200. Participation in the HAAP is optional. The HAAP is designed to reduce permanent change of station (PCS) costs and the number of PCS moves by soldiers and their families. The program has two options. Homebase assignment projects the enlisted soldier to return to the same installation upon completion of a twelve-month dependent-restricted short tour. Advance assignment projects the enlisted soldier to be assigned to a new duty station upon completion of a twelve-month dependent-restricted short tour.

Only promotable specialists and corporals through master sergeants assigned to twelve-month dependent-restricted short-tour areas are authorized to participate in the HAAP. The HAAPs will not be given to enlisted soldiers who voluntarily elect to serve a twelve-month "all others" tour when assigned to an accompanied tour area.

Compassionate Assignments

AR 614-200 establishes specific policies governing individual requests submitted by soldiers for a PCS or deletion from assignment instructions. A soldier may submit a request for any of the following reasons:

Extreme Family Problems

These are divided into problems that are temporary and can be resolved in one year and those that are not expected to be resolved in one year. Soldiers making compassionate requests are not exempt from PCS moves or temporary duty (TDY) while waiting for resolution.

Sole Surviving Son or Daughter

The sole surviving son or daughter of a family that has suffered the loss of the father, mother, or one or more sons or daughters in the military service will not be required to serve in combat. Soldiers who become sole surviving sons or daughters after their enlistment may request discharge under AR 635-200. A soldier may waive entitlement to assignment limitations, whether entitlement was based on his or her own application or the request of his or her immediate family.

Married Army Couples Program

AR 614-200 and AR 614-30 apply. Army requirements and readiness goals are paramount when considering personnel for assignment. Married Army couples desiring joint assignment to establish a common household (joint domicile) must request such assignment. The assignment desires of soldiers married to other soldiers are fully considered.

Married Army couples must be enrolled to be considered for joint assignment. Enrollment is a simple process of verifying that two soldiers are married to each other. An application within thirty days of marriage by one spouse or a separate transaction by both spouses is required, depending on location. Once enrolled, both soldiers will be continuously considered for joint assignments, and the PCS orders will indicate if joint assignment is approved.

Army Exceptional Family Member Program (AR 608-75)

The Exceptional Family Member Program (EFMP) is based on Public Law 94-142, which entitles handicapped children to free education and all medically related services in pursuit of education. The EFMP includes all family members with special medical and educational needs.

Soldiers enroll through their local Army medical treatment facility. The military sponsor and the attending medical or educational specialist complete enrollment forms. When HRC nominates a soldier enrolled in the EFMP for assignment, the assignment manager coordinates with the gaining command to determine if needed medical services are available. When services are not available, HRC considers alternative assignment locations based on existing assignment priorities or sends the soldier in an unaccompanied status.

Assignment of Female Soldiers

In recent years, the opportunities for female soldiers to serve in previously closed positions has grown significantly. The Department of Defense rescinded the direct combat exclusion rule in January 2013, and as recently as August 2015, the first two females graduated Ranger training. In December 2015, the Secretary of Defense announced the lift of the ban on female soldiers in all combat units, including infantry and special operations units. As of this writing, over 100 females have volunteered for positions among the roughly 220,000 jobs now available within those career fields. They will begin arriving in 2017 to those units when their training is successfully completed.

Exchange Assignments

AR 614-200-5-11-6 applies. For mutual convenience, CONUS-assigned soldiers may request an exchange assignment with a soldier within CONUS; a soldier assigned overseas may request an exchange assignment with a soldier within his or her same overseas command. AR 614-200, paragraph 5-11 contains detailed requirements for requests for an exchange assignment. These include time on station and time remaining upon arrival requirements, commander approval at each location, ordinary leave and travel costs, and so on.

CAREER DEVELOPMENT PROGRAM ASSIGNMENTS

A career development program is a system of intensive management of selected MOSs or CMFs. Career development programs are established to ensure that there are enough highly trained and experienced soldiers to fill positions that require unique or highly technical skills. To develop soldiers with the required proficiency, career fields within each program often require the following:

- Frequent movement from one job to another to gain required experience.
- An above-average frequency of advanced training.
- Lengthy or frequent training periods.

In applying for career programs and related training, applicants should consult DA Pam 611-21 for the prerequisites and standards of performance requirements for each program.

Chapter 6 of AR 614-200 contains the minimum requirements (subject to change) for each career program. Attaining the prerequisites does not automatically ensure entry into a career program. The appropriate career management branch selects the best-qualified soldiers for a career program.

Waivers are not granted for remaining service requirements for formal training. Waivers for other eligibility requirements or selection standards are considered unless otherwise stated in AR 614-200. Waivers cannot be implied. Each must be specifically requested. In the application for entry into the program or training requested, the applicant must include the reason for the waiver.

Career development programs include the following:

- Intelligence Career Program.
- Explosive Ordnance Disposal Career Program.
- Technical Escort Career Program.
- Army Bandsman Career Program.

ASSIGNMENT TO SPECIFIC ORGANIZATIONS AND DUTY POSITIONS

Chapter 8 and chapter 9, section III, AR 614-200 contains specific policies and procedures for nomination, evaluation, selection, and assignment of enlisted soldiers to the following:

1. Presidential support activities.
2. Observer controller at combat training centers.
3. U.S. Military Entrance Processing Command.
4. Motor transport operator (88M), U.S. Army Field Band
5. Enlisted aides to general officers.
6. Inspector general positions.
7. Drill Sergeant Program.
8. Advanced individual training (AIT) platoon sergeant.
9. Assignment as instructors at uniformed service schools.
10. Assignment to certain international, joint, defense, and departmental-level organizations and agencies.
11. Reserve component or ROTC duty (*Note:* This duty is covered in chapter 6).
12. Selection and assignment of first sergeants.

OVERSEAS SERVICE

Many Americans work very hard all their lives, and then in their declining years, when they at last have the leisure and money to travel, they see the world. Soldiers not only see the world when they are young, but they also have the unique opportunity to live among foreign peoples for extended periods and learn about their cultures from firsthand experience.

There are two ways that you can approach your first overseas tour. You can go kicking and screaming and spend your time isolated in the American community of some foreign country, never venturing very far outside the cocoon of familiar surroundings, counting the dreary days until you rotate; or you can approach foreign service as a thrilling adventure to be experienced to the fullest, and you can be a goodwill ambassador for the United States of America.

Running afoul of the law in a foreign country can be very dangerous. In countries where a Status of Forces Agreement (SOFA) exists between the U.S. government and the foreign government, soldiers may be tried for offenses under the laws of the country concerned.

Most major overseas commands operate orientation programs for newly arrived personnel in the command. These courses attempt to expose soldiers to the culture in which they will be living in order to lessen the effect of culture shock that some people experience the first time they encounter a foreign society. When you receive overseas assignment instructions, it would be a good idea for you (and your spouse, if you have one) to study the language of the country to which you will be going. Some special assignments require extensive formal language training, but most Army installations do provide some language instruction for soldiers and their dependents who are bound overseas. Learning the rudiments of a foreign language can be fun, and speaking a foreign language is a valuable skill to have once you arrive at your overseas duty station.

Standards of living overseas vary, depending on the country. Germany's standard of living is very high, and your money will not go far there; other countries are beset with substantial economic problems, and the standards of living in those places can sometimes be so low that only the very rich can afford luxuries that are considered common in the United States, and you won't be able to afford them at local prices.

As with everything else, what you get out of your situation is what you make of it. And remember that your overseas tour will not last forever; sooner or later, you must leave to come home. Emotional attachments are very hard to break off, so be warned if you establish any kind of relationship with a foreign man or woman. What usually starts as a casual, fun-filled lark, a pleasant way to pass the time, frequently develops into a serious involvement. If it is not consummated by marriage, its termination can be an emotional trauma that will be painful for both of you.

Policies

AR 614-30 lays out detailed policies regarding service outside of the continental United States (OCONUS). Some of the key policies are below. The chief consideration in selecting a soldier for service overseas is that a valid authorization exists for his or her military qualifications. Equitable distribution is made, within a given MOS and grade, of overseas duty assignments, considering both desirable and undesirable locations. All reasonable efforts are made to minimize periods of forced separations and any adverse effects of overseas service encountered by soldiers and their families.

Consistent with Army needs, soldiers are retained as long as possible in CONUS. Among individuals who have previous overseas service, those with the earliest date of return from overseas normally will be selected first. Subject to personnel requirements in short-tour areas, soldiers who have completed a normal overseas service tour in a short-tour area will not be assigned to another short-tour area on their next overseas assignment. Table 3-1 of AR 614-30 lays out roughly fifty criteria concerning eligibility for assignments OCONUS.

Kinds of Overseas Tours

Personnel accompanied or joined by their dependents at government expense must have enough remaining service to serve the tour prescribed for those "with dependents."

Army personnel married to each other and serving in the same overseas area serve tours in accordance with AR 614-30. They must extend or reenlist, if necessary, to have enough time in service to serve the tour prescribed by the table before compliance with orders directing movement.

The "all others," or "short," tour is served by soldiers who meet the following criteria:

- Elect to serve overseas without dependents.
- Are serving in an area where dependents are not permitted.
- Do not have dependents (this rule does not apply in areas where personnel who have dependents must serve "with dependents" tours).
- Are divorced or legally separated and pay child support.

Tours are normally the same for all personnel at the same station. Where there are personnel of more than one service, the service having the main interest (normally, the most personnel in the area) develops a recommended tour length that is coordinated with the other services. Tour length may vary within any given country or area, depending on the specific duty station. AR 614-30 lists overseas duty tours for military personnel.

Short-Tour and Long-Tour Eligibility

AR 614-30 chapters 3 and 7 apply. Personnel are assigned to short-tour overseas assignments according to the following priorities:

- Volunteers who have completed a minimum of twelve months' time on station or are not otherwise stabilized.

1. Intertheater consecutive overseas tour (COT) volunteers after completion of current outside continental United States (OCONUS) tour.
2. From CONUS
   a. HQDA approved volunteers.
   b. No previous OCONUS service.

   c. No previous short tour and last outside continental United States (OCONUS) assignment was a "with-dependents" tour.

   d. Last OCONUS assignment was a "with-dependents" tour in a long-tour area and has previously served a short tour.

   e. Last OCONUS tour was a short tour in accompanied status.

   f. No previous short tour and last assignment was an "all-others" tour.

   g. Serving in a long-tour area of Alaska or Hawaii and completed the prescribed thirty-six-month tour.

   h. If CONUS and last OCONUS tour was a short tour in an unaccompanied status.

Deferments and Deletions

AR 614-30 chapter 6, section IV applies. Because of the possible adverse effect on command operational readiness, granting of deferments for overseas service is strictly controlled and held to an absolute minimum. The need of the service is the major determining factor in granting deferments.

Normally, once an application has been submitted, the soldier will be retained at the home station, pending a final decision. When a soldier requests deferment and it results in his or her having less remaining time in service than the length of the prescribed tour, the individual will continue on the overseas assignment. Unless he or she voluntarily reenlists or extends to be eligible to complete the prescribed tour, the individual must sign a counseling statement, which is a bar to reenlistment. Applications are initiated by the individual concerned on DA Form 4187.

The following conditions normally warrant deferments or deletion from overseas assignment:

- A recent severe psychotic episode involving a spouse or child after a soldier receives assignment instructions.
- The soldier's children being made wards of the court or being placed in an orphanage or a foster home because of family separation. This separation must be because of military service and not because of neglect or misconduct on the part of the soldier.
- Adoption cases in which the home study (deciding whether a child is to be placed) has been completed and a child is scheduled to be placed in the soldier's home within ninety days.
- Illness of a family member (see AR 614-30 for details).
- Terminal illness of a family member where death is anticipated within one year.
- Death of a soldier's spouse or child after receipt of assignment instructions.
- Prolonged hospitalization of more than ninety days when the soldier's presence is deemed essential to resolve associated problems.
- Documented rape of the soldier's spouse or child within ninety days of the scheduled movement date, when the soldier's presence is deemed essential to resolve associated problems.

- Selection to attend the basic or advanced NCO courses or OCS, where attendance will delay overseas travel more than ninety days.
- Enrollment in the Drug and Alcohol Abuse Residential Rehabilitation Treatment Program.
- Pregnancy or related complications exceeding ninety days.

Curtailment of Overseas Tours

AR 614-30, chapter 5 applies to tour curtailments. Overseas commanders may curtail overseas tours when military requirements dictate. They may also disapprove curtailment requests.

When curtailments of more than sixty days are considered, commanders must recommend curtailments and request reassignment instructions from HRC as early as possible, not later than forty-five days before the departure date. Curtailing a tour must not cause an emergency requisition to fill the vacated position.

Overseas commanders may, at any time, curtail the tour of a soldier who has discredited or embarrassed or may discredit or embarrass the United States or jeopardize the commander's mission. They may also curtail tours when family members are moved to the United States because of criminal activity, a health problem, or death in the immediate family living with the sponsor. In exceptional cases, the commander may waive advance Headquarters Department of the Army (HQDA) coordination and attach the soldier to the nearest personnel assistance point for issue of PCS orders. These exceptions are as follows: potential defectors, extreme personal hardship, and expeditious removal of a soldier in the best interests of the service (e.g., when a soldier causes an embarrassment to the command in its relationship with a foreign government).

Pregnant soldiers are not curtailed from their overseas tours solely because of pregnancy. If noncombatant evacuation is ordered, however, pregnant soldiers who have reached the seventh month of pregnancy will be curtailed and evacuated. Such a curtailment does not, however, preclude reassigning the soldier overseas again after completion of the pregnancy and discharge from inpatient status.

Change in Overseas Tour Status

Change of tour requests are normally approved, provided the government has not expended funds for shipment of household goods or movement of dependents, and the gaining command has concurred with the change. Additionally, a soldier may be required to extend or reenlist to meet tour length requirements. Requests are normally not favorably considered if the government has expended funds for shipment of household goods or movement of family members. Exceptions to policy are considered under extenuating circumstances. Army Regulation 55-46, *Travel of Dependents and Accompanied Military and Civilian Personnel to, from, or between Overseas Areas*, the Joint Travel Regulations (JFTR), and AR 614-30, *Overseas Service*, are the applicable regulations.

Consecutive Outside Continental U.S. (OCONUS) Tours

Regulatory guidance pertaining to consecutive overseas tours (COTs) is found in AR 614-30, *Overseas Service*, chapter 4. Soldiers who volunteer to serve two full consecutive

OCONUS tours are authorized government-paid travel for themselves and command-sponsored family members to leave locations equal to the distance to the soldier's home of record. Soldiers may travel greater distances provided they pay the additional travel costs. The leave location is not restricted to CONUS and must normally be between the two tours. The government-paid travel is the only benefit associated with a COT; any leave used is chargeable to the soldier.

To be eligible for a COT, soldiers must complete their current prescribed tour plus any voluntary extensions and agree to serve another full tour plus leave and travel time between tours. COTs fall into two categories: OCONUS tours that involve a permanent change of station and OCONUS tours that do not involve a PCS.

Concurrent and Deferred Travel
Soldiers being transferred overseas should seek command sponsorship of their family members, as well as concurrent or deferred travel for family members. Sponsorship of soldiers' families is dependent upon the availability of government or economy housing. If housing will be available within 60 days, concurrent travel is normally authorized; if housing will not be available until between 61 days and 140 days, deferred travel is normally authorized.

SPONSORSHIP
Every new assignment raises questions and concerns for the soldier and his or her family. The sponsorship program (AR 600-8-8) assists soldiers and their families in establishing themselves at a new duty station and guides soldiers while they adjust to their new work environment.

A "sponsor" is an individual designated by name at a gaining organization to assist incoming members and their families in making a smooth transition into the unit and community environment. Sponsors should be a grade equal to or higher than that of the incoming soldier; be the same sex, marital status, and MOS; be familiar with the surrounding area; and not have received assignment instructions.

Commanders are responsible for ensuring that sponsors are provided enough time from their duties to help new soldiers. In addition, commanders arrange transportation so that sponsors can meet new members and their dependents at the point of arrival and bring them back to the unit (overseas only). Sponsorship is mandatory for first-term soldiers. When a soldier receives assignment instructions, he or she will complete a DA Form 5434, *Sponsor Program Counseling and Information Worksheet*, during the reassignment process. The gaining battalion CSM and assigned sponsor will generate a welcome letter to the soldier within ten days of receipt of the worksheet/appointment as sponsor, informing them of important facts and coordinating support information for the move. Each soldier is different, and your needs may be unique. Letting the gaining command know of any situations that need additional attention ahead of time will help for a smooth transition.

As the incoming soldier, you should answer the sponsor's letter immediately and do the following:

- Inform the sponsor of your time, date, and point of arrival (including flight numbers). Any changes to the itinerary should be reported to the sponsor immediately.
- Provide the sponsor a unit mailing address and telephone number (commercial or DSN).
- Inform the sponsor of the expected departure date from the losing duty station.
- If desired, provide the sponsor with leave addresses and telephone numbers.

Orientation Program

Commanders and supervisors are responsible for conducting a thorough and timely orientation to start new arrivals off properly. These orientations should make the new soldier feel needed and wanted and instill in them the motivation to contribute to the unit's mission. As you can see, a lot of effort is made by the Army to ensure that your move is as smooth and positive as possible. It is up to you to be proactive and do your part in what can be one of the most exciting times of your Army experience.

13

Promotion and Reduction

A promotion to the next rank should be one of the most exciting and humbling experiences you have while in uniform, in addition to the honor of serving your country. The Army goes to great lengths to ensure that all promotions are based on demonstrated merit and potential to serve at the next higher level, so you know you will have earned it. It never ceases to amaze me, though, how few soldiers know about the actual rules and regulations that detail the process. Of all the things you can take the time to learn as a soldier, knowing the steps to best prepare yourself and your record for promotion consideration should be at or near the top of the list. The more rank you acquire, the more soldiers you can help and the more you can help your unit and the Army as well. Adding to your bank account each month doesn't hurt either. Knowing where the best opportunities (and hurdles) are is critical to ensuring that you do get that promotion when your time is due. AR 600-8-19 is the regulation that governs promotions and reductions (a part of the regulation you can hopefully avoid), and the HRC Enlisted Promotions Branch has a web page with reams of information as well. Keeping abreast of current policy and then changes as they occur will ensure your best chances for success, and the sections below outline some of the critical rules and recommendations for you on this important topic. Soldiers are recommended for promotion only after they develop the skills, knowledge, and behavior to perform the duties and assume the responsibility of the next higher grade. Generally, if soldiers do well in their present grades, they will work well in the next higher grades.

The automated DA Form 3355, *Promotion Point Worksheet*, provides standard promotion scoring with predetermined promotion point factors, so corporals, specialists, and sergeants can measure whether they qualify for promotion. They can set goals to increase their promotion potential and then judge their qualifications when compared with those of other soldiers in their MOS. The Army promotes soldiers with the highest point totals who have met all prerequisites, are fully qualified, and who will accept Army-wide assignments.

Commanders at the grades indicated may promote soldiers, subject to authority and delegation of responsibility by higher commanders.

- *Specialist (SPC) and below.* Unit commanders may advance or promote assigned soldiers to private E-2, private first class, and SPC. When soldiers are fully eligible, promotions to PVT, PFC, and SPC are automatic unless the commander submits DA Form 4187 blocking the promotion no later than the twentieth of the preceding month.

- *Sergeant (SGT) and staff sergeant (SSG).* Field-grade commanders lieutenant colonel or higher may promote soldiers attached or assigned or on temporary duty (TDY) to their command or installation.
- *Sergeant first class (SFC) and above.* Headquarters, Department of the Army.
- *Hospitalized soldiers.* Commanders of medical facilities and those of Warrior Transition Battalions (WTBs) may promote hospitalized soldiers to SSG and below and those assigned to a WTB. For those not yet recommended at the time of hospitalization or WTB assignment, the local medical holding facility selection board may recommend promotion.
- *Students.* Commandants and commanders of training installations and activities.
- *Posthumous promotion.* Human Resources Command.

PROMOTION OF PRIVATES TO PRIVATE FIRST CLASS
Active Army personnel are advanced to the rank of private E-2 when they have completed six months of active federal service, unless it is stopped by the commander. National Guard and Army Reserve personnel on initial active-duty training are advanced to private E-2 when they complete six months of service from the day of entry, unless it is stopped by the commander. To recognize outstanding performance, local commanders may advance to private E-2 a limited number of soldiers who have at least four but less than six months' active service.

Under normal conditions, unit commanders may advance soldiers to private first class who qualify with twelve months' time in service and four months' time in grade. To recognize outstanding performance, unit commanders may advance a limited number of soldiers with a minimum of six months in service and two months' time in grade.

PROMOTION TO SPECIALIST OR CORPORAL
Normally, commanders may advance to specialist or corporal those soldiers who meet the following qualifications:

- Twenty-four months in service.
- Six months' time in grade.
- Security clearance appropriate for the MOS in which promoted; advancement may be based on granting an interim security clearance.

To recognize outstanding performance, commanders may advance soldiers on an accelerated basis, providing advancements do not cause more than the percent announced in the monthly cutoff score message from HRC of the total number of assigned specialists and corporals to have less than twenty-four months' time in service, and providing that soldiers meet the following qualifications:

- Eighteen months in service.
- Three months' time in grade.

- Security clearance required for the MOS in which advanced; may be based on an interim clearance.

Calculation of waiver percentages allowed is covered in detail in AR 600-8-19, chapter 2.

PROMOTION TO SERGEANT AND STAFF SERGEANT

Field-grade commanders and the Department of the Army both play a part in promotions to SGT and SSG. The normal sequence from recommendation to promotion to SGT and SSG is as follows:

1. *The soldier meets requirements* as decribed in the paragraphs below (see paragraph 7 for education and training requirements). The time-in-service requirement for attaining eligibility for promotion to SGT is thirty-six months active federal service for the primary zone and eighteen months for the secondary zone. The time-in-grade requirement for attaining eligibility for promotion to SGT is eight months as a corporal/specialist (CPL/SPC), waiverable to four months for those recommended in the secondary zone. Soldiers in the secondary zone may appear before a promotion board with eighteen months' time in service and four months' time in grade as of the first day of the board month.

   The time-in-service requirement for attaining eligibility for promotion to SSG is eighty-four months active federal service for the primary zone and forty-eight months for the secondary zone. The time-in-grade requirement for attaining eligibility for promotion to SSG is ten months as a SGT, waiverable to five months for those recommended in the secondary zone. Soldiers in the secondary zone may be boarded with forty-eight months' time in service and five months' time in grade as of the first day of the board month.

   Once a soldier reaches primary zone eligibility, the commander must either recommend that he or she appear before a promotion board or, if a soldier is fully eligible but not recommended, complete the DA Form 3355, *Promotion Point Worksheet*, with counseling documents, and forward them to the promotion authority for final decision. After forty-eight months' service and twelve months in the grade of E4, soldiers are put on the promotion list unless denied by the commander (see Command List Integration below).

2. *Soldier's chain of command recommends for promotion.* Soldiers may compete for promotion only in their career progression military occupational specialty (CPMOS), as outlined in DA PAM 611-21. Eligible CPLs/SPCs and SGTs compete Army-wide by a three-character MOS, and their relative standing is determined by the points attained on an 800-point system. If a soldier is in the primary zone for promotion and is not selected for appearance before the board, he or she must be counseled in writing about why they were not selected to appear.

3. *Points computed (800 points available).* See the points allocated for SGT and SSG, 600-8-19, chapter 3, section IV, Promotion Points. *Battalion commander convenes promotion board.* Although AR 600-8-19, *Enlisted Promotions*, states

that officers may serve as members of the promotion board with an officer as president, in all but the rarest of cases, the board is composed of senior NCOs with the battalion command sergeant major sitting as president. If a command sergeant major is not available, a serving sergeant major may sit as president. Rules for conduct of the promotion board are found in AR 600-8-19.

4. *Board recommends soldier for promotion with a Go or a No Go decision.* Based on a competing soldier's personal appearance, self-confidence, bearing, oral expression and conversational skill, knowledge of world affairs, awareness of military programs, and knowledge of basic soldiering and attitude, the board makes the recommendation to the promotion authority (normally the battalion commander) if he or she should be approved for integration onto the promotion standing list.

5. *Total promotion points computed (800 total points available).* Once the board has recommended a soldier and the commander approves, the total points accumulated in the Soldier Record Brief are tallied and the point areas are calculated to provide a promotion point score. The breakdown of maximum points by area are in the "Where the Points Come From" section below.

6. *Education requirements met.* Effective 1 January 2016, soldiers must be a graduate of SSD-1 to be recommended for promotion. They must graduate the Basic Leader Course (BLC) prior to promotion to SGT. Those who are recommended for SGT but do not graduate BLC prior to pin-on date will be passed over on the promotion list until the next time a need in their MOS is indicated by the Army announced points lowering to their total points. Soldiers competing for promotion to SSG must complete SSD-2 to be recommended for promotion to SSG. They must be graduates of the Advanced Leader Course (ALC) prior to promotion pin-on. Those SGT(P) that are recommended but do not graduate BLC or ALC prior to promotion pin-on date will be passed over until a need in their MOS is again announced. (*Note:* For National Guard soldiers, a twenty-four-month window after selection is allowed for completion of required NCOES, and thirty-six months where the NCOES consists of three or more phases.)

7. *DA sets monthly promotion points.* Each month the Department of the Army establishes the total number of soldiers to be promoted based on strength needs (number of soldiers needed) and budget constraints. The number of promotions are allocated by primary military occupational specialty (PMOS) within these parameters. Department of the Army promotion cutoff scores are announced monthly. (See the section on cutoff scores in this chapter.)

8. *Soldiers' points meet or exceed DA established points.* The month after approval by the promotion authority (usually the battalion commander), soldiers who meet or exceed the announced cutoff score are promoted if otherwise eligible. Each soldier promoted to SSG must have a minimum of twelve months, active federal service remaining at the time of promotion. For promotion to SGT, there is no service obligation.

9. Congratulations!

Your Key to Success

Become familiar with AR 600-8-19, chapters 1 and 3, the Monthly Cutoff Scores published by HRC, and applicable military personnel (MILPER) messages (which are available at the battalion or brigade S-1 promotion section and on HRC online at *https://www .hrc.army.mil/milper/*).

The breakdown of individual point categories and maximum points for competition to SGT and SSG are listed separately for active-duty and USAR soldiers and then combined for National Guard in the three sections below.

WHERE THE POINTS COME FROM (TO SGT)
(CHAPTER 3 AR 600-8-19)

Military Training Points	Maximum Allowable	How Achieved	Individual Points
Maximum allowed	340		
Weapons Qualification	**160**	**dependent upon number of targets hit.**	
Physical Readiness Test	**180**	**Score ranges from 40 to 180 dependent upon APFT Score**	

Awards: MAXIMUM	155 (125+30 for Airborne Advantage)	
Soldier's Medal or higher award		35
Bronze Star Medal (BSM); Purple Heart		30
Defense Meritorious Service; Medal Meritorious Service Medal (MSM)		25
Air Medal; Joint Service Commendation Medal; Army Commendation Medal (ARCOM)		20
Joint Service Achievement Medal; Army Achievement Medal (AAM)		15
Good Conduct Medal; Army Reserve Component Achievement Medal		10
Combat Infantry Badge; Combat Field Medical Badge, Combat Action Badge		15
Expert Infantry Badge; Expert Field Medical Badge; Basic U.S. Army Recruiter Badge (additional badges 5 each); Ranger Tab; Special Forces Tab; Drill Sergeant Identification Badge		10
Parachutist Badge; Air Assault Badge; Parachute Rigger Badge; Divers Badge; Explosive Ordnance Disposal Badge; Pathfinder Badge; Aircraft Crewman Badge; Nuclear Reactor Operator Badge; Awards of higher skill badge count as subsequent awards and will receive points (senior parachutist, master diver, additional recruiting badges); Driver and Mechanic Badge (maximum 5 points); Tomb Guard Identification Badge		5
Campaign Service Star		5
Southwest Asia Medal (max 12 points)		3
Soldier/NCO of the Quarter—Brigade (BDE) Level		10
Soldier/NCO of the Quarter—Installation/Division		15
Soldier/NCO of the Year—Major Army Command (MACOM)		25

WHERE THE POINTS COME FROM (TO SGT) *continued*
(CHAPTER 3 AR 600-8-19)

Awards	Maximum Allowable	How Achieved	Individual Points
Certificate of Achievement awarded by commanders/deputy commanders serving in positions authorized in the grade of lieutenant colonel (LTC) or higher or any general officer, or command sergeant major (CSM) at the brigade or higher level. (max 20)			5
Soldiers receiving incentive pay for parachute duty (Airborne Advantage)			30
Military Education	**200**		
Basic Leader Course Commandant's List			20
Basic Leader Course Distinguished Leadership/Distinguished Honor Graduate			40
Resident Military Training (ATRRS Courses/Tab Producing courses			
Maximum of 80 points allowed			
Computer Based Training (ACCP, DL & Army e-Learning courses – no points for sub-course completion):			
Maximum of 80 points allowed			
Civilian education	**135**		
For each semester hour earned of business/trade school/college/CLEP			2
Technical Certifications (limited to 5 cents for points)			10
Defense Language Proficiency Test (DLPT) –certify annually			25
completed degree after enlistment			20
Total Possible Points			800

WHERE THE POINTS COME FROM (TO SSG)
(CHAPTER 3 AR 600-8-19)

Military Training Points	Maximum Allowable	How Achieved	Individual Points
Total allowed	255		
Weapons Qualification	110	**dependent upon number of targets hit.**	
Physical Readiness Test	145	**Score ranges from 145 to 15 dependent upon APFT Score**	

Awards: MAXIMUM	195 (165 + 30 for Airborne Advantage)	
Soldier's Medal or higher award		35
Bronze Star Medal (BSM); Purple Heart		30
Defense Meritorious Service; Medal Meritorious Service Medal (MSM)		25
Air Medal; Joint Service Commendation Medal; Army Commendation Medal (ARCOM)		20

Joint Service Achievement Medal; Army Achievement Medal (AAM)	15
Good Conduct Medal; Army Reserve Component Achievement Medal	10
Combat Infantry Badge; Combat Field Medical Badge, Combat Action Badge	15
Expert Infantry Badge; Expert Field Medical Badge; Basic U.S. Army Recruiter Badge (additional badges 5 each); Ranger Tab; Special Forces Tab; Drill Sergeant Identification Badge	10
Parachutist Badge; Air Assault Badge; Parachute Rigger Badge; Divers Badge; Explosive Ordnance Disposal Badge; Pathfinder Badge; Aircraft Crewman Badge; Nuclear Reactor Operator Badge; Awards of higher skill badge count as subsequent awards and will receive points (senior parachutist, master diver, additional recruiting badges); Driver and Mechanic Badge (maximum 5 points); Tomb Guard Identification Badge	5
Campaign Service Star	5
Southwest Asia Medal (max 12 points)	3
Soldier/NCO of the Quarter—Brigade (BDE) Level	10
Soldier/NCO of the Quarter—Installation/Division	15
Soldier/NCO of the Year—Major Army Command (MACOM)	25

WHERE THE POINTS COME FROM (TO SSG) *continued* (CHAPTER 3 AR 600-8-19)

Awards Points	Maximum Allowable	How Achieved	Individual Points
Distinguished Leadership Award			10
Commandants List			5
Certificate of Achievement awarded by commanders/deputy commanders serving in positions authorized in the grade of lieutenant colonel (LTC) or higher or any general officer, or command sergeant major (CSM) at the brigade or higher level. (max 20)			5
Soldiers receiving incentive pay for parachute duty (Airborne Advantage)			30
Military Education	**220**		
Advanced Leaders Course Commandant's List			20
Advanced Leaders Course Distinguished Leadership/Distinguished Honor Graduate			40
Resident Military Training (ATRRS Courses/Tab Producing courses Maximum of 90 points allowed			
Computer Based Training (ACCP, DL & Army e-Learning courses – no points for sub-course completion): Maximum of 90 points allowed			
Civilian education	**160**		
For each semester hour earned of business/trade school/college/CLEP Tests			2
Technical Certifications (limited to 5 cents for 50 points)			10
Defense Language Proficiency Test (DLPT) –must certify annually			25
Completing a degree after current promotion to SGT			20
Total Possible Points			800

WHERE THE POINTS COME FROM (NATIONAL GUARD)
(CHAPTER 3 AR 600-8-19)

Performance Evaluation and Military Training Points	Maximum Allowable	How Achieved	Individual Points
Duty Performance	150	Unit Commander	
a. Competence			30
b. Military Bearing			30
c. Leadership			30
d. Training			30
e. Responsibility and Accountability			30
Weapons Qualification	**50**	**Score ranges from 50 to 14 dependent upon number of targets hit.**	
Physical Readiness Test	**50**	**Score ranges from 50 to 5 dependent upon APFT Score**	

Administrative Points

Awards: MAXIMUM	100		
Soldier's Medal or higher award			35
Bronze Star Medal (BSM); Purple Heart			30
Defense Meritorious Service; Medal Meritorious Service Medal (MSM)			25
Air Medal; Joint Service Commendation Medal; Army Commendation Medal (ARCOM)			20
Joint Service Achievement Medal; Army Achievement Medal (AAM)			15
Good Conduct Medal; Army Reserve Component Achievement Medal			10
Combat Infantry Badge; Combat Field Medical Badge, Combat Action Badge			15
Expert Infantry Badge; Expert Field Medical Badge; Basic U.S. Army Recruiter Badge (additional badges 5 each); Ranger Tab; Special Forces Tab; Drill Sergeant Identification Badge			10
Parachutist Badge; Air Assault Badge; Parachute Rigger Badge; Divers Badge; Explosive Ordnance Disposal Badge; Pathfinder Badge; Aircraft Crewman Badge; Nuclear Reactor Operator Badge; Awards of higher skill badge count as subsequent awards and will receive points (senior parachutist, master diver, additional recruiting badges); Driver and Mechanic Badge (maximum 5 points); Tomb Guard Identification Badge			5
Soldiers receiving incentive pay for parachute duty: Parachutist			20
		Senior	25
		Master	30
Campaign Service Star			5
Southwest Asia Medal (max 12 points)			3
Soldier/NCO of the Quarter—Brigade (BDE) Level			10
Soldier/NCO of the Quarter—Installation/Division			15
Soldier/NCO of the Year—Major Army Command (MACOM)			25
Distinguished Honor Graduate			15

WHERE THE POINTS COME FROM (NATIONAL GUARD) *continued*
(CHAPTER 3 AR 600-8-19)

Performance Evaluation and Military Training Points	Maximum Allowable	How Achieved	Individual Points
Distinguished Leadership Award			10
Commandants List			5
Certificate of Achievement awarded by commanders/deputy commanders serving in positions authorized in the grade of lieutenant colonel (LTC) or higher or any general officer, or command sergeant major (CSM) at the brigade or higher level. (max 20)			5
Military Education	200		
Active component (AC) PLDC			16
PLDC Equivalency (as approved by HRC-A)	To be determined		(TBD)
AC Advanced Leaders Course			40
Additional completed ALC (per week)			4
Ranger School			32
Special Forces Qualification Course			60
Battalion level or higher training certified by a DA Form 87, "Certificate of Training" signed by a LTC or above (per week)			4
Completion of military correspondence, extension, or nonresident subcourses (per five hours)			1
Other courses of at least one week duration (40 hours)			4
Civilian education	100		
For each semester hour earned of business/trade school/college			1.5
Any soldier completing a degree while on active duty			10
CLEP Tests (for each semester hour earned)			1.5
Promotion Board	150		
Personal Appearance			25
Oral Expression			25
Awareness of World Affairs			25
Knowledge of Military Programs			25
Basic Soldiering			25
Soldier's Attitude			25
Total Possible Points			800

Promotable soldiers must monthly review the recommended list. This is the most important document you have to refer to after undergoing any type of promotion board or point adjustment action. If you disagree with the promotion points data reflected, bring it to the attention of your first sergeant and BNS1, and be prepared to document all promotion-related requests.

Records Check

Soldiers are responsible for maintaining individual personnel documents that have a direct impact on their career. These documents are essential to the promotion process of establishing promotion points for SGT/SSG and for establishing the Official Military Personnel File (OMPF). Ultimately, the soldier, along with the chain of command, are responsible for accuracy of promotion paperwork, submission of the data into the Total Army Personnel Database (TAPDB) and follow-up of action requests. However, you're the one who cares most about your own career, so the burden of action and proof is yours to manage.

You can review your OMPF online by logging on to the Human Resources Command website or the "Self Service" tab at Army Knowledge Online (AKO).

Recommended List

After completion of all promotion actions during the month, a recommended list is published. It lists all soldiers of the organization who have been selected but not yet promoted. Names are listed by grade and zone in ascending MOS and descending promotion point score order.

Soldiers are promoted from the current recommended list by MOS. Promotions are made on the first calendar day of the month in which they are authorized. Promotion orders may be published with future effective dates.

Soldiers are eligible for promotion on the first day of the second month following date of selection; for example, a soldier recommended in January becomes eligible for promotion on 1 March.

A soldier's name on the secondary zone list for promotion to sergeant is transferred to the primary zone list on the first day of the month in which he or she completes thirty-three months of active service. The soldier becomes eligible for promotion in the primary zone on the first day of the month in which he or she completes thirty-six months of active service.

A soldier's name on the secondary zone list for promotion to staff sergeant is transferred to the primary zone on the first day of the month in which he or she completes eighty-one months of active service.

Cutoff Scores

When a soldier's number of promotion points is known, many wonder why he or she cannot be promoted immediately if the cutoff is low enough. In the first place, soldiers may be selected for promotion one month before they have the required time in service.

Second, reports from the field reflecting the number of soldiers on promotion lists, their number of points, and their zones and MOSs arrive at HQDA about the middle of the month following the month in which the soldier appeared before the promotion board.

At this point, MOS and grade vacancies are computed. The total number of promotions for a particular grade (regardless of MOS) is determined by comparing the number of personnel projected to be in that grade against the number allowed in the Army budget for the month in which promotions are to be made. This projection includes losses, those promoted in and out of the grade, and reductions. Available promotions are distributed to MOSs based on the percentage of fill.

Promotions go to those MOSs with the greatest need first. Secondary zone (waiver) promotions are limited, so they go to MOSs with the greatest need after the primary zone (no waiver) promotions are distributed. At this time—which is one to two months after the soldier appeared before the promotion board—the soldier's number of promotion points comes into the process. For example, if vacancies and budget permit the promotion of one hundred soldiers from the primary zone of a particular MOS, a promotion cutoff score is established by going down the scores until the hundred limit is reached. That is, if the top one hundred sergeants in an MOS have 716 or more points, the cutoff score would be 716. If the top one hundred have 796 or more, the cutoff would be 796.

Improving Your Cutoff Scores
To ensure you have the best score and therefore the best possible chance for promotion, there are important things you need to do. First, don't wait until you are recommended for the board to start earning points. As discussed several times in other sections of this guide, the earlier you start on your Structured Self Development (SSD) course, college courses, Army correspondence courses, PRT improvement, and so forth, the sooner you will be able to pin on sergeant and staff sergeant! Second, ensure that you are clear on how to negotiate the DA Form 3355, *Automated Promotion Point Worksheet*. This document keeps track of all data input through ATRRS (training courses), the Official Military Personnel File (OMPF) and your Soldier Record Brief (SRB), and more. The more consistent you are in keeping that up to date and verifying the accuracy of what you have accomplished against what the worksheet shows, the better your chances of promotion. Things like the weapons qualification, APFT, and other areas that you cannot input onto the worksheet yourself are especially important to check. Just because you went to the range last week is no guarantee that the score was entered into the system by your unit. Those who take charge and manage their own careers will always be in a better position than those who just move along blindly and trust that everyone will do the right thing on time, every time. So take that time to manage and upkeep your file, and talk with your team, section, or squad leader if you have any doubts. During your scheduled counseling sessions, this is a great topic to cover each time to ensure that all your efforts are not only helping the team, but your own career as well.

Command List Integration (CLI)
This policy is designed to assist the Army in filling vacant sergeant and staff sergeant authorizations/positions. Each month, soldiers meeting the established criteria for list integration will be added to the recommended list with a minimum of 39 or 14 promotion points, based on rank, unless previously denied. Commanders may block automatic integration by informing their S-1/MPD which soldiers not to integrate

Soldiers in the rank of corporal/specialist (CPL/SPC) not earlier recommended for promotion will be automatically integrated onto the SGT recommended list upon meeting the following criteria:

• Forty-six months' time in service.

- Ten months' time in grade.
- Completed Structured Self Development 1.
- Not denied integration by the commander.
- Otherwise not ineligible (AR 600-8-19).

Sergeants who have not been recommended previously will be added to the SSG recommended list upon meeting the following criteria:

- Eighty-two months' time in service.
- Ten months' time in grade.
- Completed Structured Self Development 2.
- Not denied integration by the commander.
- Otherwise not ineligible (AR 600-8-19).

The existing rules provide for an SPC/CPL or sergeant to be fully eligible for promotion recommendation for a year before CLI use. This allows the chain of command one full year past the fully eligible point to recommend a soldier under the existing means—that is, by board appearance.

The only avenue for soldiers who are automatically integrated onto the list to increase their promotion points is to appear before the promotion board. Soldiers are only promoted from the Command List Integration (CLI) to SGT when their score meets the announced cutoff score and they have seniority over others within their primary military occupational specialty (PMOS) listed on the CLI.

Recommended List Removals

Soldiers may be removed from promotions lists for the following reasons:

- Failure to qualify, for cause, for the security clearance required for the MOS in which the soldier is recommended. Those who fail to qualify for a security clearance through no adverse reason are reclassified and remain on the list in the new MOS.
- Failure to reenlist or extend to meet a service-remaining obligation.
- Being barred to reenlist.
- Reclassification from an MOS because of inefficiency or misconduct.
- Erroneous listing due to not meeting the criteria for promotion.
- Enrollment in the weight-control program.
- Failure to pass reclassification training.
- Reduction in grade after being placed on the recommended list.

A removal board is convened when required to determine whether a soldier should be removed from a recommended list. The board will be constituted as for promotion boards. The soldier being considered for removal has certain rights and must be informed of a removal action in writing. The soldier may choose to do the following:

- Appear before the board in person or waive appearance.
- Challenge any member of the board for cause.
- Request an available witness whose testimony is pertinent to his case.

- Elect to remain silent, to make an unsworn statement, to make a sworn statement, or to be verbally examined by the board.
- Question any witness appearing before the board.
- Present written affidavits and depositions of witnesses.

Failure on the part of a soldier to exercise these rights is not a bar to the board proceedings or its findings and recommendations. The promotion authority is the final approval or disapproval authority on the board's recommendations. This action is final.

A soldier removed from a list and later exonerated is reinstated to the current local recommended list as soon as possible, but not more than ten days after being completely exonerated.

REDUCTIONS IN GRADE

Commanders at the grades indicated may administratively reduce the grade of assigned soldiers:

- Specialist or corporal and below—company, troop, battery, and separate detachment commanders.
- Sergeant and staff sergeant—field-grade commanders of any organization that is authorized a lieutenant colonel or higher-grade commander. For separate detachments, companies, or battalions, the reduction authority is the next senior headquarters within the chain of command authorized a lieutenant colonel or higher-grade commander.
- Sergeant first class and higher—commanders of any organization that is authorized a colonel or higher-grade commander. For separate detachments, companies, or battalions, the reduction authority is the next senior headquarters within the chain of command authorized a colonel or higher-grade commander.

Erroneous Enlistment Grades

Soldiers in higher grades than authorized upon enlistment or reenlistment in the Regular Army or Army Reserve will be reduced to the one to which they are entitled. Authorized grades are prescribed in AR 601-210, AR 140-11, or AR 140-158.

Misconduct

For reductions imposed by court-martial, see the *Manual for Courts-Martial*. Sergeants first class and above cannot be reduced under the provision of Article 15, UCMJ.

Inefficiency

Inefficiency is defined as "demonstration of characteristics which show that the person cannot perform the duties and responsibilities of the grade and MOS" (AR 6008-19, chapter 7). It may include any act or conduct that shows a lack of abilities and qualities required and expected of a person of that grade and experience. Commanders may consider misconduct, including conviction by civil court, as bearing on efficiency.

A soldier may be reduced under the authority of chapter 7, AR 600-8-19, for long-standing unpaid personal debts that he or she has not made a reasonable attempt to pay.

An assigned soldier who has served in the same unit for at least ninety days may be reduced one grade for inefficiency. The commander starting the reduction action documents the soldier's inefficiency. The documents should establish a pattern of inefficiency rather than identify a specific incident.

The commander reducing a soldier informs him or her, in writing, of the action contemplated and the reasons. The soldier must acknowledge receipt of the letter, by endorsement, and may submit any pertinent matters in rebuttal. Sergeants and above may request to appear before a reduction board. If appearance is declined, it must be done in writing and is considered acceptance of the reduction action. A reduction board, when required, must be convened within thirty days after the individual is notified in writing.

Reduction Boards

Hopefully, you will never be in a position to personally deal with this section. However, when required, reduction boards are convened to determine whether an enlisted soldier's grade should be reduced. This convening authority must ensure that the following conditions exist:

- The board consists of officers and enlisted personnel of mature judgment and senior in grade to the person being considered for reduction.
- For inefficiency cases, at least one member must be thoroughly familiar with the soldier's specialty.
- The board must consist of at least three voting members and will comprise both officer and enlisted voting members.
- The board has an officer or senior enlisted member (or both) of the same sex as the soldier being considered for reduction.
- The composition of the board represents the ethnic population of soldiers under its jurisdiction.
- No soldier with direct knowledge of the case is appointed to the board.

A soldier who is to appear before the board will be given at least fifteen working days' written notice before the date of the hearing so that the soldier or his or her counsel has time to prepare the case.

The convening authority may approve or disapprove any portion of the recommendation of the board, but their action cannot increase the severity of the board's recommendation. If the convening authority approves a recommended reduction, he or she may direct it. When the board recommends a reduction and the convening authority approves it, the soldier will be reduced without regard to any action taken to appeal the reduction.

The soldier has the right to:

- Decline, in writing, to appear before the board.
- Have a military counsel of his or her own choosing, if reasonably available, or may employ a civilian counsel at his or her own expense, or both.
- Appear in person, with or without counsel, at all open proceedings of the board.
- If the soldier appears before the board without counsel, have the president counsel him or her on the action being contemplated, the effect of such action on his or her future in the Army, and the right to request counsel.

- Challenge (dismiss) any member of the board for cause.
- Request any reasonably available witness whose testimony the soldier believes to be pertinent to the case. When requested, the soldier must tell the nature of the information the witness will provide.
- Submit to the board written affidavits and depositions of witnesses who are unable to appear before the board.
- Employ the provisions of Article 31, UCMJ (prohibition against compulsory self-incrimination) or submit to an examination by the board.
- Have his or her counsel question any witness appearing before the board. Failure of the soldier to exercise his or her rights is not a bar to the board proceedings or its findings and recommendations.

Appeals
Appeals from reduction for misconduct are governed by Article 15, UCMJ; paragraph 135, *Manual for Courts-Martial* (MCM); and AR 27-10.

Appeals based on reduction for failure to complete training will not be accepted.

Appeals from staff sergeants and below based on reduction for inefficiency or conviction by civil court are allowed. They must be submitted in writing within thirty workdays from the date of reduction. The officer having general court-martial jurisdiction, or the next higher authority, may approve, disapprove, or change the reduction if he or she determines that the reduction was without sufficient basis, should be changed, or was proper. His or her action is final.

14

Pay and Entitlements

This chapter may be the most important one in the guide, as it explains the basic facts about your Army pay and benefits and provides you a quick reference for questions that may come up in your day-to-day duties.

Soldiers do not enlist in the Army to get rich, or at least they shouldn't. However, when you factor in the actual cash value of benefits beyond your basic pay, like housing, medical insurance (TRICARE), education, and more, the total compensation package for a soldier is nothing to sneeze at. There are a lot of other monetary benefits that escape the casual eye for soldiers and their families too, like paid vacation (leave and passes), subsistence pay (for food), and purchases at the Post Exchange (PX) and commissary that have no taxes applied. The key is to understand what compensation benefits you are receiving.

PAY AND ALLOWANCES
Military pay consists of basic pay, special and incentive pay, and allowances. Pay is computed on the basis of a thirty-day month, and soldiers are paid twice a month (on the fifteenth and the thirtieth of each month).

While some soldiers find that they can get along quite well with one lump-sum payment at the end of the month, the Army made the decision to pay all soldiers twice a month. This makes it a bit easier to manage your pay with bills and makes it easier for the Army to pay all soldiers on the same pay schedule. So you know when you are getting paid, but you also need to ensure that you report discrepancies in your pay immediately. To do that, you must know what you are authorized. The basic pay, drill pay, and other pays are announced at the beginning of each calendar year, and you can access those pay charts by going to MyPay through AKO or directly to the Defense Finance Accounting and Accounting Service (DFAS) website and then clicking on the current year. The page for military pay charts is at *http://www.dfas.mil/militarymembers/payentitlements/military-pay-charts.html*.

Leave and Earnings Statement
The Leave and Earnings Statement (LES) is an automated monthly statement of account for each soldier paid. The LES shows all entitlements earned, collections affected, and payments made during the period covered by the statement. In addition, this statement

provides the soldier a complete record of transactions that affect his or her leave account for the period of the statement. It also serves as the official leave record. You can access your LES at the MyPay website at *https://mypay.dfas.mil/mypay.aspx.*

Content of the Leave and Earnings Statement
The LES reflects a soldier's earnings information and also involvement in the Thrift Savings Plan (TSP). The TSP information is found in the blocks located directly above the "Remarks" area of the LES. The four entitlement categories are Base Pay (blocks 63 and 64 on sample), Special Pay (blocks 65 and 66), Incentive Pay (blocks 67 and 68), and Bonus Pay (blocks 69 and 70). There are two new blocks for each of four entitlement categories. The blocks containing the word "Rate" reflect the percentage rate of the monthly entitlement that the soldier elects to contribute to TSP. The blocks that contain the word "Current" reflect the dollar amount designated by the soldier. The "TSP YTD [year-to-date] Deductions" block (72) is simply what a soldier has contributed to date. The "Deferred" block (73) will contain the amount of TSP YTD contributions that are tax deferred. There is a yearly maximum for tax-deferred contributions, and once a soldier reaches the yearly maximum, the system generates a stop transaction and creates a remark with a stop date. The "Exempt" block (74) contains the amount of YTD tax-exempt TSP contributions. Deductions for TSP contributions and loan payments appear in the "Deductions" block (11) of the LES. If a soldier receives a TSP loan payment and any TSP contribution refund, the "Entitlements" block (10) of the LES will denote the amount.

Additionally, two blocks advise the soldier on his or her retirement status. These blocks are located on the far right side of the document, under the "EOM Pay" block. The "DIEMS" (date initially entered military service) block (23) reflects the date used to establish the soldier's retirement plan. The "RET Plan" block (24) indicates the retirement plan a soldier is under, based on the DIEMS date shown in the preceding block.

Study your LES very carefully. Should you discover any item you believe to be in error or should there be an entry recorded thereon that you do not understand, consult with your S-1 or local finance office immediately. If, during a routine audit of your pay record, it should be discovered that you have been overpaid at some time in the past, the government will collect what is due.

Duty in a Combat Zone/Combat Zone Tax Exclusion (CZTE)
As an enlisted member, if you serve in a combat zone for any part of a month, all of your military pay for that month is excluded from your income for income tax reporting purposes. You also can exclude military pay earned if you are ever hospitalized as a result of wounds, disease, or injury incurred in the combat zone. The exclusion of your military pay while you are in a hospital extends to two years past the termination of hostilities in the designated combat zone. The hospitalization does not have to be in the combat zone.

Online Finance
The Defense Finance and Accounting Service (DFAS) MyPay website at *https://mypay .dfas.mil/mypay.aspx* allows soldiers to access their pay record and update certain payroll

information directly, without having to fill out any paper forms. It also allows you to review or make changes to your federal and state tax information, financial allotments, home or correspondence address, savings bonds, and direct deposit or electronic funds transfer (EFT) information without the problems involved with paperwork. When you make a change, the system saves the transaction and sends it to the payroll system the next day for update. This system also allows you to view and print your Leave and Earnings Statement online.

Collections of Erroneous Payments

Overpayments for two months in a row are collected from a soldier's next month's pay. If these payments are two or more months old, collection is delayed to allow time for unit commanders to arrange for prorated collection, if necessary, before computer collection action is initiated.

Normally, the amount deducted for any period will not exceed an amount equal to two-thirds of a soldier's pay. Monthly installments may be increased or decreased to reflect changes in pay.

Soldiers may appeal the validity of a debt, the amount, or the rate of payment. If an enlisted soldier's appeal is denied, the chief of personnel operations, Department of the Army, may consider his or her case for remission or cancellation of the indebtedness.

Advance Payments

An advance of pay is authorized upon permanent change of station to provide a soldier funds for expenses, such as transportation, temporary storage of household goods, packing and shipping costs, and securing new living quarters. Advance payments are limited to no more than one month's advance pay of basic pay less deductions or, if warranted, not more than three months' basic pay less deductions at the old station, en route, or within sixty days after reporting to a new station.

Requests for advance pay from soldiers in pay grades E-1 through E4 must be approved by their commander, and this approval must be indicated in the *Pay Inquiry Form* (DA Form 2142), together with a statement that the circumstances in the individual's case warrant advancing the amount requested and that advancing a lesser amount would result in hardship to the soldier or his or her family.

The commander's approval for an advance of pay is not required for soldiers in pay grades E-5 through E-9, but advances are not made to senior-grade personnel when it is apparent that the tour of duty (obligated service) will terminate before completion of the scheduled repayment of the advance.

Lump-Sum Payments

A lump-sum payment is made to pay bonuses and accrued leave paid on immediate reenlistments. Lump-sum payments are always made in even dollar amounts. The maximum amount that may be paid is the gross amount of the enlistment minus the estimate of federal and, when applicable, state taxes. When the computation of payment results in a new amount due in dollars and cents, the amount paid will either be the lesser full dollar amount or will be rounded to the next higher dollar.

BASIC PAY—EFFECTIVE JANUARY 1, 2016

Pay Grade	2 or less	Over 2	Over 3	Over 4	Over 6	Over 8	Over 10	Over 12	Over 14	Over 16	Over 18
O-10											
O-9											
O-8	9,946.20	10,272.00	10,488.30	10,548.60	10,818.60	11,269.20	11,373.90	11,802.00	11,924.70	12,293.40	12,827.10
O-7	8,264.40	8,648.40	8,826.00	8,967.30	9,222.90	9,475.80	9,767.70	10,059.00	10,351.20	11,269.20	12,043.80
O-6	6,267.00	6,885.30	7,337.10	7,337.10	7,365.00	7,680.90	7,722.30	7,722.30	8,161.20	8,937.00	9,392.70
O-5	5,224.50	5,885.70	6,292.80	6,369.60	6,624.00	6,776.10	7,110.30	7,356.00	7,673.10	8,158.50	8,388.90
O-4	4,507.80	5,218.20	5,566.50	5,643.90	5,967.00	6,313.80	6,745.80	7,081.50	7,314.90	7,449.30	7,526.70
O-3	3,963.60	4,492.80	4,849.20	5,287.20	5,540.70	5,818.80	5,998.20	6,293.70	6,448.20	6,448.20	6,448.20
O-2	3,424.50	3,900.30	4,491.90	4,643.70	4,739.40	4,739.40	4,739.40	4,739.40	4,739.40	4,739.40	4,739.40
O-1	2,972.40	3,093.90	3,740.10	3,740.10	3,740.10	3,740.10	3,740.10	3,740.10	3,740.10	3,740.10	3,740.10
O-3E				5,287.20	5,540.70	5,818.80	5,998.20	6,293.70	6,543.30	6,686.70	6,881.40
O-2E				4,643.70	4,739.40	4,890.30	5,145.00	5,341.80	5,488.50	5,488.50	5,488.50
O-1E				3,740.10	3,993.60	4,141.50	4,292.40	4,440.60	4,643.70	4,643.70	4,643.70
W-5											
W-4	4,095.90	4,406.10	4,532.40	4,656.90	4,871.10	5,083.20	5,298.00	5,620.80	5,904.00	6,173.40	6,393.90
W-3	3,740.40	3,896.40	4,056.30	4,108.80	4,276.20	4,605.90	4,949.10	5,110.80	5,297.70	5,490.30	5,836.50
W-2	3,309.90	3,622.80	3,719.40	3,785.40	4,000.20	4,333.80	4,499.10	4,661.70	4,860.90	5,016.30	5,157.30
W-1	2,905.50	3,218.10	3,302.10	3,479.70	3,690.00	3,999.60	4,144.20	4,346.10	4,545.00	4,701.60	4,845.30
E-9							4,948.80	5,060.70	5,202.30	5,368.20	5,536.20
E-8						4,050.90	4,230.00	4,341.00	4,473.90	4,618.20	4,878.00
E-7	2,816.10	3,073.50	3,191.40	3,347.10	3,468.90	3,678.00	3,795.60	4,004.70	4,178.70	4,297.50	4,423.80
E-6	2,435.70	2,680.20	2,798.40	2,913.60	3,033.60	3,303.30	3,408.60	3,612.30	3,674.40	3,719.70	3,772.50
E-5	2,231.40	2,381.40	2,496.60	2,614.20	2,797.80	2,989.80	3,147.60	3,166.20	3,166.20	3,166.20	3,166.20
E-4	2,046.00	2,150.40	2,267.10	2,382.00	2,483.40	2,483.40	2,483.40	2,483.40	2,483.40	2,483.40	2,483.40
E-3	1,847.10	1,963.20	2,082.00	2,082.00	2,082.00	2,082.00	2,082.00	2,082.00	2,082.00	2,082.00	2,082.00
E-2	1,756.50	1,756.50	1,756.50	1,756.50	1,756.50	1,756.50	1,756.50	1,756.50	1,756.50	1,756.50	1,756.50
E-1	1566.90										

Notes:

1. Basic pay for an O-7 to O-10 is limited by Level II of the Executive Schedule which is $15,125.10. Basic pay for O-6 and below is limited by Level V of the Executive Schedule in effect during 2016, which is $12,516.60.
2. While serving as Chairman, Joint Chief of Staff/Vice Chairman, Joint Chief of Staff, Chief of Staff, Chief of Navy Operations, Commandant of the Marine Corps, Army/Air Force Chief of Staff, Chief of the National Guard Bureau Commander of a unified or specified combatant command, basic pay is $21,147.30. *(See note 1 above)*.
3. Applicable to O-1 to O-3 with at least 4 years and 1 day of active duty or more than 1460 points as a warrant and/or enlisted member. See Department of Defense Financial Management Regulations for more detailed explanation on who is eligible for this special basic pay rate.
4. For the Master Chief Petty Officer of the Navy, Chief Master Sergeant of the AF, Sergeant Major of the Army or Marine Corps or Senior Enlisted Advisor of the JCS, basic pay is $7,997.10. Combat Zone Tax Exclusion for O-1 and above is based on this basic pay rate plus Hostile Fire Pay/Imminent Danger Pay which is $225.00.
5. Applicable to E-1 with 4 months or more of active duty. Basic pay for an E-1 with less than 4 months of active duty is $1,449.00.
6. Basic pay rate for Academy Cadets/Midshipmen and ROTC members/applicants is $1,040.70.

BASIC PAY—EFFECTIVE JANUARY 1, 2016

Pay Grade	Over 20	Over 22	Over 24	Over 26	Over 28	Over 30	Over 32	Over 34	Over 36	Over 38	Over 40
O-10[1]	16,072.20	16,150.50	16,486.80	17,071.50	17,071.50	17,925.30	17,925.30	18,821.10	18,821.10	19,762.50	19,762.50
O-9[2]	14,056.80	14,259.90	14,552.10	15,062.60	15,062.60	15,816.00	15,816.00	16,606.80	16,606.80	17,436.90	17,436.90
O-8[3]	13,319.10	13,647.30	13,647.30	13,647.30	13,647.30	13,989.00	13,989.00	14,338.50	14,338.50	14,338.50	14,338.50
O-7[4]	12,043.80	12,043.80	12,043.80	12,105.60	12,105.60	12,347.70	12,347.70	12,347.70	12,347.70	12,347.70	12,347.70
O-6[5]	9,847.80	10,106.70	10,369.20	10,877.70	10,877.70	11,094.90	11,094.90	11,094.90	11,094.90	11,094.90	11,094.90
O-5	8,617.20	8,876.40	8,876.40	8,876.40	8,876.40	8,876.40	8,876.40	8,876.40	8,876.40	8,876.40	8,876.40
O-4	7,526.70	7,526.70	7,526.70	7,526.70	7,526.70	7,526.70	7,526.70	7,526.70	7,526.70	7,526.70	7,526.70
O-3	6,448.20	6,448.20	6,448.20	6,448.20	6,448.20	6,448.20	6,448.20	6,448.20	6,448.20	6,448.20	6,448.20
O-2	4,739.40	4,739.40	4,739.40	4,739.40	4,739.40	4,739.40	4,739.40	4,739.40	4,739.40	4,739.40	4,739.40
O-1	3,740.10	3,740.10	3,740.10	3,740.10	3,740.10	3,740.10	3,740.10	3,740.10	3,740.10	3,740.10	3,740.10
O-3[3]	6,881.40	6,881.40	6,881.40	6,881.40	6,881.40	6,881.40	6,881.40	6,881.40	6,881.40	6,881.40	6,881.40
O-2[2]	5,488.50	5,488.50	5,488.50	5,488.50	5,488.50	5,488.50	5,488.50	5,488.50	5,488.50	5,488.50	5,488.50
O-1[1]	4,643.70	4,643.70	4,643.70	4,643.70	4,643.70	4,643.70	4,643.70	4,643.70	4,643.70	4,643.70	4,643.70
W-5	7,283.10	7,652.40	7,927.50	8,232.30	8,232.30	8,644.50	8,644.50	9,076.20	9,076.20	9,530.70	9,530.70
W-4	6,608.70	6,924.60	7,184.10	7,480.20	7,480.20	7,629.60	7,629.60	7,629.60	7,629.60	7,629.60	7,629.60
W-3	6,070.50	6,210.30	6,359.10	6,561.60	6,561.60	6,561.60	6,561.60	6,561.60	6,561.60	6,561.60	6,561.60
W-2	5,325.90	5,436.60	5,524.50	5,524.50	5,524.50	5,524.50	5,524.50	5,524.50	5,524.50	5,524.50	5,524.50
W-1	5,020.50	5,020.50	5,020.50	5,020.50	5,020.50	5,020.50	5,020.50	5,020.50	5,020.50	5,020.50	5,020.50
E-9[5]	5,804.70	6,032.10	6,270.90	6,636.90	6,636.90	6,968.40	6,968.40	7,317.00	7,317.00	7,683.30	7,683.30
E-8	5,009.40	5,233.80	5,358.00	5,664.00	5,664.00	5,777.70	5,777.70	5,777.70	5,777.70	5,777.70	5,777.70
E-7	4,472.70	4,637.10	4,725.30	5,061.30	5,061.30	5,061.30	5,061.30	5,061.30	5,061.30	5,061.30	5,061.30
E-6	3,772.50	3,772.50	3,772.50	3,772.50	3,772.50	3,772.50	3,772.50	3,772.50	3,772.50	3,772.50	3,772.50
E-5	3,166.20	3,166.20	3,166.20	3,166.20	3,166.20	3,166.20	3,166.20	3,166.20	3,166.20	3,166.20	3,166.20
E-4	2,483.40	2,483.40	2,483.40	2,483.40	2,483.40	2,483.40	2,483.40	2,483.40	2,483.40	2,483.40	2,483.40
E-3	2,082.00	2,082.00	2,082.00	2,082.00	2,082.00	2,082.00	2,082.00	2,082.00	2,082.00	2,082.00	2,082.00
E-2	1,756.50	1,756.50	1,756.50	1,756.50	1,756.50	1,756.50	1,756.50	1,756.50	1,756.50	1,756.50	1,756.50

Notes:

1. Basic pay for an O-7 to O-10 is limited by Level II of the Executive Schedule which is $15,125.10. Basic pay for O-6 and below is limited by Level V of the Executive Schedule in effect during 2016, which is $12,516.60.
2. While serving as Chairman, Joint Chief of Staff/Vice Chairman, Joint Chief of Staff, Chief of Navy Operations, Commandant of the Marine Corps, Army/Air Force Chief of Staff, Chief of the National Guard Bureau, or Commander of a unified or specified combatant command, basic pay is $21,147.30. *(See note 1 above).*
3. Applicable to O-1 to O-3 with at least 4 years and 1 day of active duty or more than 1460 points as a warrant and/or enlisted member. See Department of Defense Financial Management Regulations for more detailed explanation on who is eligible for this special basic pay rate.
4. For the Master Chief Petty Officer of the Navy, Chief Master Sergeant of the AF, Sergeant Major of the Army or Marine Corps, Senior Enlisted Advisor to the Chief of the National Guard Bureau, or Senior Enlisted Advisor of the JCS, basic pay is $7,997.10. Combat Zone Tax Exclusion for O-1 and above is based on this basic pay rate plus Hostile Fire Pay/Imminent Danger Pay which is $225.00.
5. Applicable to E-1 with 4 months or more of active duty. Basic pay for an E-1 with less than 4 months of active duty is $1,449.00.
6. Basic pay rate for Academy Cadets/Midshipmen and ROTC members/applicants is $1,040.70.

DRILL PAY—EFFECTIVE JANUARY 1, 2016

Cumulative Years of Service

Pay Grade	2 or less	Over 2	Over 3	Over 4	Over 6	Over 8	Over 10	Over 12	Over 14	Over 16	Over 18	Over 20
O-7	8,264.40	8,648.40	8,826.00	8,967.30	9,222.90	9,475.80	9,767.70	10,059.00	10,351.20	11,269.20	12,043.80	12,043.80
1 Drill	275.48	288.28	294.2	298.91	307.43	315.86	325.59	335.3	345.04	375.64	401.46	401.46
4 Drills	1101.92	1153.12	1176.8	1195.64	1229.72	1263.44	1302.36	1341.2	1380.16	1502.56	1605.84	1605.84
O-6	6,267.00	6,885.30	7,337.10	7,337.10	7,365.00	7,680.90	7,722.30	7,722.30	8,161.20	8,937.00	9,392.70	9,847.80
1 Drill	208.90	229.51	244.57	244.57	245.50	256.03	257.41	257.41	272.04	297.90	313.09	328.26
4 Drills	835.60	918.04	978.28	978.28	982.00	1,024.12	1,029.64	1,029.64	1,088.16	1,191.60	1,252.36	1,313.04
O-5	5,224.50	5,885.70	6,292.80	6,369.60	6,624.00	6,776.10	7,110.30	7,356.00	7,673.10	8,158.50	8,388.90	8,617.20
1 Drill	174.15	196.19	209.76	212.32	220.80	225.87	237.01	245.20	255.77	271.95	279.63	287.24
4 Drills	696.60	784.76	839.04	849.28	883.20	903.48	948.04	980.80	1,023.08	1,087.80	1,118.52	1,148.96
O-4	4,507.80	5,218.20	5,566.50	5,643.90	5,967.00	6,313.80	6,745.80	7,081.50	7,314.90	7,449.30	7,526.70	7,526.70
1 Drill	150.26	173.94	185.55	188.13	198.90	210.46	224.86	236.05	243.83	248.31	250.89	250.89
4 Drills	601.04	695.76	742.20	752.52	795.60	841.84	899.44	944.20	975.32	993.24	1,003.56	1,003.56
O-3	3,963.60	4,492.80	4,849.20	5,287.20	5,540.70	5,818.80	5,998.20	6,293.70	6,448.20	6,448.20	6,448.20	6,448.20
1 Drill	132.12	149.76	161.64	176.24	184.69	193.96	199.94	209.79	214.94	214.94	214.94	214.94
4 Drills	528.48	599.04	646.56	704.96	738.76	775.84	799.76	839.16	859.76	859.76	859.76	859.76
O-2	3,424.50	3,900.30	4,491.90	4,643.70	4,739.40	4,739.40	4,739.40	4,739.40	4,739.40	4,739.40	4,739.40	4,739.40
1 Drill	114.15	130.01	149.73	154.79	157.98	157.98	157.98	157.98	157.98	157.98	157.98	157.98
4 Drills	456.60	520.04	598.92	619.16	631.92	631.92	631.92	631.92	631.92	631.92	631.92	631.92
O-1	2,972.40	3,093.90	3,740.10	3,740.10	3,740.10	3,740.10	3,740.10	3,740.10	3,740.10	3,740.10	3,740.10	3,740.10
1 Drill	99.08	103.13	124.67	124.67	124.67	124.67	124.67	124.67	124.67	124.67	124.67	124.67
4 Drills	396.32	412.52	498.68	498.68	498.68	498.68	498.68	498.68	498.68	498.68	498.68	498.68
O-3E				5,287.20	5,540.70	5,818.80	5,998.20	6,293.70	6,543.30	6,686.70	6,881.40	6,881.40
1 Drill				176.24	184.69	193.96	199.94	209.79	218.11	222.89	229.38	229.38
4 Drills				704.96	738.76	775.84	799.76	839.16	872.44	891.56	917.52	917.52
O-2E				4,643.70	4,739.40	4,890.30	5,145.00	5,341.80	5,488.50	5,488.50	5,488.50	5,488.50
1 Drill				154.79	157.98	163.01	171.50	178.06	182.95	182.95	182.95	182.95
4 Drills				619.16	631.92	652.04	686.00	712.24	731.80	731.80	731.80	731.80
O-1E				3,740.10	3,993.60	4,141.50	4,292.40	4,440.60	4,643.70	4,643.70	4,643.70	4,643.70
1 Drill				124.67	133.12	138.05	143.08	148.02	154.79	154.79	154.79	154.79
4 Drills				498.68	532.48	552.20	572.32	592.08	619.16	619.16	619.16	619.16

DRILL PAY—EFFECTIVE JANUARY 1, 2016

Cumulative Years of Service

Pay Grade	Over 22	Over 24	Over 26	Over 28	Over 30	Over 32	Over 34	Over 36	Over 38	Over 40
O-7	12,043.80	12,043.80	12,105.60	12,105.60	12,347.70	12,347.70	12,347.70	12,347.70	12,347.70	12,347.70
1 Drill	401.46	401.46	403.52	403.52	411.59	411.59	411.59	411.59	411.59	411.59
4 Drills	1605.84	1605.84	1614.08	1614.08	1646.36	1646.36	1646.36	1646.36	1646.36	1646.36
O-6	10,106.70	10,369.20	10,877.70	10,877.70	11,094.90	11,094.90	11,094.90	11,094.90	11,094.90	11,094.90
1 Drill	336.89	345.64	362.59	362.59	369.83	369.83	369.83	369.83	369.83	369.83
4 Drills	1,347.56	1,382.56	1,450.36	1,450.36	1,479.32	1,479.32	1,479.32	1,479.32	1,479.32	1,479.32
O-5	8,876.40	8,876.40	8,876.40	8,876.40	8,876.40	8,876.40	8,876.40	8,876.40	8,876.40	8,876.40
1 Drill	295.88	295.88	295.88	295.88	295.88	295.88	295.88	295.88	295.88	295.88
4 Drills	1,183.52	1,183.52	1,183.52	1,183.52	1,183.52	1,183.52	1,183.52	1,183.52	1,183.52	1,183.52
O-4	7,526.70	7,526.70	7,526.70	7,526.70	7,526.70	7,526.70	7,526.70	7,526.70	7,526.70	7,526.70
1 Drill	250.89	250.89	250.89	250.89	250.89	250.89	250.89	250.89	250.89	250.89
4 Drills	1,003.56	1,003.56	1,003.56	1,003.56	1,003.56	1,003.56	1,003.56	1,003.56	1,003.56	1,003.56
O-3	6,448.20	6,448.20	6,448.20	6,448.20	6,448.20	6,448.20	6,448.20	6,448.20	6,448.20	6,448.20
1 Drill	214.94	214.94	214.94	214.94	214.94	214.94	214.94	214.94	214.94	214.94
4 Drills	859.76	859.76	859.76	859.76	859.76	859.76	859.76	859.76	859.76	859.76
O-2	4,739.40	4,739.40	4,739.40	4,739.40	4,739.40	4,739.40	4,739.40	4,739.40	4,739.40	4,739.40
1 Drill	157.98	157.98	157.98	157.98	157.98	157.98	157.98	157.98	157.98	157.98
4 Drills	631.92	631.92	631.92	631.92	631.92	631.92	631.92	631.92	631.92	631.92
O-1	3,740.10	3,740.10	3,740.10	3,740.10	3,740.10	3,740.10	3,740.10	3,740.10	3,740.10	3,740.10
1 Drill	124.67	124.67	124.67	124.67	124.67	124.67	124.67	124.67	124.67	124.67
4 Drills	498.68	498.68	498.68	498.68	498.68	498.68	498.68	498.68	498.68	498.68
O-3E	6,881.40	6,881.40	6,881.40	6,881.40	6,881.40	6,881.40	6,881.40	6,881.40	6,881.40	6,881.40
1 Drill	229.38	229.38	229.38	229.38	229.38	229.38	229.38	229.38	229.38	229.38
4 Drills	917.52	917.52	917.52	917.52	917.52	917.52	917.52	917.52	917.52	917.52
O-2E	5,488.50	5,488.50	5,488.50	5,488.50	5,488.50	5,488.50	5,488.50	5,488.50	5,488.50	5,488.50
1 Drill	182.95	182.95	182.95	182.95	182.95	182.95	182.95	182.95	182.95	182.95
4 Drills	731.80	731.80	731.80	731.80	731.80	731.80	731.80	731.80	731.80	731.80
O-1E	4,643.70	4,643.70	4,643.70	4,643.70	4,643.70	4,643.70	4,643.70	4,643.70	4,643.70	4,643.70
1 Drill	154.79	154.79	154.79	154.79	154.79	154.79	154.79	154.79	154.79	154.79
4 Drills	619.16	619.16	619.16	619.16	619.16	619.16	619.16	619.16	619.16	619.16

DRILL PAY—EFFECTIVE JANUARY 1, 2016

Pay Grade	2 or less	Over 2	Over 3	Over 4	Over 6	Over 8	Over 10	Over 12	Over 14	Over 16	Over 18	Over 20
W-5												7,283.10
1 Drill												242.77
4 Drills												971.08
W-4	4,095.90	4,406.10	4,532.40	4,656.90	4,871.10	5,083.20	5,298.00	5,620.80	5,904.00	6,173.40	6,393.90	6,608.70
1 Drill	136.53	146.87	151.08	155.23	162.37	169.44	176.60	187.36	196.80	205.78	213.13	220.29
4 Drills	546.12	587.48	604.32	620.92	649.48	677.76	706.40	749.44	787.20	823.12	852.52	881.16
W-3	3,740.40	3,896.40	4,056.30	4,108.80	4,276.20	4,605.90	4,949.10	5,110.80	5,297.70	5,490.30	5,836.50	6,070.50
1 Drill	124.68	129.88	135.21	136.96	142.54	153.53	164.97	170.36	176.59	183.01	194.55	202.35
4 Drills	498.72	519.52	540.84	547.84	570.16	614.12	659.88	681.44	706.36	732.04	778.20	809.40
W-2	3,309.90	3,622.80	3,719.40	3,785.40	4,000.20	4,333.80	4,499.10	4,661.70	4,860.90	5,016.30	5,157.30	5,325.90
1 Drill	110.33	120.76	123.98	126.18	133.34	144.46	149.97	155.39	162.03	167.21	171.91	177.53
4 Drills	441.32	483.04	495.92	504.72	533.36	577.84	599.88	621.56	648.12	668.84	687.64	710.12
W-1	2,905.50	3,218.10	3,302.10	3,479.70	3,690.00	3,999.60	4,144.20	4,346.10	4,545.00	4,701.60	4,845.30	5,020.50
1 Drill	96.85	107.27	110.07	115.99	123.00	133.32	138.14	144.87	151.50	156.72	161.51	167.35
4 Drills	387.40	429.08	440.28	463.96	492.00	533.28	552.56	579.48	606.00	626.88	646.04	669.40

Pay Grade	Over 22	Over 24	Over 26	Over 28	Over 30	Over 32	Over 34	Over 36	Over 38	Over 40
W-5	7,652.40	7,927.50	8,232.30	8,232.30	8,644.50	8,644.50	9,076.20	9,076.20	9,530.70	9,530.70
1 Drill	255.08	264.25	274.41	274.41	288.15	288.15	302.54	302.54	317.69	317.69
4 Drills	1,020.32	1,057.00	1,097.64	1,097.64	1,152.60	1,152.60	1,210.16	1,210.16	1,270.76	1,270.76
W-4	6,924.60	7,184.10	7,480.20	7,480.20	7,629.60	7,629.60	7,629.60	7,629.60	7,629.60	7,629.60
1 Drill	230.82	239.47	249.34	249.34	254.32	254.32	254.32	254.32	254.32	254.32
4 Drills	923.28	957.88	997.36	997.36	1,017.28	1,017.28	1,017.28	1,017.28	1,017.28	1,017.28
W-3	6,210.30	6,359.10	6,561.60	6,561.60	6,561.60	6,561.60	6,561.60	6,561.60	6,561.60	6,561.60
1 Drill	207.01	211.97	218.72	218.72	218.72	218.72	218.72	218.72	218.72	218.72
4 Drills	828.04	847.88	874.88	874.88	874.88	874.88	874.88	874.88	874.88	874.88
W-2	5,436.60	5,524.50	5,524.50	5,524.50	5,524.50	5,524.50	5,524.50	5,524.50	5,524.50	5,524.50
1 Drill	181.22	184.15	184.15	184.15	184.15	184.15	184.15	184.15	184.15	184.15
4 Drills	724.88	736.60	736.60	736.60	736.60	736.60	736.60	736.60	736.60	736.60
W-1	5,020.50	5,020.50	5,020.50	5,020.50	5,020.50	5,020.50	5,020.50	5,020.50	5,020.50	5,020.50
1 Drill	167.35	167.35	167.35	167.35	167.35	167.35	167.35	167.35	167.35	167.35
4 Drills	669.40	669.40	669.40	669.40	669.40	669.40	669.40	669.40	669.40	669.40

DRILL PAY—EFFECTIVE JANUARY 1, 2016

Cumulative Years of Service

Grade	2 or less	Over 2	Over 3	Over 4	Over 6	Over 8	Over 10	Over 12	Over 14	Over 16	Over 18	Over 20
E-9							4,948.80	5,060.70	5,202.30	5,368.20	5,536.20	5,804.70
1 Drill							164.96	168.69	173.41	178.94	184.54	193.49
4 Drills							659.84	674.76	693.64	715.76	738.16	773.96
E-8						4,050.90	4,230.00	4,341.00	4,473.90	4,618.20	4,878.00	5,009.40
1 Drill						135.03	141.00	144.70	149.13	153.94	162.60	166.98
4 Drills						540.12	564.00	578.80	596.52	615.76	650.40	667.92
E-7	2,816.10	3,073.50	3,191.40	3,347.10	3,468.90	3,678.00	3,795.60	4,004.70	4,178.70	4,297.50	4,423.80	4,472.70
1 Drill	93.87	102.45	106.38	111.57	115.63	122.60	126.52	133.49	139.29	143.25	147.46	149.09
4 Drills	375.48	409.80	425.52	446.28	462.52	490.40	506.08	533.96	557.16	573.00	589.84	596.36
E-6	2,435.70	2,680.20	2,798.40	2,913.60	3,033.60	3,303.30	3,408.60	3,612.30	3,674.40	3,719.70	3,772.50	3,772.50
1 Drill	81.19	89.34	93.28	97.12	101.12	110.11	113.62	120.41	122.48	123.99	125.75	125.75
4 Drills	324.76	357.36	373.12	388.48	404.48	440.44	454.48	481.64	489.92	495.96	503.00	503.00
E-5	2,231.40	2,381.40	2,496.60	2,614.20	2,797.80	2,989.80	3,147.60	3,166.20	3,166.20	3,166.20	3,166.20	3,166.20
1 Drill	74.38	79.38	83.22	87.14	93.26	99.66	104.92	105.54	105.54	105.54	105.54	105.54
4 Drills	297.52	317.52	332.88	348.56	373.04	398.64	419.68	422.16	422.16	422.16	422.16	422.16
E-4	2,046.00	2,150.40	2,267.10	2,382.00	2,483.40	2,483.40	2,483.40	2,483.40	2,483.40	2,483.40	2,483.40	2,483.40
1 Drill	68.20	71.68	75.57	79.40	82.78	82.78	82.78	82.78	82.78	82.78	82.78	82.78
4 Drills	272.80	286.72	302.28	317.60	331.12	331.12	331.12	331.12	331.12	331.12	331.12	331.12
E-3	1,847.10	1,963.20	2,082.00	2,082.00	2,082.00	2,082.00	2,082.00	2,082.00	2,082.00	2,082.00	2,082.00	2,082.00
1 Drill	61.57	65.44	69.40	69.40	69.40	69.40	69.40	69.40	69.40	69.40	69.40	69.40
4 Drills	246.28	261.76	277.60	277.60	277.60	277.60	277.60	277.60	277.60	277.60	277.60	277.60
E-2	1,756.50	1,756.50	1,756.50	1,756.50	1,756.50	1,756.50	1,756.50	1,756.50	1,756.50	1,756.50	1,756.50	1,756.50
1 Drill	58.55	58.55	58.55	58.55	58.55	58.55	58.55	58.55	58.55	58.55	58.55	58.55
4 Drills	234.20	234.20	234.20	234.20	234.20	234.20	234.20	234.20	234.20	234.20	234.20	234.20
E-1 > 4 mos	1,566.90											
1 Drill	52.23											
4 Drills	208.92											
E-1 < 4 mos	1,449.00											
1 Drill	48.30											
4 Drills	193.20											

DRILL PAY—EFFECTIVE JANUARY 1, 2016

Cumulative Years of Service

Grade	Over 22	Over 24	Over 26	Over 28	Over 30	Over 32	Over 34	Over 36	Over 38	Over 40
E-9	6,032.10	6,270.90	6,636.90	6,636.90	6,968.40	6,968.40	7,317.00	7,317.00	7,683.30	7,683.30
1 Drill	201.07	209.03	221.23	221.23	232.28	232.28	243.90	243.90	256.11	256.11
4 Drills	804.28	836.12	884.92	884.92	929.12	929.12	975.60	975.60	1,024.44	1,024.44
E-8	5,233.80	5,358.00	5,664.00	5,664.00	5,777.70	5,777.70	5,777.70	5,777.70	5,777.70	5,777.70
1 Drill	174.46	178.60	188.80	188.80	192.59	192.59	192.59	192.59	192.59	192.59
4 Drills	697.84	714.40	755.20	755.20	770.36	770.36	770.36	770.36	770.36	770.36
E-7	4,637.10	4,725.30	5,061.30	5,061.30	5,061.30	5,061.30	5,061.30	5,061.30	5,061.30	5,061.30
1 Drill	154.57	157.51	168.71	168.71	168.71	168.71	168.71	168.71	168.71	168.71
4 Drills	618.28	630.04	674.84	674.84	674.84	674.84	674.84	674.84	674.84	674.84
E-6	3,772.50	3,772.50	3,772.50	3,772.50	3,772.50	3,772.50	3,772.50	3,772.50	3,772.50	3,772.50
1 Drill	125.75	125.75	125.75	125.75	125.75	125.75	125.75	125.75	125.75	125.75
4 Drills	503.00	503.00	503.00	503.00	503.00	503.00	503.00	503.00	503.00	503.00
E-5	3,166.20	3,166.20	3,166.20	3,166.20	3,166.20	3,166.20	3,166.20	3,166.20	3,166.20	3,166.20
1 Drill	105.54	105.54	105.54	105.54	105.54	105.54	105.54	105.54	105.54	105.54
4 Drills	422.16	422.16	422.16	422.16	422.16	422.16	422.16	422.16	422.16	422.16
E-4	2,483.40	2,483.40	2,483.40	2,483.40	2,483.40	2,483.40	2,483.40	2,483.40	2,483.40	2,483.40
1 Drill	82.78	82.78	82.78	82.78	82.78	82.78	82.78	82.78	82.78	82.78
4 Drills	331.12	331.12	331.12	331.12	331.12	331.12	331.12	331.12	331.12	331.12
E-3	2,082.00	2,082.00	2,082.00	2,082.00	2,082.00	2,082.00	2,082.00	2,082.00	2,082.00	2,082.00
1 Drill	69.40	69.40	69.40	69.40	69.40	69.40	69.40	69.40	69.40	69.40
4 Drills	277.60	277.60	277.60	277.60	277.60	277.60	277.60	277.60	277.60	277.60
E-2	1,756.50	1,756.50	1,756.50	1,756.50	1,756.50	1,756.50	1,756.50	1,756.50	1,756.50	1,756.50
1 Drill	58.55	58.55	58.55	58.55	58.55	58.55	58.55	58.55	58.55	58.55
4 Drills	234.20	234.20	234.20	234.20	234.20	234.20	234.20	234.20	234.20	234.20

Basic Pay

Basic pay is established by law and is that pay a soldier receives, based on grade and length of service, exclusive of any special or incentive pay or allowances.

Reserve Drill Pay

Reserve drill pay, like basic pay, is established by law. And like basic pay, reserve drill pay is pay a soldier receives based on grade and length of service. Unlike monthly basic pay, however, reserve drill pay is computed and paid for the number of days of service rendered. It is comparable to basic pay.

Other Pay

Assignment Incentive Pay

Assignment Incentive Pay is used to voluntarily fill hard-to-fill assignments and is taxable unless in a combat zone. In Afghanistan, soldiers can receive $300 per month for a three-month extension, $600 per month for a six-month extension, and $900 per month for a twelve-month extension. In South Korea, soldiers extending their twelve-month tours for an additional year receive $300 in Assignment Incentive Pay.

Reserve component soldiers assigned to Afghanistan who have completed twenty-two months of mobilization and volunteer (for Army National Guard [ARNG] with the consent of the governor) to extend on active duty beyond twenty-four months cumulative mobilization will be offered the opportunity to contract for Assignment Incentive Pay

Soldiers qualify for additional pay while in a combat zone.

(AIP). Soldiers will be offered $1,000 per month upon completion of their twenty-second month of mobilization. The AIP terminates when the soldier leaves the Central Command Area of Operations.

Experimental Stress Pay

Experimental stress duty pay is authorized for all Army personnel who, on or after 1 July 1965, performed as human experimental subjects in duties utilizing acceleration/deceleration experimental devices, in thermal stress experiments, and in low- or high-pressure chamber duty.

Foreign Duty Pay

All enlisted personnel assigned to an area outside the contiguous forty-eight states and the District of Columbia where an "accompanied by dependents" tour of duty is not authorized have entitlement to foreign duty or "overseas pay." Chapter 6, part 1, *DOD Pay Manual*, lists the places where foreign duty pay is authorized.

Hardship Duty Pay

Hardship duty pay (HDP) is payable to members entitled to basic pay, at a monthly rate not to exceed $300, while such members are performing specified hardship duty. HDP is paid to members (a) for performing specific missions, or (b) when assigned to designated locations. Except for certain restrictions, HDP is payable in addition to all other pay and allowances. Hardship duty pay for mission assignment (HDP-M) is payable to members, both officer and enlisted, for performing a designated hardship mission. HDP-M is payable at the full monthly rate, without prorating or reduction, for each month during any part of which the member performs a specified mission. Hardship duty pay for location assignment (HDP-L) is payable only to enlisted members when they are assigned to duty in designated locations.

Hostile Fire Pay/Imminent Danger Pay

Hostile fire pay or imminent danger pay is paid to soldiers permanently assigned to units performing duty in designated hostile fire areas or to soldiers assigned to temporary duty in such areas. Hostile fire pay is paid on a prorated basis, for the number of days in a given month that is served in the qualifying location. While drawing hostile fire pay or imminent danger pay, soldiers are exempt from federal and state taxes. Only one of these types of pay is authorized at a given time for assignment in an approved area.

Diving Pay

To qualify for special pay for diving duty, a soldier must be a rated diver in accordance with AR 611-75 and be assigned to a table of organization and equipment (TOE) or a table of distribution and allowances (TDA) position of MOS 00B, or to a position that has been designated diving duty by the assistant chief of staff for force development, Department of the Army.

Demolition Pay
A soldier is entitled to receive incentive pay for demolition duty for any month or portion of a month in which he or she was assigned and performed duty in a primary duty assignment.

Flight Pay
Flight pay is authorized for enlisted crew members and some other personnel who engage in frequent flight operations as a part of their primary duty.

Parachute Pay
Soldiers who have received a designation as a parachutist or parachute rigger or are undergoing training for such designations, and who are required to engage in parachute jumping from an aircraft in aerial flight and actually perform the specified minimum jump of once per three months are authorized parachute duty pay. In imminent danger areas, however, the commanding officer may determine a soldier cannot meet the minimum requirements due to the absence of jump equipment, aircraft, or military operations. In this situation the soldier may perform the required four jumps anytime in the twelve-month period. An additional amount is authorized for parachutists who are assigned to positions requiring high-altitude, low-opening (HALO) jump status.

Special Duty Assignment Pay
Special duty assignment pay is authorized on a graduated scale for enlisted members in designated specialties who are required to perform extremely demanding duties or duties demanding an unusual degree of responsibility. Qualifying jobs include career counselor, recruiter, and drill sergeant.

ALLOWANCES

Basic Allowance for Subsistence (BAS)
Basic allowance for subsistence is a separate pay for those soldiers entitled and is intended to supplement base pay with money for food and rations. Soldiers drawing BAS must pay for all their own meals, even if provided in the dining facility or otherwise by the government. BAS is for the soldier and is not intended for family members. The family subsistence supplement can be applied to family members and is discussed below. The BAS rate for enlisted personnel is $368.29 per month as of 1 January 2016.

Entitlement to BAS terminates automatically upon permanent change of station (PCS). Care should be taken during in-processing at a new duty station that entitlement is revalidated for personnel authorized separate rations.

Family Subsistence Supplemental Allowance
The family subsistence supplemental allowance is a great benefit that is voluntary and is designed to ensure that a soldier's BAS is sufficient to bring the total household income to a point that is equivalent to 130 percent of the federal poverty line amount. It is a nontaxable benefit (another great aspect of the benefit) and cannot exceed $1,100.

See your S-1 or local finance office to inquire about applying for this program if you qualify.

Basic Allowance for Housing (BAH)

The basic allowance for housing is based on rank, location, and whether the soldier is with or without dependents. The rates are based on housing costs for civilians with comparable income levels in the same area. Under this system, the annual growth in the housing allowance will be indexed in the national average monthly housing cost. This benefit is only authorized if you are not living in government quarters.

BAH terminates for married personnel when they occupy government quarters or when dependency terminates. Dependency is verified by the local finance and accounting officer. The documentary evidence that must be submitted to substantiate dependence includes the original or certified copy of a marriage certificate, the individual's signed statement (when called to active duty or active duty for training for ninety days or less), birth certificate, or a public church record of marriage issued over the signature of the custodian of the church or public records, and, if applicable, a divorce decree. Entitlements must be recertified upon permanent change of station.

RC mobilized soldiers are entitled to BAH based on their primary residence; however, they are not authorized to change the BAH from which they were ordered to active duty, regardless of whether or not their primary residence changes.

Family Separation Allowance (FSA)

A family separation allowance is paid to a soldier who has dependents and is serving in an overseas location where dependents are not permitted. It is in the amount of $250 per month.

Soldiers in a temporary change of station status may be authorized FSA Type II (T) at the rate of $250 per month when a soldier is away from his or her permanent duty station (PDS) (for mobilized reserve component (RC) personnel this is their home of residence) continuously for a period of thirty days and the soldier's dependents are not residing at or near the TCS station. Army/service married couples who were living together prior to and immediately before the deployment and single soldiers with authorized primary dependents may be paid family separation allowance for temporary duty (FSA-T). Relocation of dependents at government expense is not authorized.

Station Allowances

A list of areas where station allowances are authorized is in chapter 4, part 3, *DOD Pay Manual*, and chapter 4, part G, volume 1, *Joint Travel Regulations*. These allowances are paid to offset the high cost of living in certain geographical areas (overseas and in the United States). They consist of a housing allowance (OHA) and cost of living allowance (COLA). A temporary lodging allowance (TLA) and interim housing allowance (IHA) may also be paid in certain cases. You can calculate the amount of OHA and COLA based on location by visiting *www.defensetravel.dod.mil/site/ohaCalc.cfm* for OHA rates and *www.defensetravel.dod.mil/site/ColaCalc.cfm* for COLA rates.

Reserve component (RC) mobilized soldiers may receive COLA based on the location of their residence when ordered to active duty. CONUS COLA is normally determined by the zip code provided by the soldier for the location of their residence. Regular active-duty soldiers located in CONUS or OCONUS areas, who are authorized COLA, will continue to draw COLA as determined by the area to which they are assigned.

Clothing Maintenance Allowance

A clothing maintenance allowance, provided to help you take care of your uniforms, is another great benefit not found in most civilian career fields and is paid at two different rates:

- Initial, which covers replacement of unique military items that would normally require replacement during the first three years of service.
- Replacement, which covers the replacement of unique military items after the first three years of service.

Female personnel are also authorized an initial cash allowance established by AR 700-84 for the purchase of undergarments, dress shoes, and stockings.

A soldier receives the clothing maintenance allowance annually, on the last day of the month in which the soldier's anniversary date of enlistment falls.

Civilian Clothing Allowance

When duty assignments require soldiers to wear civilian clothing, they receive lump-sum payments under the following circumstances:

- Permanent duty requiring civilian clothing.
- Temporary duty in graduations of fifteen to thirty days and over thirty days.

Temporary Lodging Allowance (TLA)

TLA is an allowance received when arriving at an overseas base that offsets some of the expense of temporary housing and meals. The amount of the TLA depends on variables that include family size, the cost and cooking/dining facilities of quarters, and other allowances the family is receiving.

Temporary Lodging Expense (TLE)

TLE is an allowance received when arriving at a CONUS base that offsets some of the expense of temporary housing and meals. The TLE is up to $110 per day and can last up to ten days. It applies to stateside base arrivals from both CONUS and OCONUS bases.

BONUSES

The enlistment bonus is an enlistment incentive offered to those enlisting in the Regular Army for duty in a specific MOS. The objective of the bonus is to increase the number of enlistments in MOSs that are critical and have inadequate first-term manning levels. Section A, chapter 9, part 1 of the *DOD Pay Manual* gives basic conditions of entitlement, amount of the bonus, time of payment, and reduction and termination of the award.

Selective Reenlistment Bonus

The selective reenlistment bonus (SRB) is a retention incentive paid to soldiers in certain selected MOSs who reenlist or voluntarily extend their enlistment for additional obligated service. The objective of the SRB is to increase the number of reenlistments or extensions in critical MOSs that do not have sufficient retention levels to man the force in a given career field.

The SRB is established in three zones: Zone A consists of those reenlistments falling between twenty-one months and six years of active service, and zones B and C consist of those reenlistments or extensions of enlistments falling between six and fourteen years of service.

Payments are based on multiples, not to exceed six, of a soldier's monthly basic pay at the time of discharge or release from active duty, or the day before the beginning of extension, multiplied by years of additional obligated service.

The SRB is paid by installments. Up to 50 percent of the total bonus may be paid as the first installment, with the remaining portion paid in equal annual amounts over the remainder of the enlistment period.

A list of the MOSs designated for award of SRB and enlistment bonuses are announced via military personnel (MILPER) messages by Human Resources Command (HRC), and current lists are available on the HRC website.

ALLOTMENTS

An allotment is a specified amount of money withheld from military pay, normally upon the soldier's authorization, for a specific purpose. Payment is made by government check and mailed to the organization or person indicated by the soldier or directed by the government, depending on the circumstance.

Allotments are made by logging into the MyPay website at *https://mypay.dfas.mil* or by filling out DD Form 2558, *Authorization to Start, Stop, or Change an Allotment for Active Duty or Retired Personnel*. These forms are prepared by the individual's military personnel office, unit personnel office (S-1), or finance office, and by Army Emergency Relief and the American Red Cross. Preparation of allotment documents in the finance office, rather than in the personnel office, is intended to eliminate delays of one or more days. When there is a delay near the end of the processing month, the effective date of an allotment may be delayed a full month. Commanders may have DD Form 2558 prepared in the unit personnel office, if it will conserve time and ensure that there will be no delays in transmission to the finance office. Some of the reasons for using allotments include:

Repayment of Army Emergency Relief (AER) Loans. These allotments are authorized in multiples. AER allotments are established for a definite term of not less than three months (although this provision may be waived in certain cases).

Combined Federal Campaign (CFC) Contributions. This allotment is authorized to be in effect one at a time only. CFC allotments are made for a period of twelve months, beginning in January and ending in December. Military personnel who execute the *Payroll Withholding Authorization for Voluntary Charitable Contributions* (a Civil Service form) may do so in lieu of DD Form 2558.

Payment to a Dependent (SPT-V). This kind of allotment is authorized in multiples. It is paid to a soldier's dependent without regard to whether the soldier is already receiving BAH. In addition, involuntary SPT-V allotments can be administratively established. Normally, the amount of these allotments is not permitted to exceed 80 percent of a soldier's pay. Not more than one SPT-V allotment may be made to the same person.

Payment to a Financial Institution for Credit to a Member's Account (FININ). Only two of these allotments are authorized to be in effect at any one time. FININ allotments are for payment to a financial organization for credit to the allotter's savings, checking, or trust accounts. The FININ allotment may be established for an indefinite term and for any amount the soldier designates, provided he or she has sufficient pay to satisfy the deduction of the allotment.

Payment for Indebtedness to the United States (FED). FED allotments are for the purpose of payment of delinquent federal, state, and local taxes and/or indebtedness to the United States. A separate allotment is required for each debt or overpayment to be repaid.

Payment of Home Loans (HOME). Only one HOME allotment is authorized to be in effect at any one time. This allotment is authorized for repayment of loans for the purchase of a house, mobile home, or house trailer. A HOME allotment is established for an indefinite term and for any amount designated provided the soldier's pay credit is sufficient to satisfy the deduction of the allotment.

Payment of Commercial Life Insurance Premiums (INS). These allotments are authorized in multiples. INS allotments must be made payable to a commercial life insurance firm. INS allotments are not authorized for payment of insurance on the life of a soldier's spouse or children except under a family group contract or for health, accident, or hospitalization insurance. INS allotments are established for an indefinite period and in the amount of the monthly premium, as indicated by the number on DA Form 1341.

Repayment of American Red Cross Loans (REDCR). REDCR allotments are authorized in multiples to pay off this category of loans.

Class X Allotments. A Class X allotment is paid locally and is authorized in emergency circumstances when other classes of allotments are impracticable. This instance applies overseas only. Class X allotments may be ordered by a commander as a standby allotment when adequate provision for the financial support of a soldier's dependents has not been made.

PCS WEIGHT ALLOWANCE (POUNDS)

Pay Grade	With Dependents	Without Dependents
E-9	15,000	13,000
E-8	14,000	12,000
E-7	13,000	11,000
E-6	11,000	8,000
E-5	9,000	7,000
E-4	8,000	7,000
E-3 to E-1	8,000	5,000

BENEFITS

Transportation of Household Goods

Transportation of household goods at government expense is authorized for you in accordance with the table above. These shipment weight allowances are current as of October 2014 and should be checked annually for updates. For information on authorized weight limitations for other grades, see the Joint Federal Travel Regulations (JFTR).

Government Quarters and Family Housing

Unaccompanied Housing. Once you are out of basic training and advanced individual training, accommodations for single soldiers range from group living conditions provided to junior enlisted personnel in some troop units to private and well-appointed spaces offered senior NCOs in bachelor enlisted quarters, and a wide range of conditions in between.

Modern troop billets are mostly dormitory-style facilities with central air conditioning and heating; two, three, or four-person rooms; and recreational convenience facilities. The days of living in wooden barracks with footlockers and large community bath and shower facilities are a thing of the past and only exist today in old war movies and in some training environments.

Family Housing. Where it is available, family housing ranges in style from detached single-family housing to townhomes and high-rise apartment-style buildings accommodating multiple families. In most cases, the quarters you are assigned will be in excellent condition and will require little maintenance to keep them that way. Under the Residential Communities Initiative, the vast majority of family housing is managed by professional civilian contractors, which has been one of the most important improvements to quality of life made by the Army in decades. That said, it is important that you and your family maintain those quarters well and leave them in good condition when it is time to move on to the next assignment.

When reporting to some new duty stations, you will find pleasant family housing waiting for you; at other stations, you will have to wait weeks or even months to get any kind of quarters. In some areas, the waiting list for government housing is so long that you might find it necessary to buy or rent off the post. Your family housing office will be of great assistance if you should decide to occupy off-post quarters. Each installation and each major overseas command has a different family housing situation.

Because of your rank, you may very well find yourself responsible to a more senior occupant of a multiple dwelling or of a stairwell of such a dwelling. These assignments are important, and you should consider them a necessary part of living in close proximity to one another. Assist in keeping your communal living areas in good order and be considerate of your neighbors, and the time you spend in government housing will be some of your most memorable moments.

If you are fortunate enough to be assigned to a single-family dwelling, you will be expected to perform the type of self-help maintenance that is done by any prudent homeowner to conserve funds and preserve the premises, such as minor carpentry, maintenance of hardware (door hinges, etc.), touch-up and partial interior painting, caulking around doors and windows, repair of screens, repair of simple plumbing malfunctions (minor leaking, defective washers, simple drainage stoppages), and so forth. Accumulate a set of tools that you can use around the house or apartment for this minor maintenance work.

No matter where you live—family quarters or the barracks—you are expected to exercise individual initiative to preserve energy and utilities. Soldiers are among the most flagrant violators of good energy conservation, wasting water and electricity and fuel as if there were no tomorrow. Remind yourself and others to be conservation conscious.

Your quarters will be inspected by someone from the housing office before you are cleared to vacate them. This inspection can be very rigorous. The specific details will be furnished to you by the housing office. Some people prefer to hire a civilian contractor to do the work for them. You can avoid this unnecessary expense if you and your family take proper care of your quarters while you are living in them. For example, use rugs on the floors, keep the walls clean and in good repair, and keep your appliances clean.

Commissary and Post Exchange Services

Another very powerful benefit you have as a soldier is the commissary and Post Exchange. The price you pay for a grocery item in the commissary is the same price the government pays for it: If an item is sold to the government for eighty-five cents, then that is its cost to you. Even the commissary surcharge and tipping do not add as much to the cost of an item as do the standard markups found on similar items in civilian retail outlets. (The commissary surcharge pays for operating supplies, equipment, utilities, facility alterations, and new construction.)

The Post Exchange Service was designated the Army and Air Force Exchange Service (AAFES) in 1948. What originally began as an outlet "to supply troops at reasonable prices with articles of ordinary use . . . not supplied by the Government . . . to afford them the means of rational recreation and amusement" has since become a multibillion-dollar enterprise that spans the globe. Many Post Exchange stores are actually department stores designed for family shoppers, although single soldiers can buy all the necessities of barracks life. Some stores even permit personnel in uniform to be waited on first during certain hours of the day, such as the lunch hour.

Several hundred military exchanges are operated throughout the world by the Department of Defense. AAFES, headquartered in Dallas, Texas, and headed by a general officer, operates outlets worldwide. At a minimum, AAFES customers save the state sales tax, which is not charged.

IDENTIFICATION CARDS

Your Common Access Card is your *U.S. Armed Forces Geneva Conventions Identification Card* and is possibly the most important military document you possess. DD Form 1173, *Uniformed Services Identification and Privilege Card*, is equally important to military dependents. These cards identify the bearers as persons who are entitled to the wide range of entitlements, privileges, and benefits authorized for military personnel and their dependents.

A CAC is issued to the following:

- All active-duty military personnel.
- Members of the Army National Guard and the Selected Reserve.
- DOD employees and eligible contractors.

DD Form 2 (Reserve—green) is issued to individual Ready Reserves and inactive National Guard.

DD Form 2 (retired—blue) is issued to retired personnel of the uniformed services who are entitled to retirement pay. The DD Form 2A (retired) is also issued to persons who retired from ARNG or USAR at age sixty after completing federal service under Section 1331, Title 10, U.S. Code, and personnel permanently retired for physical disability.

DD Form 2 (retired Reserve—pink) is issued to members who have retired from the USAR or ARNG but are less than age sixty so not yet entitled to retirement pay.

All ID cards are the property of the U.S. government. They are not transferable. The individual (or sponsor) to whom the card is issued must turn in cards in the following circumstances:

- Expiration of the card.
- Change in eligibility status (such as change in grade or rank and changes caused by disciplinary action, discharge, death, retirement, reenlistment, age, marriage, or release to inactive duty of the sponsor).
- Replacement by another card.
- Request from competent authority.
- Demand of the installation commander, verifying activity, or issuing activity.
- Recovery of a lost card after a replacement has been issued.
- Request by the installation commander for temporary safekeeping while an individual is taking part in recreation and gymnastic activities.
- Official placement of a sponsor in a deserter status.
- Change in the status of a sponsor if it terminates or modifies the right to any benefit for which the card may be used.

A lost ID card must be reported promptly to your local security office/S-2. They will provide you the documentation necessary to serve as evidence of your report when you go to get a new card issued. Since your ID card gives you access to military installations, buildings, computer networks, and so forth, it is a very powerful access tool, so it's extremely important that you safeguard it at all times.

Any NCO who is performing his or her official duties may confiscate an ID card that is expired, mutilated, used fraudulently, or presented by a person not entitled to use it. Managers and employees of benefit and privilege activities also may confiscate any expired or obviously altered ID card or document.

Dependent ID Cards

DD Form 1173 is used throughout the Department of Defense to identify persons, other than active-duty or retired military personnel, who are eligible for benefits and privileges offered by the armed services.

Dependent ID cards are authorized for issue to lawful spouses; unremarried former spouses married to the member or former member for a period of at least twenty years, during which period the member or former member performed at least twenty years of service; children (adopted, legitimized, stepchildren, wards); parents (in special cases); and surviving spouses of active-duty or retired members. See AR 600-8-14 for specific details.

Generally, DD Forms 1173 are replaced for the same reasons that govern replacement of military ID cards.

To verify initial eligibility for issue of a dependent ID card and entry into the Defense Enrollment Eligibility Reporting System (DEERS), sponsors must be prepared to show marriage certificates, birth certificates, death certificates (in the case of unremarried widows or widowers), or any other documentation prescribed by AR 600-8-14 as required to establish dependency.

Abuse of Privileges
All CACs, DD Forms 2, DD Forms 1173, and other authorized identification documents issued to Army members and their dependents may be confiscated and overstamped for abuse of privileges in Army facilities. Medical benefits, however, cannot be suspended for these reasons.

Abuse of privileges includes the following:

- Unauthorized resale of commodities bought in Army activities to unauthorized persons, whether or not to make a profit (customary personal gifts are permissible).
- Shoplifting.
- Unauthorized access to activities.
- Misuse of a privilege (such as allowing an unauthorized person to use an otherwise valid ID card to gain access to a facility).
- Issuing dishonored checks in Army facilities.

Penalties for abuse of privileges in an appropriated or nonappropriated fund facility are a warning letter, temporary suspension of privileges, or indefinite suspension of privileges.

Thrift Savings Plan
The purpose of the Thrift Savings Plan (TSP) is to provide retirement income. It offers you the same type of savings and tax benefits that many private corporations offer their employees under so-called 401(k) plans. Under the plan, soldiers save a portion of their pay in a special retirement account administered by the Federal Retirement Thrift Investment Board. The total amount contributed is limited each year by the IRS. For 2016 the limit is $1,800, which does not include traditional contributions from tax-exempt pay earned in a combat zone.

Participation in the TSP is neither optional nor automatic. You must sign up through your finance office to participate. You contribute to the TSP from your own pay on a pretax basis, and the amount you contribute and the earnings attributable to your contributions belong to you. They are yours to keep even if you do not serve the twenty years ordinarily necessary to receive military retired pay.

While you are a member of the uniformed services, any tax-deferred money withdrawn before the age of fifty-nine and a half as a result of financial hardship is subject to the IRS 10 percent early withdrawal penalty, as well as regular income tax. With respect to post-separation withdrawals, if you separate from the service during or after the year in which you turn age fifty-five, your withdrawals are not subject to the early withdrawal penalty. If you separate before the year you reach age fifty-five, you can transfer your TSP account to an IRA or other eligible retirement plan (e.g., 401(k) plan, your civilian TSP account) or begin receiving annuity payments without penalty.

LEAVES AND PASSES

Military Leave
AR 600-8-10 governs leaves and passes. All members of the Army serving on active duty are entitled to leave with pay and allowances at the rate of two and one-half calendar days each month of active duty or active duty for training, including the following:

- Members of the Army serving in active military service, including members of the Army National Guard and the Army Reserve serving on active duty for a period of thirty days or more.
- Members of the Army National Guard and Reserve who are serving on initial active duty for training or active duty for training for a period of thirty days or more and for which they are entitled to pay.
- Members of the Army National Guard who are serving on full-time training duty for a period of thirty days or more and for which they are entitled to pay.

The following circumstances do not qualify as periods of earned leave:

- AWOL.
- Confinement as a result of a sentence of court-martial; confinement for more than one day while awaiting court-martial (providing the court-martial results in a conviction).
- When in excess leave.
- Due to alcohol or drug use resulting in more than a duty day of absence; when disease or injury is caused by misconduct; unauthorized absence as a result of detention by civil authorities.
- Absence due to misconduct.

The total accumulation of accrued leave (earned leave) at the end of a fiscal year (September 30) cannot exceed 60 days. Leave accumulated after that date is forfeited. The single exception to this policy applies to personnel who were prohibited from taking leave during the latter part of the fiscal year due to assignment or deployment to hostile fire or imminent danger pay areas. Eligible members can accumulate up to 30 additional days in excess of 60 but cannot carry over more than 120 days into the next fiscal year. Leave that begins in one fiscal year and is completed in another is apportioned to the fiscal year in which each portion falls. Upon discharge and immediate reenlistment, separation at expiration of term of service (ETS), or retirement, soldiers are authorized to settle their leave accounts for a lump-sum cash payment at the rate of one day of basic pay for each day of earned leave, up to 60 days. Public Law 94-212, 9 February 1976, limited settlement for accrued leave during a military career to a maximum of 60 days.

The following types of leave are authorized:

- *Advance leave.* Leave granted before its actual accrual, based on a reasonable expectation that it will be earned by the soldier during the remaining period of active duty.
- *Annual leave.* Leave granted in execution of a command's leave program, chargeable to the soldier's leave account. Also called "ordinary leave," as distinguished from emergency leave and special leave.
- *Convalescent leave.* A period of authorized absence granted to soldiers under medical treatment that is prescribed for recuperation and convalescence for sickness or wounds. Also called "sick leave," convalescent leave is not chargeable. Soldiers who sustain illness or injury while eligible for hostile fire pay are entitled to funded transportation per Joint Federal Travel Regulations (JFTR), paragraph U7210. Reference AR 600-8-10, paragraph 5-5.
- *Emergency leave.* Leave granted for a bona fide personal or family emergency requiring the soldier's presence. Emergency leave is chargeable.
- *Environmental and morale leave.* Leave granted in conjunction with an environmental and morale leave program established at overseas installations where adverse environmental conditions exist that offset the full benefit of annual leave programs. This leave is chargeable.
- *Excess leave.* This leave is in excess of accrued and/or advance leave, granted without pay and allowances.
- *Graduation leave.* A period of authorized absence granted, as a delay in reporting to the first permanent duty station, to graduates of the U.S. Military Academy who are appointed as commissioned officers. Not chargeable, providing it is taken within three months of graduation.
- *Leave awaiting orders.* This is an authorized absence—chargeable to accrued leave and in excess of maximum leave accrual—taken while awaiting further orders and disposition in connection with disability separation proceedings under the provisions of AR 635-40.
- *Reenlistment leave.* This leave is granted to enlisted personnel as a result of reenlistment. May be either advance leave or leave accrued or a combination thereof, and is chargeable against the soldier's leave account.
- *Rest and recuperation (R&R)—extensions of overseas tours.* This is a nonchargeable increment of R&R leave authorized for enlisted soldiers in certain specialties who voluntarily extend their overseas tours. It is authorized in lieu of $50 per month special pay. The tour extension must be for a period of at least twelve months. Options under this program include nonchargeable leaves of fifteen or thirty days.
- *Rest and recuperation leave.* Leave is granted in conjunction with rest and recuperation programs established in those areas designated for hostile fire pay, when operational military considerations preclude the full execution of ordinary annual

leave programs. R&R leave is chargeable to the normal leave account; however, the Army pays for transportation to and from the leave destination. Currently, soldiers assigned to the U.S. Central Command's Area of Responsibility (USCENT-COM AOR) may take up to 15 days of uncharged leave during their deployment, once they have accrued 270 days in designated area. The commander determines priority for personnel who are eligible for R&R leave based on the criteria above, as well as operational, safety, and security requirements.

- *Special leave.* This is leave accrual that is authorized in excess of sixty days at the end of a fiscal year for soldiers assigned to hostile fire/imminent danger areas or certain deployable ships, mobile units, or other duty.
- *Transition.* This leave is granted in connection with separation, including retirement, upon the request of the individual.

When possible, soldiers should be encouraged to take at least one annual leave period of about fourteen consecutive days or longer (paragraph 203b, AR 600-8-10). Personnel who refuse to take leave when the opportunity is afforded them should be counseled and informed that such refusal may result in the loss of earned leave at a later date.

Leave is requested on part I of DA Form 31, *Request and Authority for Leave.* Requests for leave must be processed through the individual's immediate supervisor, although this step may be waived where supervisory approval or disapproval is inappropriate. This approval authority (generally, the soldier's commanding officer) ascertains that the individual has sufficient leave accrued to cover the entire period of absence requested.

Personnel should be physically present when DA Form 31 is authenticated and when commencing and terminating leave. Commanders may, at their discretion, authorize confirmation of departure and return by telephone.

Passes

A pass is an authorized absence not chargeable as leave, granted for short periods to provide respite from the working environment or for other specific reasons, at the end of which the soldier is actually at his or her place of duty or in the location from which he or she regularly commutes to work. This provision includes both regular and special passes.

Regular passes are granted to deserving military personnel for those periods when they are not required to be physically present with their unit for the performance of assigned duties. Normally, regular passes are valid only during specified off-duty hours, not more than seventy-two hours, except for public holiday weekends and holiday periods that, by discretion of the president, are extended to the commencement of working hours on the next working day.

Special passes are granted for periods of three or four days (seventy-two to ninety-six hours) to deserving personnel on special occasions or in special circumstances for the following reasons: as special recognition for exceptional performance of duty, such as Soldier of the Month (or year); to attend spiritual retreats or to observe other major religious events; to alleviate personal problems incident to military service; to vote; or as compensatory time off for long or arduous duty away from the home station or for duty in an isolated location where a normal pass is inadequate.

Passes may not be issued to soldiers so that two or more are effective in succession or used in a series, through reissue immediately after return to duty.

Extension of a pass is authorized provided the total absence does not exceed seventy-two hours for a regular pass, seventy-two hours for a special three-day pass, and ninety-six hours for a special four-day pass. Special passes will not be extended by combination with public holiday periods or other off-duty hours in cases in which the combined total will exceed the maximum limits of a three-day or four-day pass. Passes may not be taken in conjunction with leave, and extensions beyond the authorized maximum are chargeable to leave (AR 600-8-10).

MyArmyBenefits and Military Onesource

My Army Benefits is a website with well over one hundred written reports concerning your benefits. It also provides a library of each state's benefits for veterans. You can visit it at *http://myarmybenefits.us.army.mil.*

Military Onesource is an open, user-friendly website that covers the vast majority of pay and benefits information, along with a host of other areas, discussed in this guide. It is a one-stop online shop for the military family for key support information. For the areas discussed in this chapter, simply go to the site and click on the "Financial and Legal" tab, near the top of the page. You can go directly to that page at *http://www.militaryonesource.mil/financial-and-legal/benefits.*

15

Uniforms, Insignia, and Personal Appearance

WEARING THE UNIFORM

Nothing makes more of a first impression than the way a soldier wears their uniform. Sharp, crisp, and well-fitting or sloppy with an ill-fitting look or dirty—others around you will make an immediate judgment. An old saying is that it is easy to change your hairstyle or clothes or manners, but very hard to change a first impression. Your Army uniform is the outward evidence of your profession and your standing in that profession, and a prime indicator of the degree of respect with which you regard your service to the United States of America and the Army. The condition of your uniform and the way you wear it are also a reflection of your own self-respect. When you put on your uniform each day, remember how proud you were the first time you actually wore it and what you saw when you looked in the mirror, and try to emulate that feeling. You earned that pride and should be eager to show it, through the meticulous care and wearing of the mark of our nation's defense.

Occasions When the Uniform Is Required to Be Worn

The Army uniform is worn by all personnel when on duty unless Headquarters, Department of the Army (HQDA), has authorized the wearing of civilian clothes. The following general rules apply:

- Installation commanders may prescribe the uniforms to be worn in formations; duty uniforms are generally prescribed by local commanders or heads of agencies, activities, or installations.
- The wearing of combinations of uniform items not prescribed in AR 670-1 is prohibited.
- Uniform items changed in design or material may continue to be worn until the wear-out date unless specifically prohibited by Headquarters, Department of the Army.

Occasions When the Uniform May Not Be Worn

The wearing of the Army uniform is prohibited for all Army personnel under the following circumstances:

- In connection with the promotion of any political interests or when engaged in off-duty civilian employment.
- Except as authorized by competent authority, when participating in public speeches, interviews, picket lines, marches, rallies, or public demonstrations.
- When wearing the uniform would bring discredit upon the Army.
- When specifically prohibited by Army regulations.

Wearing of Headgear

The Army uniform is not normally complete unless the proper form of hat, cap, or beret is worn with it. Headgear is worn when outdoors and indoors when under arms.

Soldiers are exempt from wearing headgear to evening social events (after retreat). The appropriate headgear is, however, worn when wearing these uniforms on all other occasions.

Headgear is not required to be worn only when it would interfere with the safe operation of military vehicles. Military headgear is not required to be worn in privately owned or commercial vehicles.

Beret

The black beret is the Army standard headgear when wearing the Army Service Uniform (ASU) and is worn by those soldiers not currently wearing the green, maroon, or tan beret. Soldiers authorized to wear the black beret may wear the beret with the Army Combat Uniform (ACU) in garrison environments when authorized by the commander for special occasions.

For enlisted soldiers, the crest of the unit to which the soldier is assigned is worn centered on the blue Army flash on the black beret. Soldiers wear the beret so that the headband is straight on the head, one inch above the eyebrows, with the flash over the left eye and the excess material draped over to the right, down to at least the top of the ear, but no lower than the middle of the ear. A dip is formed in the wool, just behind the flash stiffener, and a slight fold is formed to the right front of the beret, next to the flash. Soldiers will tie off the adjusting ribbon into a nonslip knot, cut off the excess adjusting ribbon as close to the knot as possible, and tuck the knot into the edge binding at the back of the beret. The beret is formfitting to the head when worn properly; therefore, soldiers may not wear hairstyles that distort the beret.

Optional service caps are the blue service cap for the ASU and mess dress uniform and the white service cap for the white mess dress uniform.

Patrol Cap

The patrol cap is the standard Army headgear for the ACU while in garrison and when on detail. It is worn in the field when authorized to remove the helmet. Headgear for the ACU uniform is described in more detail below. The tan, green, or maroon beret is worn with the ACU in garrison for soldiers authorized their wear (see chapter 4, DA PAM 670-1).

Uniform Appearance

The word *uniform* as used in this context means "conforming to the same standard or rule." Although absolute uniformity of appearance by all soldiers at all times cannot reasonably be expected as long as armies are composed of so many various individuals, uniformed soldiers should project a military image that leaves no doubt that they live by a common standard.

One important rule of uniformity is that, when worn, items of the uniform should be kept buttoned, zippered, and snapped; metallic devices (such as collar brass insignia) should be kept in proper luster; and shoes should be cleaned and shined. In instances where boots are worn with uniforms, soldiers will not blouse boots any lower than the third eyelet from the top.

Lapels and sleeves of coats and jackets for both male and female personnel should be roll pressed (without creasing). Trousers, slacks, and sleeves of shirts and blouses should be creased.

Care and Maintenance of the Uniform

All solid brass items (belt buckles, belt-buckle tips, collar brass insignia) should be maintained in a high state of luster at all times. These items come coated with a lacquer, and if their surfaces are kept protected and gently rubbed clean with a soft clean cloth, they will keep their shine for a long time. But when the lacquer coating becomes scratched, dirt begins to accumulate in the scratches, and the item can be kept shined only by completely removing the lacquer surface. The safest and most reliable method for removing the coating from brass items is to use Brasso polish applied with thumb and forefinger or a cloth.

Spit-shining does make shoes, boots, and equipment look sharp, but it dries out the leather.

Replace heels on shoes and boots after wear of seven-sixteenths of an inch or more. To check your footgear, ask a battle buddy to attempt to roll a pencil under the heel.

Pay attention to the removal of stains from your clothing.

Never press dirty clothing, and be careful when you do press clothing that the iron is not too hot. Use a damp cloth between the iron and the fabric when pressing wool items, dampen the surface of cotton clothing before applying the iron, and observe the various fabric settings on the iron when pressing synthetic fabric.

Frequent cleaning of uniform items will increase their longevity and maintain the neat soldierly appearance that the uniform is designed to project. Rotating items of clothing, such as shoes and boots, will contribute to their longer life.

Fitting of Uniforms

Uniform items purchased in the military clothing sales store are fitted (or should be fitted) before they are taken off the premises. Personnel who purchase uniform items through the Post Exchange or from commercial sources should pay close attention to the proper fit of the items before wearing them.

An NCO should be able to tell at a glance whether a soldier (male or female) is wearing a properly fitted uniform. Fitting instructions and alterations of uniforms are made in accordance with AR 700-84 and TM 10-227, *Fitting of Army Uniforms and Footwear.*

The Clothing Allowance System

Clothing allowances are provided so that you may maintain your initial clothing issue. Monthly clothing allowances provide you with the cost of replacement and purchase of new items or the purchase of additional clothing items, but not cleaning, laundering, and pressing. The basic allowance begins on the soldier's 181st day of active duty and is paid each month for the remainder of the first three-year period. The standard allowance begins the day after the soldier completes thirty-six months on active duty. The clothing allowance accrues monthly and is paid annually during the month of the soldier's basic active service date.

CLASSIFICATION OF SERVICE AND UTILITY FIELD UNIFORMS

Class A Army Service Uniform

For males: consists of the Army blue coat and trousers, a short-sleeved or long-sleeved white shirt with pleated pockets, a black four-in-hand tie (tied in a slipknot with the ends left hanging), and other accessories.

For females: consists of the appropriate Army blue coat and skirt or slacks, a short-sleeved or long-sleeved white shirt, a black neck tab, and authorized accessories. The Army maternity uniform (slacks or skirt) is also a Class A service uniform when the tunic is worn.

Class B Service Uniform

For males: consists of the same as for the Class A except that the service coat is not worn. The black tie is required when wearing the long-sleeved shirt and is optional with the short-sleeved shirt.

For females: consists of the same as for the Class A except that the service coat and the maternity tunic are not worn. The black neck tab is required when wearing the long-sleeved shirt and the long-sleeved maternity shirt. It is optional with the short-sleeved version of both shirts.

For soldiers wearing green, tan, or maroon berets, or those assigned to air assault coded positions or military police on duty, blousing the trousers and wearing black leather combat boots with the blue ASU is allowed.

Class C Uniforms

These are utility, field, and other organizational uniforms, such as the Army Combat Uniform (ACU), hospital duty, and food service uniforms.

Optional Dress Uniforms

The Army blue mess uniform and white mess uniform are available for optional purchase by enlisted soldiers. See chapters 16 through 19, DA PAM 670-1, for details on wear.

Male Army Service Uniform

The Army Service Uniform (Class A) consists of the blue coat and trousers, worn with either the long-sleeved or short-sleeved white, pleated-pocket shirt and a black four-in-hand necktie.

The coat should fit with a slight drape in both the front and the back. No pronounced tightness at the waist or flare below the waist is authorized. The length of the coat should extend to below the crotch.

Army Service Uniform trousers are straight-legged and reach the top of the instep, and are cut on a diagonal line to reach a point approximately midway between the top of the heel and the top of the standard shoe in the back. The trousers may have a slight break in the front.

Accessories (Class A)

The U.S. insignia disk is worn on the right lapel collar approximately one inch above the notch. The branch insignia disk is worn on the left lapel collar approximately one inch above the notch. Both are centered on the lapel collar so as to be parallel with the inside of the lapel.

Distinctive unit insignia (unit crests) of the currently assigned unit are worn centered on both shoulder loops (epaulets) of the coat between the outside edge of the shoulder loop button and the seam of the loop.

When awarded, sew-on service stripes (hash marks) are placed four inches above the bottom of the left sleeve and centered on the sleeve, one for each three years of service. Overseas bars are placed four inches above the bottom of the right sleeve, denoting each six months of service.

The nameplate is worn on the right breast pocket of the coat, centered between the top of the button and the top of the pocket. Unit awards, such as the Presidential Unit Citation, Joint Meritorious Unit Award, and so forth, are worn one-eighth inch above the right breast pocket. Regimental distinctive insignia, if awarded, are worn one-eighth inch above the right breast pocket if there are no unit awards worn, or one-quarter inch above unit awards if they are worn. The Combat Service Identification Badge (CSIB) is worn centered on the right breast pocket. If other, lower-precedence identification (ID) badges are worn, the CSIB may be worn on the right to stand alone by moving the other, lower-precedence badge to the left pocket in a similar position or by wearing both on the right pocket with the CSIB farthest to the wearer's right. See DA PAM 670-1, chapter 22, for precedence and wear details for all ID badges.

Individual decorations and service ribbons are worn one-eighth inch above the left breast pocket of the coat. When combat and special skill badges are worn, they are centered one-quarter inch above the ribbons. When more than one badge is worn above the ribbons, badges will be stacked one-half inch apart and may be aligned to the left to present a better appearance.

Marksmanship badges are worn on the left breast pocket flap one-eighth inch below the top seam of the pocket. If more than one badge is worn, they are spaced one inch apart and centered in relation to the bottom edge of the ribbons and the pocket button. When special skill badges (e.g., driver's badge) are worn on the pocket flap, they are placed to the right of the marksmanship badges.

The Army black beret, organizational berets, and drill sergeant hats are authorized for wear with the Class A and Class B uniforms.

Male Class B Uniform

The men's Class B uniform omits the coat. It consists of the long-sleeved or short-sleeved white shirt and blue trousers with black web belt and brass buckle. The black four-in-hand necktie must be worn with the long-sleeved shirt and is optional for the short-sleeved shirt. Soldiers are required to have one long-sleeved and two short-sleeved white pleated-pocket shirts.

Individual awards and decorations are authorized to be worn on the Class B uniform shirts. Their placement is as on the coat. Check DA PAM 670-1 for additional details.

Shoulder mark rank insignia is worn on the Class B uniform shirt for all NCOs and on the shirt collars for non-NCO enlisted grades.

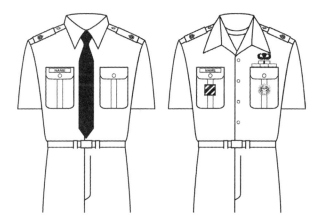

Female Class A Uniform

The female Army Service Uniform consists of the blue coat and the blue skirt or slacks, a white short-sleeved or long-sleeved shirt, and a black neck tab.

As for males, the coat should fit with a slight drape in the front and back, extending in length to a point below the crotch. The blue slacks are straight-legged and slightly flared at the bottom. The skirt length will not be more than one inch above or two inches below the crease in the back of the knee.

Accessories (Class A)

Specifications for wear of the unit crests, rank insignia, service stripes, overseas bars, and regimental crests are similar for the female Class A uniform as they are for the male Class A uniform and are described above. There are, however, some differences.

The U.S. insignia disk is centered on the right collar of the coat approximately five-eighths inch up from the notch, with the center line of the insignia parallel to the inside edge of the lapel. The branch insignia disk is centered in the same manner on the left collar.

The key to the alignment of accessories on the female Class A uniform is the place-ment of the plastic nameplate. The nameplate can be adjusted to conform to individual figure differences. The nameplate is centered horizontally on the right side between one and two inches above the top button of the coat. The regimental insignia is worn one-half inch above the nameplate or one-quarter inch above any unit or foreign awards, if worn. Individual and service ribbons are aligned on the left side parallel to the bottom edge of the nameplate. Other badges are aligned on the nameplate or the ribbons in the same manner as on the male Class A uniform, except for the Combat Service Identification Badge. It is worn parallel to the waistline on the ASU coat and then otherwise in the same manner as on the male uniform.

The Army black beret, organizational berets, and drill sergeant hats are authorized for wear with the Class A and Class B uniforms. No hair should show on the forehead below the front bottom edge of the beret or hat, which should be situated approximately one inch above the eyebrows.

Female Class B Uniforms

The female Class B uniform omits the coat. It consists of the long-sleeved or short-sleeved white shirt, which is worn with either the blue slacks or skirt. The black neck tab must be worn with the long-sleeved shirt and is optional for the short-sleeved shirt.

Soldiers are required to have one long-sleeved and two short-sleeved white shirts. Individual awards and decorations are authorized to be worn on the Class B uniform shirts. Their placement is as on the coat. Check AR 670-1 for additional details.

Shoulder mark rank insignia is worn on the Class B uniform shirt for all NCOs and on the shirt collars for non-NCO enlisted grades.

Service Dress Tropical Uniform

This alternative to the Class A uniform is composed of the Class B uniform with short-sleeved white shirt (standard or lay-flat collar) and no neck tab or necktie, but with ribbons and badges worn. It is a seasonal uniform intended for hot weather conditions for formal ceremonies, parades, and official functions, at the direction of local commanders in those climates. As an alternative to wearing all ribbons as on the Class A coat, soldiers may elect to only wear three authorized ribbons. If this option is used, ribbons must be worn in correct order of precedence (such as Army Commendation Medal, Army Achievement Medal, and Overseas Service Ribbon). ASU slacks for males and the ASU slack or skirt option for females remain unchanged for this uniform.

Maternity Uniform

A pregnant soldier is provided with a specially constructed uniform. Accessories, insignia, awards, badges, and accoutrements for the maternity uniforms follow the same regulations as those for the women's Class A and Class B uniforms.

WORK AND DUTY UNIFORMS

Army Combat Uniform

The Army Combat Uniform (ACU) is the primary uniform for daily wear as a work, utility, and field uniform. It comes in two varieties: the Universal Camouflage Pattern (UCP) and Operational Camouflage Pattern (OCP). The UCP ACU has a wear-out date of 30 September 2019 and will be replaced by the OCP with a mandatory possession date of 1 October 2019 as of this writing. The ACU is composed of a jacket, trousers, moisture-wicking T-shirt, and brown combat boots. Headgear for this uniform includes the patrol cap, the primary headgear in garrison, the beret (when directed by the commander in garrison), and the sun hat (boonie hat) for field or combat conditions when the Kevlar helmet is not worn. The patrol cap is worn level on the head, with the visor straight to the front and the name tape centered on the hook and loop fasteners at the back. No hair should be visible on the forehead under the visor. The cap band (bottom edge of the hat) should be parallel to the ground. No rolling or other modifications are authorized, and the hat should fit snugly at the largest part of the head without excessive gaps due to looseness or material distortion due to over-tightness.

Cold Weather Uniform

The Generation II, extended cold weather clothing system (ECWCS) is designed for wear by all personnel when issued as organizational clothing and prescribed or authorized by the commander. Wear is in accordance with CTA 50-900. Components of this uniform may be worn with utility and other organizational uniforms as part of a cold weather ensemble when issued and prescribed by the commander (e.g., the ACU Gore-Tex parka).

The Generation III ECWCS is designed to provide advanced protection against wet and cold conditions with a seven-layer top (upper body) kit and five-layer bottom (lower body) kit.

Male Hospital Duty Uniform

This year-round duty uniform for all male soldiers in the Army Medical Specialist Corps and those in medical, dental, or veterinary MOSs is worn in medical health-care facilities as prescribed by the medical commander. The commander may authorize the wear of this uniform in a civilian community when in support of civilian activities.

Female Hospital Duty and Maternity Uniform

This authorized year-round uniform is worn by Army Medical Specialist Corps personnel and enlisted females with medical, dental, or veterinary MOSs.

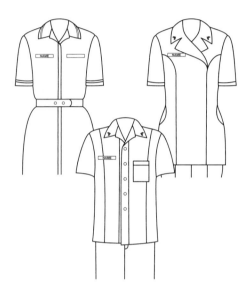

Flight Uniform

This uniform is authorized for year-round wear when on duty in a flying or standby-awaiting-flight status. Commanders may direct exceptions to wear policy.

Combat Vehicle Crewman (CVC) Uniform

The CVC is a year-round duty uniform for combat vehicle crewmen when on duty or as directed by the commander. This uniform is not for travel.

Maternity Work Uniform

This uniform is authorized for year-round on-duty wear by pregnant soldiers. It is not intended as a travel uniform, but it may be worn in transit between the individual's quarters and duty station.

Physical Fitness Uniform

The Army Physical Fitness Uniform (APFU) is the current physical fitness uniform being phased in across the force. It has a mandatory possession date of 1 October 2017. It is composed of black athletic shorts, a black long- or short-sleeved T-shirt, and a black-and-gold jacket with long, black athletic pants. It will replace the current Improved Physical Fitness Uniform (IPFU), with a phase-out date of 30 September 2017. Still authorized for wear, the IPFU has a black-and-gray running jacket, long, black running pants, black shorts, a long- or short-sleeved gray T-shirt, and a microfleece or black knit cap. The black microfleece cap also has a mandatory possession date of 1 October 2017. An optional APFU in female and unisex sizes, with an improved pant liner, is composed of different material and is optional for purchase at the soldier's expense.

OPTIONAL UNIFORMS

Other Authorized Uniforms

- Army blue mess uniform
- Army white mess uniform

OUTERWEAR

A unisex cardigan sweater (optional) replaces the individual male and female black army cardigan and may be worn buttoned or unbuttoned indoors, but must be buttoned outdoors. The old-style cardigan sweaters may no longer be worn.

A black double-breasted and belted all-weather coat replaced the unbelted black all-weather coat.

A unisex black, waist-length jacket with liner for wear with the Class B uniform is also authorized for optional purchase in clothing sales stores.

DISTINCTIVE UNIFORM ITEMS

The following uniform items are distinctive and should not be sold to or worn by unauthorized personnel: all Army headgear, badges, decorations, service medals, awards, tabs, service ribbons, appurtenances, and insignia of any design or color that have been adopted by the Department of the Army.

Headgear

The following items of headgear are authorized for Army personnel:

Item	Female Version*
Beret, black (Army)	Beret, black (Army)
Beret, green (Special Forces)	
Beret, maroon (Airborne)	
Beret, tan (Ranger)	
Cap, cold weather (AG 344)	
Cap, cold weather, utility	
Cap, food handler's, white, paper	
Cap, hot weather	
Cap, service, blue	Hat, service, blue

Hat, camouflage, desert	
Hat, drill sergeant	Hat, drill sergeant

*These are distinctively female items. Other items of headgear listed may be worn by female soldiers, as prescribed in AR 670-1.

Leader's Identification Insignia

The leader's identification (LI) insignia is a green cloth loop, one and five-eighths inches wide, worn on the center tab of the ECWCS parka (field jacket). Personnel cease to wear them when reassigned from a command position. Leaders in all units (Active Army, Army National Guard, and Army Reserves), regardless of unit category (modification table of organization and equipment [MTOE] or table of distribution and allowance [TDA]), will wear the LI insignia. The specific leaders in units authorized to wear the leader's identification insignia are commanders, deputy commanders, platoon leaders, command sergeants major, first sergeants, platoon sergeants, section leaders (when designated in TOE), squad leaders and tank commanders, and rifle squad fire team leaders.

Distinctive Unit Insignia and Heraldic Items

Distinctive unit insignia (DUI) are made of metal or metal and enamel and are usually based on elements of the design of the coat of arms or historic badge approved for a specific unit. Sometimes erroneously referred to as "unit crests," DUI are subject to the approval of the Institute of Heraldry, U.S. Army, and, like shoulder sleeve insignia, are authorized for wear on the uniform as a means of promoting esprit de corps.

When authorized, these insignia are worn by all assigned personnel of an organization, except general officers. A complete set of insignia consists of three pieces: one for each shoulder loop and one for headgear (garrison, utility, cold weather caps, or berets).

Regimental Insignia

Regimental DUI are worn by all personnel affiliated with a regiment. For males, the "unit crest" of the affiliated regiment is worn centered and one-eighth inch above the pocket seam or one-half inch above unit and foreign awards, if worn, on the Army blue uniform. Females wear the unit crest one-half inch above the nameplate or one-quarter inch above unit and foreign awards. The DUI worn on the shoulder loops of the Army blue (enlisted only) coat and jacket is always the unit of assignment. If assigned and affiliated to the same regiment, then all three crests are the same.

Distinctive Items for Infantry

Infantry personnel are authorized to wear the following distinctive items:

- A shoulder cord of infantry blue formed by a series of interlocking square knots around a center cord. The cord is worn on the right shoulder of the Army Service Uniform coat and shirt, passed under the arm and through the shoulder loop, and secured to the button on the shoulder loop.
- A plastic infantry blue disk, one and one-quarter inches in diameter, is worn by enlisted personnel of the infantry, secured beneath the branch of the service and

Adjutant General's Corps

Air Defense Artillery

Armor

Branch Immaterial

Aviation

Cavalry

Chaplain Assistant

Chemical Corps

Civil Affairs

Corps of Engineers

Field Artillery

Finance

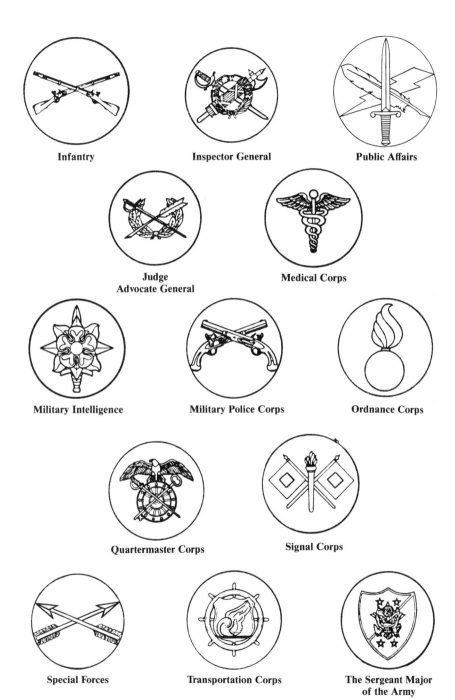

Infantry

Inspector General

Public Affairs

Judge
Advocate General

Medical Corps

Military Intelligence

Military Police Corps

Ordnance Corps

Quartermaster Corps

Signal Corps

Special Forces

Transportation Corps

The Sergeant Major
of the Army

the U.S. insignia, with a one-eighth-inch border around the insignia. It is authorized to be worn on the Army Service Uniform.

- An insignia disk of infantry blue plastic, one and three-quarter inches in diameter, is worn secured beneath the insignia on the service cap. Criteria for wear are the same as those for the infantry blue insignia disk.

Organizational Flash

This shield-shaped embroidered patch with a semicircular bottom approximately two and one-quarter inches long and one and seven-eighths inches wide is worn centered on the stiffener of the beret by personnel authorized to wear one of the organizational berets (Ranger, Special Forces, and Airborne).

Airborne Background Trimming

Background trimming is authorized for wear with the parachutist or air assault badge. When authorized, such background will be worn by personnel of an Airborne-designated organization who have been awarded one of the parachute badges or by personnel in an organization designated air assault who have been awarded the air assault badge.

PERSONAL APPEARANCE

A vital ingredient of the Army's strength and military effectiveness is the pride and discipline that soldiers bring to their service. It is the responsibility of noncommissioned officers to ensure that the military personnel under their supervision present a neat and soldierly appearance. It is the duty of each individual soldier to always take pride in his or her appearance. If you are unclear about any of the information provided in this chapter, you can be sure there is an NCO in your chain who will be happy to help ensure that you are wearing your uniform well and correctly. It is much better to ask and get guidance than to guess and get corrected on your appearance.

Standards for All

Regardless if you are a male or female soldier, there is an equal expectation that you will carry yourself, your fitness and military bearing, and your appearance equally well and with as much professionalism as is possible. Key areas that apply to all include hair color, which must look natural on the soldier. Fingernails must be neatly trimmed, and females may not exceed one-quarter inch of fingernail length and may wear only clear polish in uniform. Males may not have fingernails extending beyond the fingertip. Tinted eye color contacts are also prohibited for all soldiers in uniform, as are dreadlocks. Tattoos or brands anywhere on the head, face, and neck above the T-shirt neckline or on the wrists or the hands are prohibited. An exception is one "ring" tattoo on the joint of a finger closest to the palm. Tattoos regardless of location on the body that are extremist, indecent, sexist, or racist are prohibited, as they are prejudicial to good order and discipline within units. All soldiers are also prohibited from any type of body mutilation. This includes ear gouging, tongue splitting, ear "elfing" (pointing), intentional scarring, or any other type of mutilation. Commanders will do an annual check of all assigned soldiers to ensure they are in compliance with this policy. It is important to note that this policy, along with the section on jewelry below, is stated as punitive in chapter 3 of AR 670-1, meaning you could face UCMJ or administrative actions if found in violation. It is in your best interest to read up on chapter 3 of the regulation and also to talk with your leadership if you are not clear on the policy and before acquiring any tattoos or brands, then also definitely avoiding intentional mutilation.

Wearing of Civilian Jewelry

The wearing of a personal wristwatch, identification wrist bracelet, and no more than two rings is authorized with the Army uniform as long as they are not prohibited for safety reasons and the style is conservative and in good taste. One pedometer, heart monitor, or other fitness tracking device is also allowed, in addition to the one bracelet or watch allowed on each wrist. The wearing of a purely religious medal on a chain around the neck is authorized, provided that neither the medal nor the chain is exposed.

No jewelry, watch chains, or similar civilian items, including pens or pencils, should be allowed to appear exposed on the uniform. Exceptions are a conservative tie tack or tie clasp that may be worn with the black four-in-hand necktie, and a pen or pencil may appear exposed on the ACU coat, hospital duty uniform, food service uniform, and combat vehicle crew and flight uniforms.

Soldiers in and out of uniform are prohibited from attaching jewelry or other ornamentation to, through, or under their skin, tongue, or other body part—except for females with pierced ears. Female soldiers may wear screw-on or post-type earrings with the service, dress, or mess uniforms. Earrings may not be worn with Class C utility uniforms (utility, field, or organizational, including hospital duty and food service uniforms). Earrings must be small in diameter, six millimeters or one-quarter inch; gold, silver, or white pearl; unadorned; and spherical. They must fit snugly against the ear and must be worn as a matched pair with only one in each earlobe. Male soldiers are not authorized to wear earrings.

One electronic device is authorized for wear on the uniform in official duties. It must be no larger than a government-issued electronic device, and it and the carrying case must be black in color. Items that do not comply must be carried elsewhere. Bluetooth and other wireless earpiece devices are prohibited in uniform unless while driving a commercial or military vehicle (this includes motorcycles and bicycles).

Wearing of Civilian Clothing

Civilian clothing is authorized for wear off duty unless the clothing is prohibited by the installation commander within CONUS or the major command overseas. When on duty in civilian clothes, soldiers must conform to the appearance standards of AR 670-1 (see chapter 3), unless specifically authorized for mission requirements.

Security Badges

Security identification badges are worn in restricted areas as prescribed by local commanders. They are usually laminated plastic identification badges worn suspended from clips. They should never be worn outside the secure area for which they authorize an individual access. To prevent the possibility of losing them, some personnel suspend them from a chain worn around the neck and, when in public, under their outer garments.

Standards for Male Soldiers

Fingernail polish is not authorized for male soldiers. Many hairstyles are acceptable in the Army. The hair must be neatly groomed, and the length and bulk of the hair cannot be excessive or present a ragged, unkempt, or extreme appearance. Hair should present a tapered appearance and, when combed, should not fall over the ears or eyebrows or touch the collar. Block cuts are permitted in moderate degree, but in all cases the bulk and length of hair cannot interfere with the normal wear of headgear or protective mask. Men may shave their heads bald.

A soldier's face should be clean shaven, except that Army regulations do permit mustaches. No portion of a mustache is permitted to cover the upper lip line or extend beyond the crease of the upper and lower lips. Handlebar mustaches, goatees, and beards are not authorized. Where beard growth is prescribed by appropriate medical authority, as is sometimes necessary in the treatment of different types of skin disorders, the length required for medical treatment should be specified: "A neatly trimmed beard is authorized. The length will not exceed one-quarter inch," for example. If you have such a medical condition, be sure to keep your exemption slip handy at all times when in uniform.

Standards for Female Soldiers

Hair must be neatly groomed and is defined and explained in detail in chapter 3, AR 670-1, as short, medium, and long in terms of length. Regardless of category or style, the length and bulk of the hair should not be excessive or present a ragged, unkempt, or extreme appearance. Women may wear braids, twists, and cornrows. Wigs and extensions are allowed but must be natural in appearance and conservative in nature. Hair should not fall over the eyebrows or extend below the bottom edge of the collar. Hairstyles cannot interfere with the proper wearing of military headgear or protective masks.

Cosmetics should be applied conservatively and in good taste. Only clear fingernail polish is authorized for any uniform. Two-tone, French-tip, or multitone manicures and nail designs are prohibited.

REFERENCES

AR 600-8-22, *Military Awards.*

AR 670-1, *Uniform and Insignia.*

AR 700-84, *Issue and Sale of Personal Clothing.*

DA PAM 670-1, *Uniform and Insignia.*

FM 3-21-15 [21-15], *Care and Use of Individual Clothing and Equipment.*

16

Awards and Decorations

The Army's awards and decorations program provides tangible recognition for acts of valor, exceptional service or achievement, special skills or qualifications, and acts of heroism not involving actual combat. It is the responsibility of any soldier having personal knowledge of an act, an achievement, or a service believed to warrant the award of a decoration to submit a formal recommendation for consideration.

Under this criterion, it is possible that a private may recommend a captain for a decoration, but usually the system works the other way. As a soldier, and especially when you become an NCO, you must be alert for service or acts that warrant special recognition. The only consideration that should be used is this one: Does the person's act or service warrant an award?

CRITERIA
Award recommendations must be factual and specific, and they must clearly demonstrate that the person being recommended deserves recognition. If your narrative does not support award of a decoration—if you use clichés in place of straightforward and factual prose narrative writing—your recommendation likely will be disapproved.

TIME LIMITATION
Awards for meritorious service should be anticipated, and your recommendation should be submitted far enough in advance to ensure that the award is ready in time to be presented to the individual before his or her departure. Most units require a mandatory submission period prior to a PCS or ETS of a soldier (e.g., AAM approved at battalion level and recommendation submitted 30 days prior, ARCOM approved at brigade level 60 days prior, MSM approved at division level 90 to 120 days prior, etc.). While sometimes difficult to manage given a unit's pace, it is important to give each involved manager and leader in the award approval process time to react and move the award to the approval authority and back to the unit for presentation.

Another reason for acting quickly is that the closer you are to the act or service for which an individual is being recommended, the fresher the details will be in your memory. In any event, each recommendation for an award of a military decoration must be entered into military channels within two years of the act, achievement, or service to be honored. No recommendation except the Purple Heart is awarded more than three years after the act or period of service to be honored (with the exception of lost recommendations or those circumstances covered in paragraph 1-14, AR 600-8-22, *Military Awards*). If a soldier under your supervision deserves an award, let him or her know that you've submitted a recommendation. If the recommendation is not approved, at least the soldier will know you tried and will respect you for it.

PRECEDENCE
Decorations, the Good Conduct Medal, and service medals are ranked in the following order of precedence when worn or displayed:

U.S. military decorations.
U.S. unit awards.
U.S. nonmilitary decorations.
U.S. service (campaign) medals and service and training ribbons.
U.S. Merchant Marine awards.
U.S. nonmilitary unit awards.
Foreign military decorations.
Foreign unit awards.
Non-U.S. service awards.
State awards for Army National Guard (ARNG) soldiers.

U.S. military decorations are ranked in the following order of precedence when worn or displayed:

Medal of Honor (Army, Navy, Air Force).
Distinguished Service Cross.
Navy Cross.
Air Force Cross.
Defense Distinguished Service Medal.
Distinguished Service Medal (Army, Navy, Air Force, Coast Guard).
Silver Star.
Defense Superior Service Medal.
Legion of Merit.
Distinguished Flying Cross.
Soldier's Medal.
Navy and Marine Corps Medal.
Airman's Medal.
Coast Guard Medal.
Bronze Star Medal.
Purple Heart.
Defense Meritorious Service Medal.
Meritorious Service Medal.
Air Medal.
Aerial Achievement Medal.
Joint Service Commendation Medal.

Army Commendation Medal.
Navy Commendation Medal.
Air Force Commendation Medal.
Coast Guard Commendation Medal.
Joint Service Achievement Medal.
Army Achievement Medal.
Navy Achievement Medal.
Air Force Achievement Medal.
Coast Guard Achievement Medal.
Combat Action Ribbon.

U.S. service (campaign) medals, and service and training ribbons authorized for wear on the uniform are listed below, in their order of precedence. Personnel may wear service medals and service and training ribbons awarded by other U.S. Services on the Army uniform, except for the Air Force Longevity Service Award ribbon and Air Force, Navy, and Coast Guard marksmanship medals and ribbons. Personnel will wear service and training medals and ribbons awarded by other U.S. Services after U.S. Army service and training ribbons and before foreign awards.

Prisoner of War Medal.
Good Conduct Medal. (Good Conduct Medals from the other Services in order of precedence.)
Army Reserve Components Achievement Medal. (This medal and equivalents awarded by other Service reserve components follow the Army Good Conduct Medal and Good Conduct Medals from the other Services.)
American Defense Service Medal.
Women's Army Corps Service Medal.
American Campaign Medal.
Asiatic-Pacific Campaign Medal.
European-African-Middle Eastern Campaign Medal.
World War II Victory Medal.
Army of Occupation Medal.
Medal for Humane Action.
National Defense Service Medal.
Korean Service Medal.
Antarctica Service Medal.
Armed Forces Expeditionary Medal.
Vietnam Service Medal.
Southwest Asia Service Medal.
Kosovo Campaign Medal.
Afghanistan Campaign Medal.
Iraq Campaign Medal.
Global War on Terrorism Expeditionary Medal.
Global War on Terrorism Service Medal.
Korean Defense Service Medal.

Armed Forces Service Medal.
Humanitarian Service Medal.
Military Outstanding Volunteer Service Medal.
Army Sea Service Ribbon.
Navy Sea Service Ribbon.
Armed Forces Reserve Medal.
NCO Professional Development Ribbon.
Army Service Ribbon.
Overseas Service Ribbon.
Army Reserve Components Overseas Training Ribbon.
Coast Guard Special Operations Service Ribbon.
Air Force Combat Readiness Medal.

UNIT AWARDS

U.S. unit awards are given to an operating unit and are worn by members of that unit who participated in the cited action. Personnel who did not participate in the cited action, but who are assigned in the cited unit, are authorized temporary wear of some unit awards. U.S. unit awards authorized for wear on Army uniforms are listed below in their order of precedence:

Presidential Unit Citation (Army, Air Force).
Presidential Unit Citation (Navy).
Joint Meritorious Unit Award.
Valorous Unit Award.
Meritorious Unit Commendation (Army).
Navy Unit Commendation.
Air Force Outstanding Unit Award.
Coast Guard Unit Commendation.
Army Superior Unit Award.
Meritorious Unit Commendation (Navy).
Navy "E" Ribbon.
Air Force Organizational Excellence Award.
Coast Guard Meritorious Unit Commendation.

WEARING OF MEDALS AND RIBBONS

All individual U.S. decorations and service medals (full-size medals, miniature medals, and ribbons) are worn above the left breast pocket or centered on the left side of the coat or jacket of the prescribed uniform (with the exception of the Medal of Honor [MOH], which may be worn suspended around the neck). Decorations are worn with the highest displayed above and to the wearer's right of the others.

Full-size decorations and service medals may be worn on the Army Service Uniform when worn for social functions or when directed. They are worn in order of precedence from the wearer's right to left, in one or more lines, without overlapping within a line, with a one-eighth-inch space between lines. No line will contain fewer medals than the

Ribbons Representing
Decorations and Service Medals

1		2	
3	4		5
6	7		8
9	10		11

1. Medal of Honor
2. Distinguished Service Cross
3. Distinguished Service Medal
4. Silver Star
5. Legion of Merit
6. Distinguished Flying Cross

7. Soldier's Medal
8. Bronze Star Medal
9. Purple Heart
10. Meritorious Service Medal
11. Air Medal

one above it. The Medal of Honor is worn with the neck band ribbon around the neck, outside the shirt collar and inside the coat collar, with the medal hanging over the necktie.

Miniature decorations and service medals are authorized for wear on the mess and evening mess uniforms only. They may be worn side by side or overlapped, but the overlap will not exceed 50 percent and will be equal for all. There are no miniature medals authorized for the Medal of Honor.

Service ribbons are worn in the order of precedence from the wearer's right to left in one or more lines either without a space between rows or with a one-eighth-inch space. No row should contain more than four service ribbons. Soldiers are authorized to wear them on the Army Service Uniform.

Retired personnel and former soldiers may wear either full-size or miniature medals on appropriate civilian clothing on Veterans Day, Memorial Day, and Armed Forces Day, and at formal occasions of ceremony and social functions of a military nature.

Unauthorized Wearing of Decorations and Badges

You and your fellow soldiers and leaders, past and present, showed valor and courage and worked incredibly hard or went far above and beyond the call of duty to earn the decorations and badges worn. Federal law prescribes stiff penalties for the unauthorized wearing of U.S. decorations, badges, appurtenances, and unit awards:

> Whoever knowingly wears . . . any decoration or medal authorized by Congress for the Armed Forces of the United States or any of the service medals or badges awarded to the members of such forces, or the ribbon, button, or rosette of any such badge, decoration or medal, or any colorable imitation thereof, except when authorized under regulations made pursuant to law, shall be fined not more than $250 or imprisoned not more than six months, or both.

—62 Stat. 732, June 25, 1948, as amended 18 U.S.C. 704

The U.S. Code (18 U.S.C. 703) further prescribes:

> Whoever, within the jurisdiction of the United States, with intent to deceive or mislead, wears any naval, military, police, or other official uniform, decoration, or regalia of any foreign state, nation, or government with which the United States is at peace, or anything so nearly resembling the same as to be calculated to deceive, shall be fined not more than $250 or imprisoned not more than six months or both.

U.S. Military Decorations, Service Medals, and Ribbons

The Medal of Honor

The Army and Air Force version of the Medal of Honor (MOH) is the highest award for the risk of life "above and beyond the call of duty" involving actual conflict with an enemy; the Navy version can and has been awarded to noncombatants in peacetime, and Congress has similarly awarded special medals to honor individual exploits during peacetime.

The Medal of Honor is designed in the form of a five-pointed star, made of silver and heavily electroplated in gold. In the center of the star appears the head of Minerva—the Roman goddess whose name is associated with wisdom and righteousness in war—surrounded by the words "United States of America." An open laurel wreath, enameled in green, encircles the star, and the oak leaves at the bases of the prongs of the star are likewise enameled. The medal is suspended by a blue silk ribbon, spangled with thirteen white stars (representing the thirteen original states), and attached to an eagle supported by a horizontal bar upon which is engraved the word "Valor."

The reverse of the medal is plain so that the name of the recipient may be engraved thereon; the reverse of the bar is stamped "The Congress to . . . ."

On 21 December 1861, President Abraham Lincoln approved the Medal of Honor for enlisted men of the Navy and Marine Corps; a similar medal was established for the Army on 12 July 1862, further amended by legislation enacted on 3 March 1863, to include officers and making the provisions retroactive to the beginning of the Civil War. The first Army medals were awarded on 25 March 1863. The Medal of Honor is awarded only by the president of the United States (paragraph 3-8, AR 600-8-22).

Distinguished Service Cross

Established by legislation on 9 July 1918 (as amended 25 July 1963), the Distinguished Service Cross (DSC) evolved from the Certificate of Merit of 1847. The DSC is the second-highest decoration for valor in war and is bestowed to recognize extraordinary heroism in connection with military operations in time of war. Unlike the Medal of Honor, however, the DSC may be awarded for heroism involving several acts over a short period of time that need not have been performed in actual conflict with an enemy but must have involved extraordinary risk of life. Successive awards are denoted by oak-leaf clusters (paragraph 3-9, AR 600-8-22).

Defense Distinguished Service Medal

Established by Executive Order 11545, 9 July 1970, the Defense Distinguished Service Medal (DDSM) is awarded to any military officer who, while assigned to joint staffs and other joint activities of the Department of Defense, distinguishes himself or herself by exceptionally meritorious service in a position of unique and great responsibility. It is not awarded for a period of service for which a Distinguished Service Medal or similar decoration is awarded. Subsequent awards are denoted by oak-leaf clusters (paragraph 2-3, AR 600-8-22).

Distinguished Service Medal

Established by an act of Congress of 9 July 1918, the Distinguished Service Medal (DSM) is awarded to any person who, while serving in any capacity with the U.S. Army, has distinguished himself or herself by exceptionally meritorious service in a duty of great responsibility. Awards may be made to persons other than members of the armed forces of the United States for wartime services only, and then only under exceptional circumstances with the approval of the president. Successive awards are denoted by oak-leaf clusters (paragraph 3-10, AR 600-8-22).

Silver Star

Established by an act of Congress of 9 July 1918 (as amended by an act of 25 July 1963), the Silver Star (SS) is the third-ranking U.S. decoration for heroism in wartime.

When first established, the SS was worn in the form of a small silver star, three-sixteenths inch in diameter, upon the respective service medal and ribbon to indicate each separate citation for gallantry in action earned during the campaign for which the service medal was authorized. These stars were known as "citation stars."

The current version of the SS is gilt bronze in the shape of a star one and one-quarter inches across. On the obverse is a laurel wreath, within which is a silver star three-sixteenths inch in diameter; on the reverse are inscribed the words "For Gallantry in Action." The SS may be awarded by any commander who has the authority to award the DSC, and the SS, like the DSC, may be awarded for acts of heroism that take place over a period of time. Successive awards are denoted by oak-leaf clusters (paragraph 3-11, AR 600-8-22).

Defense Superior Service Medal

Established by Executive Order 11904, 6 February 1976, the Defense Superior Service Medal (DSSM) may be awarded to U.S. personnel who give superior meritorious service in a position of significant responsibility. It is not awarded to any individual for a period of service for which a Legion of Merit or similar decoration is awarded. Successive awards are denoted by oak-leaf clusters (paragraph 2-4, AR 600-8-22).

Legion of Merit

Established by an act of Congress of 20 July 1942, the Legion of Merit (LM) is awarded to any member of the armed forces of the United States or a friendly foreign country who distinguishes himself or herself by outstanding meritorious conduct in the performance of outstanding services and achievements. Successive awards are denoted by oak-leaf clusters (paragraph 3-12, AR 600-8-22).

Distinguished Flying Cross
Established by an act of Congress of 2 July 1926, the Distinguished Flying Cross (DFC) may be awarded, in war or peace, to U.S. military personnel who distinguish themselves by heroism or extraordinary achievement while participating in aerial flight. Such awards are made only to recognize single acts of heroism or extraordinary achievement that are not sustained operational activities against an armed enemy. An act of heroism must be evidenced by voluntary action above and beyond the call of duty. Achievement awards must have resulted in an accomplishment so exceptional and outstanding as to clearly set the individual apart from other persons in similar circumstances. Awards to foreign personnel serving with the U.S. armed forces may be made only in connection with actual wartime operations. Successive awards are denoted by oak-leaf clusters (paragraph 3-13, AR 600-8-22).

Soldier's Medal
Established by an act of Congress of 2 July 1926, the Soldier's Medal (SM) is awarded to U.S. and foreign military personnel in recognition of heroism not involving actual conflict with an enemy. The performance must have involved personal hazard or danger and voluntary risk of life of approximately the same degree as that required for award of the Distinguished Flying Cross, but awards of the SM are not made solely on the basis of having saved a life. Subsequent awards of this decoration are denoted by oak-leaf clusters (paragraph 3-14, AR 600-8-22).

Bronze Star Medal
Originally established by Executive Order 9419 of 4 February 1944 (superseded by Executive Order 11046 of 26 August 1962), the Bronze Star Medal (BSM) can be awarded to U.S. and foreign personnel, both military and civilian, for acts that display heroism, meritorious achievement, or service performed in connection with military operations against an armed force. A bronze V device is worn to denote awards for heroism, and successive awards are denoted by oak-leaf clusters (paragraph 3-15, AR 600-8-22).

Purple Heart
Originally established by General George Washington on 7 August 1782, the Purple Heart (PH) is the oldest U.S. military decoration. The PH is awarded in the name of the president to any member of the armed forces or any civilian of the United States who, while serving under competent authority in any capacity with one of the U.S. armed services after 5 April 1917, has been wounded or killed or who has died or may die after being wounded.

A "wound" is defined as any injury (not necessarily one that breaks the skin) caused by an outside force or agent. Multiple injuries suffered at the same moment from the same agent are considered as one wound. Specific examples of injuries that would be authorized the award of the PH are those incurred while making a parachute landing from an aircraft that had been brought down by enemy fire, or injuries received as the result of a vehicle accident caused by enemy fire. Subsequent awards of the PH are denoted by oak-leaf clusters (paragraph 2-8, AR 6008-22).

Defense Meritorious Service Medal

Established by Executive Order 12019 of 3 November 1977, the Defense Meritorious Service Medal (DMSM) is awarded in the name of the secretary of defense to any member of the armed forces who, while serving in any joint activity of the Department of Defense on or after 3 November 1977, for a period of sixty days or more, demonstrates incontestably exceptional service or achievement of a magnitude that clearly places him or her above his or her peers. Subsequent awards of the DMSM are denoted by oak-leaf clusters (paragraph 2-5, AR 600-8-22).

Meritorious Service Medal

Established by Executive Order 1144.8 on 16 January 1969, the Meritorious Service Medal (MSM) is awarded to any member of the armed forces of the United States who, while serving in a noncombat area after 16 January 1969, distinguished himself or herself by outstanding meritorious achievement or service. The achievement or service must have been comparable to that required for the Legion of Merit but in a position of lesser, though considerable, responsibility. This decoration is the equivalent of the Bronze Star Medal for recognition of outstanding meritorious noncombat achievement or service and takes precedence with, but after, the BSM when both are worn on the uniform. It is currently authorized as an exception to policy for award in a combat theater (since 11 September 2001) for meritorious achievement or service in noncombat duty for the global war on terrorism era. The MSM will not be used as an upgrade or downgrade from a recommended BSM, and any downgrades will be to an ARCOM. This decoration is not awarded to foreign personnel. Subsequent awards are denoted by oak-leaf clusters (paragraph 3-16, AR 600-8-22).

Air Medal

Established by Executive Order 9242-A, 11 September 1942, the Air Medal (AM) is awarded to any person who, while serving in any capacity in or with the Army, shall have distinguished himself or herself by meritorious achievement while participating in aerial flight. Awards may be made in recognition of single acts of merit or heroism or for meritorious service. A system of denoting successive awards of the medal was devised using bronze Arabic numerals instead of oak-leaf clusters. Therefore, an individual holding fifteen awards of the AM wears the numeral "14" on the suspension ribbon and service ribbon (paragraph 3-17, AR 600-8-22).

Joint Service Commendation Medal

The Joint Service Commendation Medal (JSCM) is awarded to any member of the armed forces who distinguishes himself or herself by meritorious achievement or service while serving in any joint assignment. Awards made for acts or services involving direct participation in combat operations on or after 25 June 1963 may be denoted by the bronze V device. Subsequent awards of the JSCM are denoted by oak-leaf clusters (paragraph 2-6, AR 600-8-22).

Army Commendation Medal

The Army Commendation Medal (ARCOM) is awarded to any member of the armed forces who distinguishes himself or herself by heroism, meritorious achievement, or meritorious service. The ARCOM may also be awarded to a member of the armed forces of a friendly foreign nation who distinguishes himself or herself by an act of heroism, extraordinary achievement, or meritorious service that has been of mutual benefit to a friendly nation and the United States. Awards of the ARCOM may be made for acts of valor performed under circumstances described above that are of lesser degree than those required for award of the Bronze Star Medal and may include acts that involve aerial flight. Awards may also be made for noncombat acts of heroism that do not meet the requirements for award of the Soldier's Medal. This decoration is primarily awarded to company-grade officers, warrant officers, and enlisted personnel (paragraph 3-18, AR 600-8-22).

Joint Service Achievement Medal

The Joint Service Achievement Medal (JSAM) is awarded to any member of the armed forces of the United States, below the grade of full colonel, who distinguishes himself or herself by meritorious achievement or service while serving in any joint activity after 3 August 1983. Military personnel on temporary duty to a joint activity for at least sixty days are also eligible. The required achievement or service, while of lesser degree than that required for award of the Joint Service Commendation Medal, must have been accomplished with distinction. Subsequent awards are designated by oak-leaf clusters (paragraph 2-7, AR 600-8-22).

Army Achievement Medal

The Army Achievement Medal (AAM) is awarded to any member of the armed forces of the United States, or to any member of the armed forces of a friendly foreign nation, who, while serving in any capacity with the Army in a noncombat area on or after 1 August 1981, distinguishes himself or herself by meritorious service or achievement of a lesser degree than that required for award of the Army Commendation Medal. Subsequent awards are designated by oak-leaf clusters (paragraph 3-19, AR 600-8-22).

Prisoner of War Medal

The Prisoner of War Medal (POWM) is authorized for all U.S. military personnel who were taken prisoner of war after 6 April 1917, during an armed conflict and who served honorably during the period of captivity (paragraph 2-9, AR 600-8-22).

Good Conduct Medal

The Good Conduct Medal (GCM) is awarded to enlisted personnel for exemplary behavior, efficiency, and fidelity to active federal military service. Generally, the qualifying period is three years of continuous active service completed on or after 26 August 1940.

Exceptions are for those who separated from the service by reason of physical disability incurred in the line of duty, who died or were killed before completing one year of service, or who separated after more than one year but less than three years (draftees). Those exceptions apply only to the first award.

Isolated examples of nonjudicial punishment are not necessarily automatically disqualifying but must be considered on the basis of the soldier's whole record; consideration as to the nature of the infraction, the circumstances under which it occurred, and when it occurred must be duly weighed by the individual's commander. Conviction by court-martial terminates a period of qualifying service; a new period begins following the completion of the sentence imposed by court-martial.

The first award is the actual medal itself. Successive awards of the GCM are identified by clasps, or bars, one-eighth inch by one and three-eighths inches, of bronze, silver, or gold, with loops (also called knots) that indicate each period of service for which the medal is authorized (chapter 4, sections 1 and 2, AR 600-8-22).

Army Reserve Components Achievement Medal

The Army Reserve Components Achievement Medal (ARCAM) may be awarded upon recommendation of the unit commander for three years of honest and faithful service on or after 28 March 1995. Service must have been consecutive, in the grade of colonel or below, and in accordance with the standards of conduct, courage, and duty required by law and customs of the service of an active-duty member of the same grade. The reverse of this medal is struck in two designs for award to personnel whose service has been primarily in the Army Reserve or primarily in the National Guard (chapter 4-14, AR 600-8-22).

Unit Awards

Unit awards are authorized in recognition of group heroism or meritorious service, usually during a war, as a means of promoting esprit de corps. They are of the following categories: unit decorations, infantry and medical streamers, campaign streamers, war service streamers, and campaign silver bands.

U.S. unit decorations, in order of precedence listed in this section, have been established to recognize outstanding heroism or exceptionally meritorious conduct in the performance of outstanding services. These awards may be worn permanently by those who served with the unit during the cited period. The Presidential Unit Citation (Army), the Valorous Unit Award, the Meritorious Unit Commendation, and the Army Superior Unit Award may be worn temporarily by those serving with the unit subsequent to the cited period.

Presidential Unit Citation

The Presidential Unit Citation is awarded to units of the armed forces of the United States and cobelligerent nations for extraordinary heroism in action against an armed enemy occurring on or after 7 December 1941. The unit must display such gallantry, determination, and esprit de corps in accomplishing its mission under extremely difficult and hazardous conditions as to set it apart from and above other units participating in the same campaign. The degree of heroism required is the same as that which would warrant award of a Distinguished Service Cross to an individual. The Presidential Unit emblem (Army) is a blue ribbon set in a gold-colored metal frame of laurel leaves (paragraph 7-13, AR 600-8-22).

Joint Meritorious Unit Award
The Joint Meritorious Unit Award is awarded to joint activities of the Department of Defense for meritorious achievement or service, superior to that normally expected, during combat with an armed enemy of the United States, during a declared national emergency, or under extraordinary circumstances that involve the national interest (paragraph 7-15, AR 600-8-22).

Valorous Unit Award
Criteria for the Valorous Unit Award are the same as those for the Presidential Unit Citation except that the degree of valor required is that which would merit award of the Silver Star to an individual. The emblem is a scarlet ribbon with the Silver Star color design superimposed in the center, set in a gold-colored metal frame with laurel leaves (paragraph 7-14, AR 600-8-22).

Meritorious Unit Commendation
The Meritorious Unit Commendation is awarded for at least six months of exceptionally meritorious conduct in support of military operations to service and support units of the armed forces of the United States and cobelligerent nations. The degree of achievement is that which would merit the award of the Legion of Merit to an individual. The emblem is a scarlet ribbon set in a gold-colored metal frame with laurel leaves (paragraph 7-15, AR 600-8-22).

Army Superior Unit Award
The Army Superior Unit Award is given for outstanding meritorious performance of a difficult and challenging mission under extraordinary circumstances by a unit during peacetime. The emblem is a scarlet ribbon with a vertical green stripe in the center, on each side of which is a narrow yellow stripe, set in a gold-colored metal frame with laurel leaves (paragraph 7-16, AR 600-8-22).

U.S. Service Medals
Service or campaign medals denote honorable performance of military duty within specified limited dates in specified geographical areas. With the exception of the Humanitarian Service Medal, the Armed Forces Reserve Medal, the Army Reserve Component Achievement Medal, the Army Service Ribbon, and the NCO Professional Development Ribbon, they are awarded only for active federal military service.

Service medals are worn in order by the date when the person became eligible for the award, not by the date of entry in the records or the date upon which the award was established. Foreign military service medals are worn following authorized U.S. decorations. Not more than one service medal is awarded for service involving identical or

DECORATIONS, AWARDS, AND SERVICE MEDALS

U.S. ARMY AND DEPARTMENT OF DEFENSE MILITARY DECORATIONS

**Medal of Honor
(Army)**

**Distinguished Service
Cross (Army)**

**Defense
Distinguished Service
Medal**

**Distinguished Service
Medal (Army)**

Silver Star

**Defense
Superior Service
Medal**

Legion of Merit

**Distinguished Flying
Cross**

**Soldier's Medal
(Army)**

**Bronze Star
Medal**

Purple Heart

**Defense
Meritorious Service
Medal**

**Meritorious Service
Medal**

Air Medal

Joint Service Commendation Medal

Army Commendation Medal

Joint Service Achievement Medal

Army Achievement Medal

Prisoner of War Medal

**Good Conduct Medal
(Army)**

**Army Reserve
Components
Achievement Medal**

**National Defense Service
Medal**

**Antarctica Service
Medal**

**Armed Forces
Expeditionary Medal**

**Vietnam Service
Medal**

**Southwest Asia Service
Medal**

**Kosovo Campaign
Medal**

**Afghanistan Campaign
Medal**

**Iraq Campaign
Medal**

**Global War on Terrorism
Expeditionary
Medal**

**Global War on Terrorism
Service Medal**

Korean Defense Service Medal

Armed Forces Service Medal

Humanitarian Service Medal

Military Outstanding Volunteer Service Medal

Armed Forces Reserve Medal

U.S. ARMY SERVICE AND TRAINING RIBBONS

NCO
Professional
Development
Ribbon

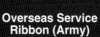

Army Service
Ribbon

Overseas Service
Ribbon (Army)

Army Reserve
Components
Overseas Training
Ribbon

U.S. ARMY AND DEPARTMENT OF DEFENSE
UNIT AWARDS

Presidential Unit
Citation (Army)

Joint Meritorious
Unit Award

Valorous Unit
Award

Meritorious Unit
Commendation
(Army)

Army Superior Unit
Award

ARMY SERVICE UNIFORM

Class A Uniform

Class B Uniform

NON-U.S. SERVICE MEDALS

**United Nations
Medal**

NATO Medal

**Multinational
Force and Observers
Medal**

**Republic of Vietnam
Campaign Medal**

**Kuwait Liberation Medal
(Kingdom of *Saudi
Arabia*)**

**Kuwait Liberation Medal
(Government of
Kuwait)**

U.S. ARMY BADGES AND TABS

Combat and Special Skill Badges

Combat Infantryman Badge
1st Award

Combat Medical Badge
1st Award

Combat Infantryman Badge
2nd Award

Combat Medical Badge
2nd Award

Combat Infantryman Badge
3rd Award

Combat Medical Badge
3rd Award

Expert Infantryman Badge

Expert Field Medical Badge

Combat Action Badge

**Master Aviator
Badge**

**Basic Aviator
Badge**

**Senior Aviator
Badge**

**Master
Flight Surgeon
Badge**

**Basic
Flight Surgeon
Badge**

**Senior
Flight Surgeon
Badge**

**Master
Aircraft Crewman
Badge**

**Basic
Aircraft Crewman
Badge**

**Senior
Aircraft Crewman
Badge**

**Basic
Military Free Fall
Parachutist Badge**

**Jumpmaster
Military Free Fall
Parachutist Badge**

**Basic Parachutist
Badge**

**Senior Parachutist
Badge**

**Master Parachutist
Badge**

**Combat Parachutist
Badge (1 Jump)**

**Combat Parachutist
Badge (2 Jumps)**

**Combat Parachutist
Badge (3 Jumps)**

**Combat Parachutist
Badge (4 Jumps)**

**Combat Parachutist
Badge (5 Jumps)**

Air Assault Badge

Glider Badge

**Special Forces Tab
(Metal Replica)**

**Ranger Tab
(Metal Replica)**

Sapper Tab

**Presidents Hundred
Tab**

**Pathfinder
Badge**

**Salvage Diver
Badge**

**Second Class Diver
Badge**

**First Class Diver
Badge**

**Master Diver
Badge**

**Scuba Diver
Badge**

**Special Operations
Diver Badge**

**Special Operations
Diving Supervisor
Badge**

**Basic Explosive
Ordnance Disposal
Badge**

**Master Explosive
Ordnance Disposal
Badge**

**Senior Explosive
Ordnance Disposal
Badge**

**Nuclear Reactor
Operator Badge
(Basic)**

**Nuclear Reactor
Operator Badge
(Second Class)**

**Nuclear Reactor
Operator Badge
(First Class)**

**Nuclear Reactor
Operator Badge
(Shift Supervisor)**

**Parachute Rigger
Badge**

**Driver and Mechanic
Badge**

Marksmanship Badges

Marksman

Sharpshooter

Expert

Identification Badges

Presidential Service

Vice-Presidential Service

Secretary of Defense

Joint Chiefs of Staff

Army Staff

**Guard,
Tomb of the Unknown Soldier**

Drill Sergeant

**U.S. Army Recruiter, Basic
(Active Army)**

**U.S. Army Recruiter, Basic
(Army National Guard)**

**U.S. Army Recruiter
(U.S. Army Reserve)**

U.S. Army Instructor, Basic

overlapping periods of time, except that each of the following groups of service medals may be awarded to an individual provided he or she meets the criteria prescribed by chapter 5, AR 600-8-22. For information concerning the criteria for the award of any service medal not listed below, see chapter 5, AR 600-8-22.

Army of Occupation Medal
Established by the War Department General Orders 32, 1946, this medal is awarded for service for thirty consecutive days at a normal post of duty with the Army of Occupation of Berlin during the period 1945–1990. This medal was previously authorized for post–World War II occupation duty in Germany, Austria, Italy, Japan, and Korea (see paragraph 5.1, AR 600-8-21, *Soldier Application Program*, 1995). Berlin service does not authorize the wearing of a clasp on either the service medal or the service ribbon (paragraph 5-11, AR 600-8-22).

National Defense Service Medal
This medal is awarded for honorable active service for any period between the periods 27 June 1950, to 27 July 1954; 1 January 1961, to 14 August 1974; 2 August 1990, to 30 November 1995; and 11 September 2001, to a date to be later determined. Subsequent award of the NDSM is denoted by a bronze service star (paragraph 2.10, AR 600-8-22).

Antarctica Service Medal
The Antarctica Service Medal is awarded to any member of the armed forces of the United States who participates in or has participated in scientific, direct support, or exploratory operations in Antarctica under sponsorship and approval of the U.S. government. This includes flights as a member of the crew of an aircraft flying to or from the Antarctic continent or as a member of a U.S. ship operating south of latitude sixty degrees south in support of U.S. programs in Antarctica (paragraph 2.11, AR 600-8-22).

Armed Forces Expeditionary Medal
The Armed Forces Expeditionary Medal is authorized for U.S. military operations, U.S. operations in direct support of the United Nations, and U.S. operations of assistance for friendly foreign nations. Operations are defined as military actions or the carrying out of strategic, tactical, service, training, or administrative military missions and the process of carrying on combat, including movement, supply, attack, defense, and maneuvers needed to gain the objectives of any battle or campaign. Designated areas and dates of service for eligibility are in AR 600-8-22. Subsequent awards of this medal are denoted by bronze service stars (paragraph 2-12, AR 600-8-22).

Vietnam Service Medal
The Vietnam Service Medal is awarded to all members of the armed forces who served in Vietnam and contiguous waters or airspace after 3 July 1965 and through 28 March 1973. Members of the armed forces in Thailand, Laos, or Cambodia or the airspace thereover who during the same period served in direct support of operations in Vietnam are also eligible. See AR 600-8-22, appendix B, for authorized campaigns and dates. One bronze

service star (or a combination of bronze and silver stars, as applicable) may be worn on the suspension ribbon and bar representing this medal (paragraph 2-13, AR 600-8-22).

Southwest Asia Service Medal

The Southwest Asia Service Medal (SWASM) is awarded to U.S. military personnel who served in the Persian Gulf area between 2 August 1990 and 30 November 1995. Subsequent awards of the SWASM are denoted by service stars affixed to the medal (paragraph 2-14, AR 600-8-22).

Kosovo Campaign Medal

The Kosovo Campaign Medal is awarded to recognize the accomplishments of military servicemembers who participated in or were in direct support of the conflict in Kosovo. Members authorized the Kosovo Campaign Medal must have participated in or served in direct support of the Kosovo operation after 24 March 1999. Servicemembers must be bona fide members of a unit that participated in or engaged in direct support of the operation for thirty consecutive days in the area of eligibility, or for sixty nonconsecutive days provided this support involved entering the area of eligibility. One bronze service star is worn on the suspension and service ribbon of the Kosovo Campaign Medal for qualified participation during the campaign period. Meeting the qualification in each of the two campaigns would warrant the medal and two bronze service stars (paragraph 2-15, AR 600-8-22).

Afghanistan Campaign Medal

The Afghanistan Campaign Medal (ACM) is awarded to soldiers who deployed to Afghanistan in direct support of Operation Enduring Freedom (OEF) on or after 11 September 2001 to 31 December 2014, and Operation Freedom's Sentinel from 1 January 2015 to a date to be determined or the cessation of OEF. The area of eligibility encompasses all land area of the country of Afghanistan and all airspaces above the land. A bronze service star is worn on the campaign and suspension ribbons for a day or more of participation for each campaign phase. Appendix B, AR 600-8-22, lists the campaign phases (paragraph 2-16, AR 600-8-22).

Iraq Campaign Medal

The Iraq medal is awarded to soldiers who deployed to Iraq in direct support of Operation Iraqi Freedom (OIF) or Operation New Dawn (OND) on or after 19 March 2003 until 31 December 2011. The area of eligibility encompasses all land area of the country of Iraq and the contiguous water area out to twelve nautical miles, and all airspaces above the land area of Iraq and above the contiguous water area out to twelve nautical miles. A bronze service star is awarded on the campaign and suspension ribbons for a day or more of participation for each period of service. Only one of the following awards are allowed for the same service, action, or time period: Iraq Campaign Medal, Global War on Terrorism Expeditionary Medal, Global War on Terrorism Service Medal, and Armed Forces Expeditionary Medal. Appendix B, AR 600-8-22, lists the campaign phases for OIF (paragraph 2-16, AR 600-8-22).

Global War on Terrorism Expeditionary Medal
The Global War on Terrorism Expeditionary Medal (GWOTEM) is awarded to service-members who served in military expeditions to combat terrorism on or after 11 September 2001. Starting 30 April 2005, the Global War on Terrorism Expeditionary Medal was no longer authorized to be awarded for service in Afghanistan or Iraq. The GWOTEM is still authorized for service in the other geographical areas of eligibility (paragraph 2-18, AR 600-8-22).

The Global War on Terrorism Service Medal
The Global War on Terrorism Service Medal (GWOTSM) is awarded to servicemembers who have participated in or served in support of Global War on Terrorism Operations outside the designated areas of eligibility (AOE) for the Global War on Terrorism Expeditionary Medal on or after 11 September 2001 to a date to be determined. All soldiers serving on active duty between 11 September 2001 and March 2004 are authorized the GWOTSM. After March 2004, battalion commanders—the award approval authority—must determine if a soldier serving on active duty has qualified for the GWOTSM. Soldiers will not receive more than one of the following medals for the same act, time period, or service: Afghanistan Campaign Medal, Iraq Campaign Medal, Global War on Terrorism Expeditionary Medal, or Armed Forces Expeditionary Medal (paragraph 2-19, AR 600-8-22).

Korea Defense Service Medal
The Korea Defense Service Medal (KDSM) is authorized to members of the armed forces who have served on active duty in support of the defense of the Republic of Korea from 28 July 1954 to a date to be determined. The area of eligibility encompasses all the land area of the Republic of Korea, the contiguous water out to twelve nautical miles, and all airspaces above the land and water areas. Effective 3 February 2004, the Overseas Service Ribbon (OSR) is no longer authorized for overseas tours in the Republic of Korea (paragraph 2-20, AR 600-8-22).

Armed Forces Service Medal
The Armed Forces Service Medal is awarded to members of the armed forces, who as of 1 June 1992 are participating or have participated as members of U.S. military units in a U.S. military operation, which is deemed to be a significant activity, and are encountering or have encountered no foreign armed opposition or imminent threat of hostile action.

Servicemembers must be bona fide members of a unit participating for one or more days in the operation or engaged in direct support in the area of eligibility, or for sixty nonconsecutive days—provided this support involves entering the area of eligibility or participating as a regularly assigned aircrew member of an aircraft flying into, out of, within, or over the area of eligibility in support of the operation. Second and subsequent awards are denoted by bronze service stars (paragraph 2-21, AR 600-8-22).

Humanitarian Service Medal
The Humanitarian Service Medal is authorized to be awarded to any armed forces personnel who directly participated in a Department of Defense–approved humanitarian act

or operation, except when a by-name eligibility list is published. No more than one award of this medal may be made for the same act or operation. Subsequent awards are designated by bronze numerals. Operations for which award of the Humanitarian Service Medal have thus far been approved are listed in appendix C, AR 600-8-22 (paragraph 2-15, AR 600-8-22).

Military Outstanding Volunteer Service Medal

Received by members of the armed forces of the United States who subsequent to 31 December 1992 performed outstanding volunteer community service of a sustained, direct, and consequential nature. To be eligible, an individual's service must (1) be to the civilian community, including the military family community; (2) be significant in nature and produce tangible results; (3) reflect favorably on the military service and the Department of Defense; and (4) be of a sustained and direct nature. The Military Outstanding Volunteer Service Medal (MOVSM) is intended to recognize exceptional community support over time and not a single act or achievement. Further, it is intended to honor direct support of community activities (paragraph 2-23, AR 600-8-72).

Armed Forces Reserve Medal

Awarded for honorable and satisfactory service as a member of one or more of the reserve components of the armed forces of the United States for a period of ten years within a twelve-year period. Subsequent ten-year awards are denoted by a bronze hourglass. A gold hourglass is awarded on completion of the fourth ten-year period.

Awarded for mobilization on or after 1 August 1990 to members called to active duty or volunteered and served on active duty in support of U.S. military operations or contingencies designated by the secretary of defense. The "M" device is worn to indicate mobilization. Subsequent mobilizations are denoted by the wearing of a number to indicate the number of times mobilized. No hourglass is worn unless authorized under the above paragraph (paragraph 5-8, AR 600-8-22, and MILPER msg. 96-196).

NCO Professional Development Ribbon

Established by the secretary of the Army on 10 April 1981 and effective 1 August 1981, the NCO Professional Development Ribbon is awarded to members of the U.S. Army, Army National Guard, and Army Reserve for successful completion of designated NCO professional development courses. The ribbon is awarded for the first of the four levels of professional development and the corresponding numeral is affixed to the ribbon for each level of schooling accomplished above that as follows: Basic Leader Course (BLC), Advanced Leader Course (ALC) (2), Senior Leader Course (SLC) (3), and the Sergeants Major Academy (USASMA) (4) (paragraph 5-6 and table 5-1, AR 600-8-22).

Army Service Ribbon

Established by the secretary of the Army on 10 April 1981 and effective 1 August 1981, the Army Service Ribbon is awarded to members of the U.S. Army, Army National Guard, and Army Reserve who have successfully completed initial entry training. Enlisted persons are eligible upon completion of initial MOS-producing courses. For those enlisted persons assigned an MOS based on civilian or other service-acquired skills, it is awarded after four months of honorable active service (paragraph 5-5, AR 600-8-22).

Overseas Service Ribbon
Established by the secretary of the Army on 10 April 1981 and effective 1 August 1981, the Overseas Service Ribbon is awarded to all members of the U.S. Army, Army National Guard, and Army Reserve credited with a normal overseas tour completed in accordance with AR 614-30. A soldier who has overseas service credited by another armed service is also eligible for this ribbon. The ribbon is not authorized for completion of an overseas tour of duty for which a service medal has been authorized (paragraph 5-4, AR 600-8-22).

Army Reserve Components Overseas Training Ribbon
Established by the secretary of the Army on 11 July 1984, the ribbon is awarded to members of the U.S. Army reserve components for successful completion of annual training or active-duty training for a period of not less than ten days on foreign soil (paragraph 5-3, AR 600-8-22).

Non-U.S. Service Medals

United Nations Medal
This medal may be awarded to personnel who have been in the service of the United Nations for a period of not less than six months with one of the units designated in paragraph 9-17, AR 688-8-2. The United Nations has, to date, cast medals for eleven different operations. Effective 13 October 1995, soldiers awarded any of these medals may wear the first medal and ribbon for which they qualify. Not more than one UN Medal may be worn. Award of a medal in a different UN mission is denoted by a bronze service star on the one UN Medal (paragraph 9-10, AR 600-8-22).

NATO Medal
Qualifying periods of service for the NATO medal are thirty days (continuous or accumulated) in designated NATO operations. Tours are normally 180 days in length. Dates of eligibility for the Former Republic of Yugoslavia, Kosovo-related operations, Balkans operations, national training–related operations in Iraq, and other NATO operations qualifying for the NATO Medal are detailed in AR 600-8-22. As of this writing, current operations eligible for award include International Security Assistance Force in Afghanistan (1 June 2003 to a date to be determined) and operations related to Africa, Operations Allied Provider, Allied Protector, and Ocean Shield (1 January 2008 to a date to be determined). In the event two NATO Medals are earned simultaneously based on location or duty, the NATO chain of command will determine the one medal awarded based on qualifying conditions. Subsequent awards for separate NATO operations, contingent on secretary of defense approval, will be denoted by a bronze service star on the service ribbon and suspension ribbon of the medal (paragraph 9-11, AR 600-8-22).

Multinational Force and Observers Medal
To qualify for this medal, a soldier must have served with the Multinational Force and Observers at least ninety days after 3 August 1981. Subsequent awards for each completed six-month tour are indicated by an appropriate numeral, starting with numeral "1" (paragraph 9-13, AR 600-8-22).

Republic of Vietnam Campaign Medal
Authorized for acceptance by Department of Defense instructions 1348.17, 31 January 1974, this medal is worn by members of the armed forces who served in the Republic of Vietnam for six months during the period 1 March 1961 to 28 March 1973, inclusive, or served outside the geographical limits of the Republic of Vietnam and contributed direct combat support to the Republic of Vietnam Armed Forces for six months. Such persons must meet the criteria established for the Armed Forces Expeditionary Medal (Vietnam) or the Vietnam Service Medal during the period of service required to qualify for the Republic of Vietnam Campaign Medal. Soldiers who served under the above conditions for less than six months but who were wounded by hostile forces, captured, or killed in action or otherwise in the line of duty are also authorized this medal. Soldiers assigned on 28 January 1973 are eligible if they served sixty days as of that date or served sixty days between 28 January 1973 and 28 March 1973, inclusive (paragraph 9-14, AR 600-8-22).

Kuwait Liberation Medal (Kingdom of Saudi Arabia)
Awarded by the Kingdom of Saudi Arabia to members of the armed forces of the United States, who served within the designated war zone of Operation Desert Storm during the period 17 January 1991, through 28 February 1991 (parapraph 9-15, AR 600-8-22).

Kuwait Liberation Medal (Government of Kuwait)
Awarded by the government of Kuwait to U.S. military personnel who were assigned to one of several designated areas in and around Kuwait from 2 August 1990 to 31 August 1993. To be eligible, personnel must have been attached to or regularly served for one day or more with an organization participating in ground and/or shore operations; with a naval vessel directly supporting military operations; or as a crew member in one or more aerial flights that directly supported military operations in the designated areas. Temporary duty for thirty or sixty nonconsecutive days supporting such operations during the designated period also qualifies for award of the medal. The time requirement may be waived for temporary duty (TDY) soldiers who actually participated in combat operations (paragraph 9-16, AR 600-8-22).

Foreign Individual Awards
Decorations received from a foreign government in recognition of active field service in connection with combat operations or for outstanding or unusually meritorious performance may be accepted and worn upon approval of the Department of the Army. Without this approval, they become the property of the United States and must be deposited with the Department of the Army for use or disposal.

Qualification and special skill badges may be accepted if awarded in recognition of meeting the criteria, as established by the awarding foreign government, for the specific award.

Foreign badges are authorized for wear only on service and dress uniforms. The German marksmanship award (Schutzenschnur) may be worn only by enlisted personnel, on the right side of the uniform with the upper portion attached under the center of the shoulder loop and the bottom portion attached under the lapel.

U.S. Army Badges and Tabs

Badges and tabs are appurtenances of the uniform. In the eyes of their wearers, several badges have a significance equal to or greater than all but the highest decorations. There is no established precedence with badges as there is with decorations and service medals or ribbons. The badges are of three types: combat and special skill badges, marksmanship badges and tabs, and identification badges. Badges are awarded in recognition of attaining a high standard of proficiency in certain military skills. Subdued combat and special skill badges and the Sapper, Ranger, and Special Forces tabs are authorized on field uniforms.

Combat and Special Skill Badges

The following badges are awarded to denote excellence in performance of duties under hazardous conditions and circumstances of extraordinary hardship as well as for special qualifications and successful completion of prescribed courses of training (see chapter 8, AR 600-8-22, for details).

Combat Infantryman Badge (CIB). Awarded to infantry personnel in the grade of colonel or below who, after 6 December 1941, satisfactorily perform duty while assigned or attached as a member of a Ranger, Special Forces, or infantry brigade, regiment, or smaller unit during any period that such unit is engaged in active ground combat and the soldier is personally present and under fire while serving in a unit engaged in direct combat to close with and destroy the enemy with direct fire. The soldier must be serving in a primary duty position of infantry or Special Forces (paragraph 8-6, AR 600-8-22).

Combat Medical Badge (CMB). Awarded to medical personnel under the operational control, attached or assigned by appropriate orders to combat arms units of brigade, regimental, or smaller size—or to a medical unit of company or smaller size organic to a combat arms unit of brigade or smaller size—during any period the infantry unit is engaged in actual ground combat. Such medical personnel are eligible for award of the badge, provided they are personally present and under fire during such ground combat.

Global War on Terror: Medical personnel assigned or attached to or under operational control of any ground combat arms units, including Combat Aviation Units of brigade or smaller size are eligible for the Combat Medical Badge if they have satisfactorily performed medical duties while the unit is engaged in active ground combat, provided they are personally present and under fire. Retroactive awards are not authorized for service prior to 18 September 2001 (paragraph 8-7, AR 600-8-22).

Combat Action Badge. Awarded to any soldier performing assigned duties in an area where hostile fire pay or imminent danger pay is authorized, who is personally present and actively engaging or being engaged by the enemy, and performing satisfactorily in accordance with the prescribed rules of engagement. The soldier also must not be assigned/attached to a unit that would qualify the soldier for the CIB/CMB (paragraph 8-8, AR 600-8-22).

Stars for Combat Infantryman Badge, Combat Medical Badge, and Combat Action Badge. The second and succeeding awards of the CIB, CMB, and the CAB, made to recognize participation and qualification in additional declared wars, are indicated by the addition of stars to the basic badges (chapter 8, section II, AR 600-8-22).

Expert Infantryman Badge. Awarded to infantry personnel of the active Army, ARNG, and USAR who satisfactorily complete prescribed proficiency tests (paragraph 8-9, AR 600-8-22).

Expert Field Medical Badge. Awarded to Army medical service personnel who satisfactorily complete prescribed proficiency tests (paragraph 8-10, AR 600-8-22).

Army Astronaut Badges. The Army Astronaut Badge is an authorized special skill badge, but the requirements for award of this badge are not stated in the regulations. These badges are awarded in three degrees: basic, senior, and master.

Army Aviation Badges. There are nine badges relating to Army aviation—three each for Army aviators, flight surgeons, and aircraft crewmen—in the degrees of basic, senior, and master (paragraph 8-27, AR 600-8-22).

Master Army Aviator Badge, Senior Army Aviator Badge, and Army Aviator Badge. Awarded upon satisfactory completion of prescribed training and proficiency tests as outlined in AR 600-105 (paragraph 8-17, AR 600-8-22).

Master Flight Surgeon Badge, Senior Flight Surgeon Badge, and Basic Flight Surgeon Badge. Awarded upon satisfactory completion of prescribed training and proficiency tests as outlined in AR 600-105 while serving as a Medical Service Corps officer (AR 600-105, paragraph 8-18).

Master Aviation Badge, Senior Aviation Badge, and Basic Aviation Badge (previously the Aircraft Crewman Badges). Authorized for award to enlisted personnel who meet the prescribed requirements (paragraphs 8-28–8-30, AR 688-8-22).

Glider Badge. This badge is no longer awarded but is still authorized for wear by individuals who were previously awarded the badge (paragraph 8-33, AR 600-8-22).

Space Badge. This badge is awarded to those soldiers assigned to the Space and Missile Defense Command for the prescribed number of months, who have received the requisite space-related training and education and are performing in assigned cadre duty. There are three levels of badges for this category: basic, senior, and master (paragraph 8-31, AR 600-8-22).

Parachutist Badges. To be awarded the Master Parachutist Badge, an individual must meet the following criteria: have participated in sixty-five jumps, twenty-five with combat equipment, four at night, and five mass tactical jumps; have graduated as jumpmaster or served as jumpmaster on one or more combat jumps or on thirty-three noncombat jumps; have been rated excellent in character and efficiency; and have served on jump status for not less than thirty-six months (paragraph 8-14, AR 600-8-22).

For the Senior Parachutist Badge, an individual must meet the following criteria: have been rated excellent in character and efficiency with participation in thirty jumps, including fifteen jumps made with combat equipment, two night jumps, and two mass tactical jumps; have graduated from a jumpmaster course or served as jumpmaster on one or more combat jumps or fifteen noncombat jumps; and have served on jump status for not less than twenty-four months (paragraph 8-13, AR 600-8-22).

The Parachutist Badge is awarded for satisfactory completion of the course given by the Airborne Department of the Infantry School or while assigned or attached to an Airborne unit or for participation in at least one combat jump (paragraph 8-12, AR 600-8-22).

Military Freefall Parachutist Badge. This badge is awarded to those armed forces personnel who qualify, in two categories: jumpmaster and basic badges. The basic badge requires completion of an Army-approved course of instruction in military free-fall or a minimum of one free-fall combat jump. The jumpmaster badge requires completion of an Army-approved military free-fall jumpmaster program (paragraph 8-16, AR 600-8-22).

Combat Parachutist Badges. Participation in a combat parachute jump entitles the individual to wear a bronze star, or stars, affixed to the Parachutist Badge (paragraph 8-11, 600-8-22).

Parachute Rigger Badge. Awarded to any individual who successfully completes the Parachute Rigger Course conducted by the U.S. Army Quartermaster School and who holds a parachute rigger MOS or skill identifier (paragraph 8-15, AR 600-8-22).

Pathfinder Badge. Awarded upon successful completion of the Pathfinder course conducted at the Infantry School (paragraph 8-25, AR 600-8-22).

Air Assault Badge. Awarded to personnel who have satisfactorily completed either the Training and Doctrine Command (TRADOC) prescribed training course or the standard air assault course while assigned or attached to the 101st Air Assault Division since 1 April 1974 (paragraph 8-26, AR 600-8-23).

Diver Badges. Awarded after satisfactory completion of prescribed proficiency tests (AR 611-75). Five badges are authorized for enlisted personnel (paragraph 8-19, AR 600-8-22).

Driver and Mechanic Badge. Awarded only to enlisted personnel to denote a high degree of skill in the operation and maintenance of motor vehicles (paragraph 8-32, AR 600-8-22).

Explosive Ordnance Disposal Badges. There are three badges under this heading, any of which may be awarded to soldiers: Master Explosive Ordnance Disposal Badge, Senior Explosive Ordnance Disposal Badge, and Explosive Ordnance Disposal Badge. They are awarded to individuals assigned to duties involving the removal and disposition of explosive ammunition under hazardous conditions (paragraph 8-21, AR 600-8-22). This is now a Group 3 badge.

Nuclear Reactor Operator Badges. The Shift Supervisor Badge, the Operator First Class Badge, and the Operator Basic Badge were awarded upon completing the Nuclear Power Plant Operators Course or equivalent training and after operating nuclear power plants for specific periods. These badges are no longer awarded but are still authorized for wear by individuals to whom they were previously awarded (paragraph 8-34, AR 600-8-22).

Physical Fitness Training Badge. This badge is awarded to soldiers who obtain a minimum score of 270 on the Army Physical Fitness Test (APFT), scoring a minimum of 90 in each of the three graded areas, and who meet the weight-control requirements of AR 600-9. The badge is only maintained by achieving this level or higher on subsequent record APFT and weigh-in (paragraph 8-51, AR 600-8-22).

Special Forces Tab

The commander, U.S. Army John F. Kennedy Special Warfare Center (USAJFKSWC), Fort Bragg, North Carolina, may award the Special Forces Tab to any individual who has successfully completed the Special Forces Qualification Course or the Special Forces Officer Course. The Special Forces Tab may be awarded to any person on active duty, active status in the reserve components, in retired status, or honorably discharged who meets the appropriate criteria (paragraph 8-49, AR 600-8-22).

Ranger Tab. Awarded to any person who successfully completes a Ranger course conducted by the Infantry School or who was awarded the Combat Infantryman Badge (CIB) while serving during World War II as a member of the 1st through 6th Ranger Battalions or the 5307th Composite Group (paragraph 8-48, AR 600-8-22).

Sapper Tab. Awarded by successful completion of a Sapper Leaders Course conducted by the U.S. Army Engineer School. Retroactively, the Sapper tab may be awarded to any person successfully completing the Sapper Leaders Course on or after 14 June 1985 (paragraph 8-50, AR 600-8-14).

Marksmanship Badges and Tabs

These badges and tabs include basic marksmanship qualification badges and the President's Hundred Tab.

Only members of the armed forces of the United States and civilian citizens of the United States are eligible for these qualification badges. Qualification badges for marksmanship are of three types: basic qualification, excellence in competition, and distinguished designation. Basic qualification badges (including Expert, Sharpshooter, and Marksman Badges) are awarded to those individuals who attain the qualification score prescribed in the appropriate field manual for the weapon concerned (paragraph 8-47, AR 600-8-22).

President's Hundred Tab. Awarded to each person who qualifies among the top one hundred contestants in the President's Match held annually at the National Rifle Matches (paragraph 8-53, AR 600-8-22).

Identification Badges

Identification badges are worn to signify special duties.

Presidential Service Identification Badge. The Presidential Service Certificate and the Presidential Service Badge were established by Executive Order 11174, 1 September 1964. They are awarded in the name of the president of the United States as public evidence of deserved honor and distinction to members of the armed forces who have been assigned duty in the White House for at least one year after 20 January 1961. Once the badge is awarded, it may be worn as a permanent part of the uniform (paragraph 8-36, AR 600-8-22).

Vice-Presidential Service Identification Badge. The Vice-Presidential Service Badge was established by Executive Order 11544, 8 July 1970. It may be awarded upon recommendation of the military assistant to the vice president and may be worn as a permanent part of the uniform (paragraph 8-37, AR 600-8-22).

Secretary of Defense Identification Badge. Military personnel who have been assigned to duty and have served not less than one year after 13 January 1961, in the office of the secretary of defense are eligible for this badge. Once awarded, it may be worn as a permanent part of the uniform. It also is authorized for temporary wear by personnel assigned to specified offices of the secretary of defense (paragraph 8-38, AR 600-8-22).

Joint Chiefs of Staff Identification Badge. This badge may be awarded to military personnel who have been assigned to duty and who have served not less than one year after 16 January 1961 in a position of responsibility under the direct cognizance of the Joint Chiefs of Staff. Once awarded, the badge may be worn as a permanent part of the uniform (paragraph 8-39, AR 600-8-22).

Army Staff Identification Badge. This badge has been awarded by the Army since 1920 and is the oldest of the five types of identification badges now authorized for officers. It was instituted to give a permanent means of identification to those commissioned officers who had been selected for duty on the War Department General Staff, with recommendation for award based upon performance of duty. It has been continued under the present departmental organization.

Between 30 September 1979 and 28 May 1985, the badge could be awarded to the sergeant major (SGM) of the Army and to other senior NCOs (SGM E-9) assigned to duty with the same staff units. Effective 28 May 1985, qualifying service must be of at least one year while assigned to permanent duty on the Army General Staff or assigned to the office of the secretary of the Army. All soldiers assigned today are authorized wear, provided they meet the criteria in DA Memo 672-1. Once awarded, this badge may be worn as a permanent part of the uniform (paragraph 8-40, AR 600-8-22).

Guard, Tomb of the Unknown Soldier Identification Badge (paragraph 8-41, AR 600-8-22).

Identification Badge (paragraph 8-42, AR 600-8-22).

U.S. Army Recruiter Identification Badge (paragraph 8-43, AR 600-8-22).

Army National Guard Recruiter Identification Badge (paragraph 8-45, AR 600-8-22).

U.S. Army Reserve Recruiter Identification Badge (paragraph 8-46, AR 600-8-22).

Career Counselor Badge (paragraph 8-44, AR 600-8-22).

Army Instructor Badge (basic, senior, master; TRADOC Regulation 600-21).

Appurtenances
Appurtenances are devices affixed to service or suspension ribbons or worn in place of medals or ribbons. They are worn to denote additional awards, participation in a specific event, or other distinguished characteristics of the award.

Oak-Leaf Cluster
A bronze or silver twig of four oak leaves with three acorns on the stem, thirteen-thirty-seconds inch in length for the suspension ribbon and five-sixteenths inch in length for the service ribbon, is issued in lieu of a decoration for second or succeeding awards of decorations (other than the Air Medal) and service medals. A silver oak-leaf cluster is issued to be worn in lieu of five bronze clusters. Five one-sixteenth-inch oak-leaf clusters, joined together in series of two, three, and four clusters, are authorized for optional purchase and wear on service ribbons.

Numerals
Arabic numerals three-thirteenths inch high are issued in lieu of a medal or ribbon for second and succeeding awards of the Air Medal, the Humanitarian Service Medal, the Multinational Force and Observers Medal, the Army Reserve Components Overseas Training Ribbon, and the Overseas Service Ribbon. The numeral worn on the NCO Professional Development Ribbon denotes the highest completed level of NCO development. The numerals are worn centered on the suspension ribbon of the medal or the ribbon bar.

V Device
The V device is a bronze letter V, one-quarter inch high with serifs at the top of the members (i.e., the little strokes at the tops of the arms of the V that look like little rectangles). The V device denotes awards of a medal for heroism and may be awarded with the Bronze Star Medal, the Air Medal, the Joint Service Commendation Medal (when the award is for acts or services involving direct participation in combat operations), and the Army Commendation Medal.

Clasps
Clasps are authorized to be worn on the Good Conduct Medal, the Army of Occupation Medal, and the Antarctica Service Medal.

Service Stars
The service star is a bronze or silver five-pointed star three-sixteenths inch in diameter. Three-sixteenths-inch service stars joined together in a series of two, three, and four stars are authorized for optional purchase and wear on service ribbons. Service stars, signifying participation in a combat campaign, are authorized for wear on the Armed Forces Expeditionary Medal and the Vietnam Service Medal. (*Note:* Bronze and silver stars are worn on U.S. Navy decorations in the same manner as oak-leaf clusters are worn on Army and Air Force decorations.)

Arrowhead
The arrowhead is a bronze replica of a Native American arrowhead, one-quarter inch high. It denotes participation in a combat parachute jump, combat glider landing, or amphibious assault landing, while assigned or attached as a member of an organized force carrying out an assigned tactical mission. It is worn on the service and suspension ribbons of the Vietnam Service Medal, Armed Forces Expeditionary Medal, and Global War on Terrorism Expeditionary Medal.

Service Ribbons
Service ribbons are identical to the suspension ribbons of the medals they represent and are mounted on bars equipped with attaching devices; they are issued for wear in place of medals. The service ribbon for the Medal of Honor is the same color as the neck band, showing five stars in the form of a letter M.

Miniature Medals
Miniature replicas of all medals except the Medal of Honor are authorized for wear on specified uniforms, such as the blue and white mess uniforms, in lieu of the issued medals. Miniatures of decorations are issued only to foreign nationals. Awards issued by the secretary of defense include miniature medals.

Lapel Buttons
Lapel buttons are authorized for wear on the left lapel of civilian clothing only. They are available for service ribbons and other decorations and badges. Included in this category are the Army Lapel Button, which is awarded to any soldier (except retirees) who completed nine months' honorable active federal service after 1 April 1984, and the U.S. Army Retired Lapel Button.

Gold Star Lapel Button. Authorized for wear on the Army Service Uniform (ASU) of soldiers who have lost a family member to combat. Members that authorize the wear of the Gold Star Lapel Button include a spouse, parent, child, or stepchild. The pin is centered vertically and horizontally on the left lapel of the ASU for enlisted soldiers.

Next of Kin Button. Authorized for wear by soldiers who lost a spouse or child or who are the primary next of kin of a soldier who lost his or her life while serving in uniform on active duty or while assigned to the ARNG or USAR.

CERTIFICATES AND LETTERS
Officers and senior NCOs may write and sign letters of appreciation and commendation for other enlisted personnel. Frequently, soldiers will ask for these accolades. Remember that a letter or certificate from an overseas commander or brigade or higher command sergeant major (CSM) is worth 5 promotion points.

Certificates and letters may be nothing more than pats on the back. Nevertheless, they go a long way toward boosting the morale of most recipients, and their judicious use is a good way to recognize faithful and competent service.

Certificate of Achievement

Commanders may recognize periods of faithful service, acts, or achievements that do meet the standards required for decorations by issuing to individual military personnel a Certificate of Achievement, DA Form 2442.

Certificates of Achievement are awarded under local criteria and may be used for awarding the Good Conduct Medal, for participation in the Department of the Army Suggestion Program, or to recognize meritorious acts or service.

Letters of Commendation and Appreciation

Acts or services that do not meet the criteria for decorations or a Certificate of Achievement may be recognized by written expressions of commendation or appreciation. These letters are typed on letterhead stationery and should not contain formalized printing, seals, or other distinguishing features that depart from normal letter form (paragraph 10-13, AR 600-8-22).

17

Military Justice

A fact of military life is that, despite the availability of information on the subject and the effort of commanders to keep their soldiers informed, many individuals simply do not know very much about the military justice system. Specific provisions pertaining to administration of the military justice system are in the *Manual for Courts-Martial* and AR 27-10, *Military Justice*. While it is understandable that many soldiers would avoid this topic like the plague, it is important to have a basic understanding as a professional, so you are aware and understand the discussions around you and how they are affecting soldiers in your unit. When you become an NCO, you will have to have an intimate understanding of all facets of military justice, so getting a head start in understanding can do nothing but help. Questions on this topic can be fully expected at Soldier of the Month and promotion boards as well, so let's take a look.

NONJUDICIAL PUNISHMENT

Article 15 of the Uniform Code of Military Justice (UCMJ) provides commanding officers the authority and procedures to impose disciplinary punishments for minor offenses without a court-martial. Punishment without court-martial is called "nonjudicial" punishment. Such punishments may be in addition to or in lieu of admonition or reprimand. Unless the accused is embarked on a vessel, Article 15 punishment may not be imposed if the accused demands trial by court-martial.

Punishments authorized under Article 15 are less severe than court-martial punishments. Unlike a special or general court-martial, Article 15 is not considered a federal conviction for a criminal offense. Article 15 is intended to provide a swift, efficient, and relatively easy method for punishing those committing minor offenses, for maintaining discipline, and for deterring future offenses. Under Article 15, commanders have wide latitude in punishments that may be imposed, ranging from oral reprimand to reduction in pay grades, fines, restriction, extra duty, or a combination of these.

It is a mistake to disregard the effect of an Article 15 on a soldier's career, although those received when in the junior enlisted grades can generally be overcome. The original copy of DA Form 2617, *Record of Proceedings under Article 15, UCMJ*, may be filed either in the Official Military Personnel File performance portion of the permanent record or in the restricted portion. Records of Article 15 punishments can be used in a wide variety of personnel decisions and can lead to an involuntary administrative discharge.

Under Article 15 proceedings, legal rules of evidence do not apply, and providing defense counsel at the hearing is not mandatory. Nevertheless, the accused does have protection against arbitrary use of Article 15. In addition to the right to demand trial by court-martial in lieu of Article 15 punishment, the accused has the right to consult with counsel to decide whether to accept the punishment; if the accused accepts Article 15 and considers the punishment too harsh, they may appeal it. Other rights include the right to remain silent, to fully present his or her case in the presence of the imposing commander, to call witnesses, to present evidence, to be accompanied by a spokesperson, to request an open hearing, and to examine available evidence.

In order to find the soldier guilty, the commander must be convinced beyond a reasonable doubt that the soldier committed the offense. The maximum punishment depends on the type of Article 15 imposed (summary, company, or field grade), rank of the commander imposing punishment, and the rank of the soldier being punished.

Purposes of Nonjudicial Punishment
Nonjudicial punishment may be imposed in appropriate cases for the following purposes:

- To correct, educate, and reform offenders who have shown that they cannot benefit by less stringent measures.
- To preserve, in appropriate cases, an offender's record of service from unnecessary stigmatization by record of court-martial conviction.
- To further military efficiency by disposing of minor offenses in a manner requiring less time and personnel than trial by court-martial.

Generally, the term *minor offenses* includes misconduct not involving any greater degree of criminality than is involved in the average offense tried by summary court-martial.

Nonpunitive measures usually deal with misconduct resulting from simple neglect, forgetfulness, laziness, inattention to instructions, sloppy habits, immaturity, difficulty in adjusting to disciplined military life, and similar deficiencies. These measures are primarily tools for teaching proper standards of conduct and performance and do not constitute punishment. Some examples include denial of pass or other privileges, counseling, administrative reduction in grade, extra training, bar to reenlistment, and MOS reclassification. Certain commanders have the authority, apart from any under Article 15, to reduce enlisted persons administratively for inefficiency or other reasons. *Nonpunitive measures and nonjudicial punishment should not be confused.*

A written admonition or reprimand should contain a statement indicating that it has been imposed merely as an administrative measure and not as punishment under Article 15. Conversely, admonitions and reprimands that are imposed as punishment under Article 15 should be clearly stated to have been imposed as punishment under that article.

Commanding officers also have the authority to impose restraints or restrictions on a soldier for administrative purposes, such as to ensure the soldier's presence within the command. This authority exists apart from the authority to impose restriction as nonjudicial punishment. These nonpunitive measures may also include, subject to any applicable regulation, administrative withholding of privileges.

MAXIMUM PUNISHMENTS
FOR ENLISTED MEMBERS UNDER ARTICLE 15*

Note: The maximum punishment imposable by any commander under summarized proceedings cannot exceed extra duty for fourteen days, restriction for fourteen days, oral reprimand, or any combination thereof.

Punishment	Imposed by Company Grade Officers	Imposed by Field Grade or General Officers
Admonition/Reprimand	Yes	Yes
and		
Extra Duties[1]	14 days	45 days
and		
Restriction	14 days	60 days
or		
Correctional Custody[2]	7 days	30 days
(PV1, PV2, PFC)		
or		
Reduction		
(PV1, PV2, PFC, SPC, CPL)	One grade in peacetime[3]	One grade or more
(SGT, SSG)	One grade	
and		
Forfeiture[4]	7 days' pay	Half of 1 month's pay for 2 months

---

1   Combinations of extra duties and restriction cannot exceed the maximum allowed for extra duty.
2   Subject to limitations imposed by superior authority and presence of adequate facilities. If punishment includes reduction to private first class or below, reduction must be unsuspended.
3   Only if imposed by a field grade commander of a unit authorized to have a commander who is a lieutenant colonel or higher.
4   Amount of forfeiture is computed at the reduced grade, even if suspended, if reduction is part of punishment.

Extra training or instruction is one of the most effective nonpunitive measures available to a commander. It is used when a soldier's duty performance has been substandard or deficient. For example, a soldier who fails to maintain proper attire may be required to attend classes on the wearing of the uniform and stand inspection until the deficiency is corrected.

Summarized Proceedings

Summarized proceedings under Article 15 may be used if, after a preliminary inquiry, a commander determines that the punishment for an offense should not exceed extra duty or restriction for fourteen days, oral reprimand or admonition, or any combination of these punishments. The record of these proceedings is made on DA Form 2627-1. Generally, summarized proceedings are conducted like proceedings for more serious cases prosecuted under nonjudicial punishment, except that the individual normally is allowed twenty-four hours to decide whether to demand trial by court-martial and to gather matters in defense, extenuation (unique points about the incident or offense), and/or mitigation (reasons why any punishment should be lessened). Because of the limited nature of the punishments imposed under these proceedings, the soldier has no right to consult with legally qualified counsel nor the right to a spokesperson.

Nature of Punishments

Nonjudicial punishments include the following actions:

Admonition and Reprimand. An admonition or reprimand may be imposed in lieu of or combined with Article 15 punishments.

Restriction. The severity of this type of restraint is dependent upon its duration and geographical limits specified when the punishment is imposed. A soldier undergoing restriction may be required to report to a designated place at specified times if it is considered reasonably necessary to ensure that the punishment is being properly executed.

Extra Duties. This form of punishment involves the performance of duties in addition to those normally assigned to the person undergoing the punishment. Extra duties may include fatigue duties. In general, extra duties that would demean his or her position as a noncommissioned officer may not be assigned to a corporal or above.

Reduction in Grade. This form involves the following considerations:

- Promotion authority. The grade from which a soldier is reduced must be within the promotion authority of the imposing commander or the officer to whom authority to punish under Article 15 has been delegated.
- Lateral appointments or reductions of corporal to specialist are not authorized. An NCO may be reduced to a lower pay grade, provided the lower grade is authorized in his or her primary MOS.
- Date of rank. When a soldier is reduced in grade as a result of unsuspended reduction, the date of rank in the grade to which reduced is the date the punishment of reduction was imposed.
- Entitlement to pay. When a soldier is restored to a higher pay grade because of a suspension or when a reduction is mitigated to a forfeiture, entitlement to pay at the higher grade is effective on the date of the suspension or mitigation.

- Senior noncommissioned officers: Sergeants first class and above may not be reduced under the authority of Article 15.

Forfeiture of Pay. Pay refers to basic pay of the individual plus any foreign duty pay. Forfeitures imposed by a company-grade commander may not be applied for more than one month, while those imposed by a field-grade commander may not be applied for more than two months. The maximum forfeiture of pay to which a soldier is subject during a given month—because of one or more actions under Article 15—is one-half of his or her pay per month. Article 15 forfeitures cannot deprive a soldier of more than two-thirds of his or her pay per month.

FORFEITURES OF PAY AUTHORIZED UNDER ARTICLE 15

Maximum monthly authorized forfeitures of pay under Article 15, UCMJ, may be computed using the applicable formula below:

1. Upon enlisted persons:

$$\frac{(\text{monthly basic pay}^{1,2} + \text{foreign pay}^{1,3})}{2} = \begin{array}{l} \text{maximum forfeiture per month} \\ \text{if imposed by major or above} \end{array}$$

$$\frac{(\text{monthly basic pay}^{1,2} + \text{foreign pay}^{1,3}) \times 7}{30} = \begin{array}{l} \text{maximum forfeiture if imposed} \\ \text{by captain or below} \end{array}$$

2. Upon commissioned and warrant officers when imposed by an officer with general court-martial jurisdiction or by a general officer in command:

$$\frac{(\text{monthly basic pay}^{2})}{2} = \begin{array}{l} \text{maximum authorized forfeiture} \\ \text{per month} \end{array}$$

---

1   Amount of forfeiture is computed at the reduced grade, even if suspended, if reduction is part of the punishment imposed.
2   At the time punishment is imposed.
3   If applicable.

Combination and Apportionment
No two or more punishments involving deprivation of liberty may be combined in the same nonjudicial punishment to run either consecutively or concurrently, but other punishments may be combined. Restriction and extra duty may be combined in any manner to run for a period not in excess of the maximum duration imposable for extra duty by the imposing commander.

Suspension, Mitigation, Remission, and Setting Aside

Suspension. The purpose of suspending punishment is to grant a deserving soldier a probational period during which the individual may show that he or she deserves a remission of the suspended portion of his or her nonjudicial punishment. If—because of further misconduct within this period—it is determined that remission of the suspended punishment is not warranted, the suspension may be vacated and the suspended portion of the punishment executed.

Mitigation. Often there are factors other than the facts and circumstances of the offense that show that the accused should receive a light punishment. Examples include lack of past criminal record, good duty performance, and family hardship.

Remission. Remission can cancel any portion of the unexecuted punishment. Remission is appropriate under the same circumstances as mitigation.

Setting Aside and Restoration. Under this action, the punishment or any part or amount thereof, whether executed or unexecuted, is set aside, and any property, privileges, or rights affected by the portion of the punishment set aside are restored. The basis for this action is ordinarily a determination that under all the circumstances of the case, the punishment has resulted in a clear injustice.

Notification and Explanation of Rights

The imposing commander must ensure that the soldier is notified of the intention to dispose of the matter (offense/misconduct) under Article 15. The imposing commander may delegate notification authority to another officer, warrant officer, or senior NCO, providing that person outranks the person being notified. If an NCO is selected, that person should normally be the unit first sergeant or another NCO who is the senior enlisted person in the command in which the accused is serving.

The soldier must be given a "reasonable time" to consult with counsel, including time off from duty, if necessary, to decide whether to demand trial. The amount of time granted is normally forty-eight hours.

Before deciding to demand trial, the accused is not entitled to be informed of the type or amount of punishment he or she will receive if nonjudicial punishment is imposed. The imposing commander will inform the soldier of the maximum punishment allowable under Article 15 and the maximum allowable for the offense if the case proceeds to a trial by court-martial and conviction for the offense.

Right to Demand Trial

The demand for trial may be made at any time before imposition of punishment. The soldier will be told that if trial is demanded, it could be by summary, special, or general court-martial. The soldier will also be told that he or she may object to trial by summary court-martial and that at a special or general court-martial he or she would be entitled to be represented by qualified military counsel or by civilian counsel obtained at the soldier's expense.

Appeals

Only one appeal is permitted under Article 15 proceedings. An appeal not made within a "reasonable time" may be rejected as untimely by the superior authority. The definition of what constitutes a "reasonable time" varies according to the situation. Generally, an appeal, including all documentary matters, submitted more than five calendar days (including weekends and holidays) after punishment is imposed will be presumed to be untimely. If, at the time of imposition of punishment, the soldier indicates a desire not to appeal, the superior authority may reject a subsequent election to appeal, even if it is made within the five-day period.

Appeals are made on DA Form 2627, *Record of Proceedings under Article 15 (UCMJ*, or DA Form 2627-1, *Summarized Record of Proceedings under Article 15, UCMJ*, and forwarded through the imposing commander or successor-in-command to the superior authority. The superior must act on the appeal unless otherwise directed by competent authority. A soldier is not required to state the reasons for the appeal, but he or she may present evidence or arguments proving innocence or why the sentence should be mitigated or suspended. Unless an appeal is voluntarily withdrawn, it must be forwarded to the appropriate superior authority. A timely appeal does not terminate because a soldier is discharged from the service but must be processed to completion.

Announcement of Punishment

The punishment may be announced at the next unit formation after punishment is imposed or, if appealed, after the decision. It also may be posted on the unit bulletin board. The purpose of announcing the results is to avert the perception of unfairness of punishment and to deter similar misconduct by others.

Records of Punishment

DA Forms 2627 are prepared in an original and six copies. What happens to those copies, especially the original, is of the utmost importance to soldiers who receive punishment under nonjudicial proceedings.

Original. For enlisted soldiers in the grade of CPL/SPC and below, prior to the punishment being imposed, the original copy is filed locally, in the nonjudicial punishment files, for two years. at which time it is destroyed. For SGT and above, the original copy is forwarded to the U.S. Army Enlisted Records and Evaluation Center, Fort Knox, Kentucky. The decision on where in the punished soldier's Official Military Personnel File (OMPF) this copy will be placed is made by the imposing commander at the time punishment is imposed, and is final. The imposing commander will decide whether it is to be filed in the performance fiche or the restricted fiche of the individual's OMPF.

Other Copies. Copy one of the form is also maintained in unit files, ensuring that there is a local form for those SGT and above, with the original sent to the OMPF. For those Articles 15 filed in the performance fiche of the OMPF, copy one is placed in the unit nonjudicial punishment files. This copy is maintained permanently and is forwarded to the gaining command upon the NCOs transfer, unless the original is transferred from the performance to the restricted fiche, at which time it is destroyed. Otherwise, it is kept in the unit personnel files and destroyed two years from the date of punishment or on the soldier's transfer, whichever occurs first. Copy two is forwarded to the finance office if there is a reduction in grade or any unsuspended forfeiture of pay. Copy three is provided to the military personnel office/division. Copy four is provided to the soldier, and copy five is maintained by the unit paralegal office.

COURTS-MARTIAL

Courts-martial are the agencies through which Army magistrates try personnel accused of violations of the punitive articles of the Uniform Code of Military Justice (UCMJ). These are Articles 77 through 134 of the UCMJ and are designed to provide punishment of three broad groups of crimes and offenses:

- Crimes common to both the military and civilian law, such as murder, rape, sodomy, arson, burglary, larceny, and fraud against the United States.
- Crimes and offenses peculiar to the military services, such as desertion, disobedience, misbehavior before the enemy, and sleeping on post.
- General offenses that are prosecuted under Article 134, the General Article, which covers "all disorders and neglects to the prejudice of good order and discipline in the armed forces, all conduct of a nature to bring discredit upon the armed forces, and crimes and offenses not capital."

During peacetime, courts-martial may impose sentences ranging from simple forfeiture of pay to confinement and forfeiture of all pay and allowances to even death. (See appendix 12 of *Manual for Courts-Martial* for the "Maximum Punishment Chart.") During time of war, a general court-martial may impose any penalty authorized by law, including death.

Who May Prefer Charges

Charges are initiated by anyone bringing to the attention of the military authorities information concerning an offense suspected to have been committed by a person subject to the UCMJ. This information may be received from anyone, whether subject to the UCMJ or not.

Action by Immediate Commander

Upon receipt of information that an offense has been committed, the commander exercising immediate jurisdiction over the accused under Article 15, UCMJ, must make a preliminary inquiry into the charges in order to permit an intelligent disposition of them.

Based on the outcome of the preliminary inquiry, a commander may decide that all or some of the charges do not warrant further action, and those charges may be dismissed. The commander may also decide, based on the preliminary investigation, that the offenses committed warrant punishment under Article 15, UCMJ, or he or she may refer more serious charges to higher authority for trial by court-martial.

Effective Dates of Sentences

Whenever a sentence includes a forfeiture of pay or allowances in addition to confinement, the forfeiture applies to pay or allowances becoming due on or after the date the sentence is approved by the convening authority.

Confinement included in a sentence begins to run from the date of sentencing by the court-martial. Reductions are effective on the date the sentence is approved. All other sentences of courts-martial are effective on the date they are ordered executed.

REFERENCES

AR 27-10, *Military Justice*, 2011.

Manual for Courts-Martial, 2012.

Servicemember's Legal Guide, 5th edition, by Lt. Col. Jonathan P. Tomes, U.S. Army, Ret. (Stackpole Books).

18

Personal Affairs

In the preceding chapters of this guide, the broader focus and message is on two key areas of competence: tactical and technical competence, knowing how to soldier and knowing your job. The third leg of the competency stool that provides for a well-rounded professional is personal competence, taking care of all of your personal life responsibilities. This chapter places the focus there and provides recommendations and sources to ensure you have the resources you need. Soldiers often allow their personal responsibilities to pile up under more pressing professional matters. Doing so can be costly to you, and especially to your loved ones.

Consider, for example, that neglecting to get life insurance and a last will and testament can cause surviving family members to be left out in the cold, financially and otherwise. Consider, too, that medical bills for unforeseen illnesses and injuries can devastate your financial future. What can you do about portions of major bills disallowed by TRICARE or TRICARE Dental? Do you really understand your family's medical and dental benefits, and how and under what circumstances TRICARE supplements are strongly recommended?

What happens, for example, when you deploy to a combat zone or elsewhere overseas and your spouse and children remain behind in local quarters? Do your family members have what they need to achieve a decent quality of life and standard of living in their new environment? Where can they turn for help when problems arise?

What if, for some reason beyond your control and ability to rectify, your end-of-month Leave and Earnings Statement reads "No Pay Due" and you must pay rent and meet other living expenses? Who can help fully or partially defray necessary payments to landlords, banks, and other creditors until your pay is sorted out?

Are your personal affairs in order? To what extent? Do you keep records? Where are they? Who else knows where your vital records are kept? Does your spouse or significant other know important account numbers and first and supplemental points of contact? You must make the effort to consider and take charge of your personal affairs. It is your responsibility to plan for your personal needs and those of your family. Remember that deployability includes personal readiness. The most physically fit, tactically and technically competent soldier is no good to their unit if she or he cannot get on the plane to deploy because of personal issues or a failure to prepare family members.

Keep your chain of command informed on personal issues. Your superiors don't want to involve themselves in your life; however, it is much easier for your leaders to assist you prior to the explosion, rather than trying to pick up the pieces afterward. Remember, helping you with your problems is one of the things they get paid to do. If they can't help, they will surely be able to point you in the right direction.

PERSONAL AFFAIRS RECORDS

The simplest way to keep your survivors informed about arrangements you have made for them is to prepare a record of your personal affairs. At the minimum, be sure that they know the location of the following:

- Your birth certificate and those of all members of your immediate family.
- Your marriage certificate.
- Divorce papers or previous spouse's death certificate, if applicable.
- Your life insurance policies.

If you put the original of your will and other key documents in a safe-deposit box, be sure that your spouse or executor has access to it. If you die and no one has access to the box, a court order must be obtained to open it.

A personal affairs record is a necessity for the married soldier because it serves as a vital source of information for his or her family. A personal affairs record can be detailed, but make sure it includes at least the following:

- Insurance policy numbers and their amounts (include automobile and homeowner's policies).
- Previous years' tax records.
- Copies of titles and bills of sale.
- Information on bank accounts.
- A list of all pay allotments.
- Information regarding any veterans' benefits to which you may be entitled.

If you are married, be sure someone in your family knows how to pay your household bills, when they are due, and where to find them.

MILITARY RECORDS

Keep a file of all records about your military service. Keep copies of orders, discharge certificate, awards, citations, letters of appreciation and commendation, medical and dental records, Leave and Earnings Statements, and other information about your military history, even old NCOERs when you become an NCO. Information is frequently needed throughout your active service career and afterward, when you apply for certain benefits. A lot of this information will also become very useful in preparing a résumé when it is time to leave the service.

Emergency Data

Your DD Form 93, *Record of Emergency Data*, must be accurate and up-to-date at all times. This record tells your military personnel directorate (MPD) where your next of kin can be located immediately. It gives the name of the person you want to receive your pay if you are missing in action as well as other information of benefit to your dependents.

FAMILY CARE PLAN

The wrong time for you, either as dual military parents or a single parent, to begin planning who will take care of your children is when you find yourself on a short-notice deployment. AR 600-20, *Army Command Policy*, stipulates that every single-parent soldier, dual military parents, and single and dual military pregnant soldiers must develop a family care plan. The plan, DA Form 5305, at a minimum includes proof that a guardian has agreed to care for dependent children under the age of eighteen. Powers of attorney for medical care, guardianship, and the authorization to start or stop financial support should be in the packet, and the children should have military ID cards. Lastly, the regulation requires a letter of instruction to the guardian/escort. This letter should contain specific instructions needed for the guardian to ensure the best care of the dependents.

Although not required for the packet, birth certificates, Social Security cards, shot records, other medical or insurance cards, medication dosages if necessary, and lists of family member addresses and phone numbers in case of emergency should be kept in a central location (an accordion-style organizer or file cabinet special drawer is suitable) and labeled to make it easy for the guardian to find documents fast. You might also want to contact financial institutions, children's doctors, schools, and day-care providers prior to deployment, so there will not be questions when your guardian comes to sign your child out of school to take him or her to the doctor.

Power of Attorney

A power of attorney is a legal document by which you give another person the power to act as your agent, either for some particular purpose or for the transaction of your business in general. In the wrong hands, a power of attorney can ruin you because the agent who holds such a power has, within the limits granted by it, full authority to deal with your property without consulting you. Grant it only to someone you can trust, and then only when you must.

You may never need a power of attorney, or if you do need one, it may only be required to perform certain acts and no others—a limited or special power of attorney. Always consult a legal assistance officer or a lawyer before assigning a power of attorney, and cancel it as soon as it is no longer required.

Bank Accounts

If you are married, you and your spouse should decide who manages the accounts. Make them joint accounts so that if anything happens to you, your family will have ready access to funds.

Current regulations require soldiers to have guaranteed direct deposit to a financial institution. With a guaranteed direct deposit from the U.S. Army Finance Center, you do not have to bother with anything but reviewing your Leave and Earnings Statement on payday (as discussed in chapter 14).

Your Will

The importance of having a will cannot be overemphasized. You may not consider that you "own" very much, but not having a will could cause many legal complications after your death. If you were to die without a will—intestate—your estate would be distributed according to the descent and distribution laws of your state of legal residence, or in the case of real property located in another state, the laws of that state.

If you are married, both you and your spouse should have wills, even if each will makes the same distribution of property and assets. It is particularly important to have a will if you have minor children so that their interests can be protected through a guardianship of your choice in the event both you and your spouse die.

Once you have made your will, review it periodically to keep it up-to-date. As circumstances change, you may want to update it to be sure that it still expresses your desires about the distribution of your property and assets.

Keep your will in a safe place. The safest place to keep it (and other important papers) is in a safe-deposit box at your bank. It is not a bad idea to send a copy of your will together with a statement as to the location of the original to the principal beneficiary or the person named in the will as the executor.

Life Insurance

It is beyond the scope of this guide to discuss all the things to look for when you are shopping for civilian/commercial life insurance. What kind of policy to get and how much insurance you may need depends strictly upon your individual or family situation. You are particularly insurable if you are still relatively young and you have school-age children who depend upon you. Shop around. There are numerous good individual and group insurance plans available; there are some pretty bad ones available as well—and plenty of unscrupulous insurance agents willing to take your money. Be vigilant when you buy insurance, and try and talk first to a mentor you trust who may have experience or someone else you can trust on this topic (immediate family, extended relatives, etc.).

Servicemembers Group Life Insurance (SGLI)

Maximum coverage is $400,000, unless you decline coverage or request a reduced amount of coverage. DOD currently pays the premiums for servicemembers who are deployed in a designated combat zone for $150,000 of SGLI coverage. When you leave the service, your SGLI is convertible to Veterans Group Life Insurance (VGLI). Another benefit of SGLI is that those who elect the full SGLI are automatically enrolled in Family Member SGLI, and family members are automatically provided coverage. Your spouse would be covered for $100,000 unless you elect a lesser amount, which must be incrementally lowered in $10,000 amounts, and your dependent children are provided $10,000 of coverage, all at no cost to you. Finally, if you have SGLI, then you are automatically enrolled in Traumatic Injury Protection (TSGLI). This coverage provides between $25,000 and $100,000 of benefits, depending on the conditions and outcome of the traumatic injury. Regardless of any commercial insurance you may elect to take additionally, it is a good idea to seriously consider this program and be sure to talk with your chain of command before electing to decline coverage.

FAMILY CARE PLAN

For use of this form, see AR 600-20; the proponent agency is DCSPER

PRIVACY ACT STATEMENT

AUTHORITY: 10 U.S.C. Section 3013, Secretary of the Army; Army Regulation 600-20, Army Command Policy and E.O. 9397 *(SSN)*

PRINCIPAL PURPOSE: To emphasize to soldiers the significance of their responsibilities to the military service and their family members while performing required military duties.

ROUTINE USES: None

DISCLOSURE: Mandatory; Failure to maintain a Family Care Plan could subject the soldier to separation, administrative action, or disciplinary action under the UCMJ.

PART I - SOLDIER'S FAMILY CARE

	INITIALS
A. I was counseled on _____ *(date)*, and fully understand the policy on family member care responsibilities. I understand that I must arrange for care of my family members, remain available for deployment and training, and report for duty as required without interference of responsibility for family members. I assume responsibility for all obligations for such things as child care, food, adequate housing, transportation, and emergency needs of my family members regardless of age.	
B. I have made and will maintain arrangements for the care of my family members during all the following: 1. Duty 6. Temporary Duty 11. Deployment 2. Exercises/field duty 7. Unit Training Assembly 12. Other Military Duty 3. Permanent Change of Station 8. Active Duty Training 13. Emergencies 4. Alerts 9. Unaccompanied Tours 14. Leave/non-duty Time 5. Annual Training 10. Mobilization	
C. I understand the importance of ensuring the proper care for my family members, and ensuring my own readiness and deployability as well. I further understand that in light of the critical nature of both these requirements:	
1. Failure to make and maintain adequate family member care arrangements in accordance with the Army's policy is grounds for disciplinary action or separation.	
2. Nonavailability for worldwide assignment and/or unit deployment may lead to my separation from the Army.	
3. If arrangements for the care of my family members fail to work, I am not automatically excused from prescribed duties, unit deployment, or reassignment.	
4. If I fail to maintain a Family Care Plan or provide false information regarding my plan, I am subject to separation, administrative action, or disciplinary action under UCMJ.	
5. I must maintain an up-to-date Family Care Plan and revise my Plan when circumstances change. I understand that Family Care Plans may be tested at the discretion of the commander.	
6. I will receive no special consideration in duty assignments or duty stations based on my responsibilities for my family members unless enrolled in the Exceptional Family Member Program *(EFMP)* in accordance with AR 600-75.	
D. I have made all necessary arrangements *(legal, educational, financial, religious, special, etc.)* to ensure a smooth, rapid turnover of family member care responsibilities in case this plan is implemented.	
E. I have arranged for necessary travel required to transfer my family members to a designated person. If my principal designee is not in the local area, I have arranged with a nonmilitary person in the local area to assume temporary guardianship of my family members until they are transferred to my principal care designee, or that designee arrives to assume responsibility for their care.	
F. A copy of DA Form 5841-R *(Power of Attorney)* or **equivalent documents** and a copy of DA Form 5840-R *(Certificate of Acceptance as Guardian)* for each escort or guardian whether temporary or long-term is attached to this plan.	
G. The following additional required documents are completed, included in this plan, and will be put into effect as part of my Family Care Plan.	
1. DD Form 1172 *(Application for Uniformed Services Identification Card)* for each family member whether they have a currently valid ID card or not.	
2. DD Form 2558 *(Authorization to Start, Stop or Change an Allotment for Active Duty or Retired Personnel)* or other proof of financial support for expenses incurred by guardian and family members.	
3. Copies of Letters of Instruction *(which have been forwarded to designated escorts or guardians along with powers of attorney and other pertinent documents)*, outlining all special instructions concerning the care of my family members have also been included in my Family Care Plan.	
H. I have thoroughly briefed escorts and guardians on the full extent of their responsibilities and on procedures for gaining access to military/civilian facilities, services, entitlements and benefits on behalf of my family members.	
I. I am confident that my Family Care Plan is workable, and to the best of my knowledge, the guardian *(s)* and escort *(s)* I have designated will be both willing and able to carry out the responsibilities of caring for my family members.	

PART II - DESIGNATION OF GUARDIANS/ESCORTS

A. I (We) have designated the following temporary guardian to care for my (our) family member *(s)* until responsibility is transferred to escort or principal (long-term) guardian.

1. TYPED OR PRINTED NAME	2a. COMPLETE ADDRESS *(Including Street, Apartment Number, P.O. Box Number, Rural Route Number, City, State, and ZIP + 4 where applicable)*
3. TELEPHONE NUMBER *(Include Area Code)*	
	2b. E- MAIL ADDRESS

DA FORM 5305-R, APR 1999   DA FORM 5305-R, MAR 1992 IS OBSOLETE   USAPA V1.00

B. I (We) have designated the following individual(s) as principal long-term guardian(s) for my (our) family member (s). The designated guardian(s) reside in the continental United States or United States territories.

1. TYPED OR PRINTED NAME	2a. COMPLETE ADDRESS (Including Street, Apartment Number, P.O. Box Number, Rural Route Number, City, State, and ZIP + 4 where applicable)
3. TELEPHONE NUMBER (Include Area Code)	2b. E-MAIL ADDRESS

C. I (We) have designated the following individual(s) as escort for my (our) family member(s) if evacuation from OCONUS becomes necessary (applies only to persons assigned OCONUS):

1. TYPED OR PRINTED NAME	2a. COMPLETE ADDRESS (Including Street, Apartment Number, P.O. Box Number, Rural Route Number, City, State, and ZIP + 4 where applicable)
3. TELEPHONE NUMBER (Include Area Code)	2b. E-MAIL ADDRESS

PART III - DUAL MILITARY COUPLES ONLY
MILITARY SPOUSE AND COMMANDER CERTIFICATION

A. **Spouse:** We have made arrangements and will maintain arrangements for the care of our family member (s) in all circumstances required by our commitment to the military and our family.

1. SIGNATURE OF SPOUSE	2. DATE (YYYY/MM/DD)

3. TYPED OR PRINTED NAME OF SPOUSE	4. SSN

5. Recertification	a. INIT.	DATE	b. INIT.	DATE	c. INIT.	DATE	d. INIT.	DATE	e. INIT.	DATE

B. **Commander:** I have counseled the military spouse assigned to my unit, reviewed the Family Care Plan, and I am satisfied that the members have made adequate family care arrangements.

1. SIGNATURE OF COMMANDER	2. DATE	3. UNIT ADDRESS

4. TYPED OR PRINTED NAME OF COMMANDER

5. Recertification	a. INIT.	DATE	b. INIT.	DATE	c. INIT.	DATE	d. INIT.	DATE	e. INIT.	DATE

PART IV - SOLDIER AND COMMANDER CERTIFICATION

A. **Soldier:** I (We) have made arrangements and will maintain arrangements for the care of my (our) family member(s) in all circumstances required by my (our) commitment to the military and my (our) family.

1. SIGNATURE OF SOLDIER	2. DATE (YYYY/MM/DD)

3. TYPED OR PRINTED NAME OF SOLDIER	4. SSN

5. Recertification	a. INIT.	DATE	b. INIT.	DATE	c. INIT.	DATE	d. INIT.	DATE	e. INIT.	DATE

B. **Commander:** I have reviewed the Family Care Plan, and I am satisfied that the members have made adequate family care arrangements that will allow for a full range of military duties and for worldwide availability as defined here.

1. SIGNATURE OF COMMANDER	2. DATE	3. UNIT ADDRESS

4. TYPED OR PRINTED NAME OF COMMANDER

5. Recertification	a. INIT.	DATE	b. INIT.	DATE	c. INIT.	DATE	d. INIT.	DATE	e. INIT.	DATE

Servicemembers Civil Relief Act (SCRA)

This piece of federal law provides protection of rights, privileges, immunities, and benefits to servicemembers while serving on active duty. These benefits include protection against paying taxes in both the home state and the state in which servicemembers are stationed, exemption from personal property taxes when stationed in a state that is not their domicile, the ability to have civil court cases delayed, and special treatment of certain financial obligations. Servicemembers may also qualify for lowering their interest rates for obligations incurred prior to entering active service. For more information, go to *http://www.benefits.va.gov/homeloans/documents/docs/scra_notice.pd* or see a legal assistance attorney. All mobilized reserve component (RC) soldiers can receive financial support and information from the local servicing finance office or defense military pay office (DMPO).

One of the most significant provisions of the Servicemembers Civil Relief Act (SCRA) for RC soldiers is the right of reemployment. RC soldiers who are mobilized are exempt from the Uniformed Services Employment and Reemployment Rights Act (USERRA) five-year limit for retaining reemployment rights. In regard to questions about employment or reemployment rights, servicemembers can check the Employer Support of the Guard and Reserve (ESGR) website at *www.ESGR.org*.

HOUSING

Military families often must rent local housing while waiting for government quarters to become available. If you find yourself in that situation, you might want to consider renting an apartment on a month-by-month basis. Should you sign a lease for a specified period of time and then have to break it because a set of quarters unexpectedly becomes available, you typically have to forfeit your deposit (usually an amount equal to a month's rent).

Renting an apartment gives single soldiers a degree of independence and privacy not available in the barracks, and for this reason, many soldiers want to move off post. Whether a single soldier can move off post depends on the following:

- Your post commander's policy. It is also up to the commanding officer of your unit. Some commanders are liberal in granting this privilege; it depends upon your unit's mission. Commanders of headquarters units can sometimes be more liberal than those of tactical or combat support units.
- The amount and quality of troop housing available. Some small, specialized units have trouble finding adequate troop housing, especially at overcrowded installations in metropolitan areas. Where sufficient troop housing is available, however, commanders normally fill the billets up first before allowing lower-ranking single personnel to move off post.
- Nonabuse of the privilege. Your commander will revoke permission to live off post as soon as you start coming to work late, running up debts, or causing disturbances among the local population.

Be sure that you can afford to live off post. Your military pay combined with your housing and subsistence allowances may be enough, depending on the geographical area,

Guide for Obtaining Information and Assistance

	YOUR CHAIN OF COMMAND	PERSONNEL NCO OR OFFICER	REENLISTMENT NCO	JUDGE ADVOCATE	INSPECTOR GENERAL	FINANCE OFFICER	CHAPLAIN	HOUSING OFFICER	TRANSPORTATION OFFICER	AMERICAN RED CROSS	ARMY COMMUNITY SERVICES	ARMY EMERGENCY RELIEF	EDUCATION OFFICER/ADVISOR
Appeals	1	2		2	2		2						
Assignment, reassignment, MOS, and proficiency pay	1	1				2							
Reenlistment	1		1										
Personnel matters: promotion, reduction, discharge, retirement Veterans' benefits	1	1	2	2									
Complaints (requests for assistance)	1	2	2	2	2	2	2	2	2	2	2	2	
Debts and civilian creditors	1	1		2		2	2				2		
Dependents' schools	1	1									2		
Family and religious affairs	1	2					1			2	2		
Travel of dependents, shipment of POV and household goods	1	2				2			1		2		
Medical service (individual and dependents)	1	1											
Pay, allowances, and incentive pay	1	2				1							
Leaves and passes	1	2											
Insurance, all types (SGLI and commercial)	1	1				2							
Legal assistance, including U.S. and foreign law, wills, and powers of attorney	1			1									
Military education	1	2	2										
Nonmilitary education	1	2											2
PX, commissary, QM sales store	1			2									
Government quarters, off-post housing	1	2						1					
Registration/operation of privately owned vehicle (POV), registration of firearms	1												
Entry into U.S., passport, visa, naturalization, immigration, birth certificate (children born in foreign country)	1	2		1							2		
Home conditions and emergency leave	1	2					2			2	2	2	
Emergency financial assistance	1	2					1			2	2	2	
Postal service	1												
Drug and alcohol rehabilitation program	1						2				1		

1. Primary source
2. Other sources as appropriate

but just enough and no more. If supporting yourself in an apartment leaves you flat broke at the end of the month, you are better off living in the barracks.

Some soldiers find it a good idea to team up with two or three friends and rent a place by splitting all the costs. This is an excellent idea if your companions can be trusted to pay their share, take care of the communal areas, and respect your privacy and personal property.

PERSONAL PROPERTY

Joint ownership of property can have certain advantages in establishing an automatic and known passage of ownership upon the death of one owner, and can also have certain disadvantages. Inquire into federal and state laws regarding ownership of family property, and take actions that put your estate in the most favorable ownership positions.

In the event of your death, your immediate personal effects will be forwarded at government expense to the person entitled to their custody. This does not give the recipient legal title to them, but they should be retained for disposition under the law.

If you own real estate in your name and it is not paid for, show on your personal affairs record whether there is a mortgage or a deed of trust against it, along with the name of the person or organization to whom you are indebted. Also include information about property taxes and insurance.

Transfer of automobile ownership is sometimes complicated because of varying state laws. Remember that joint titling may make you or your spouse subject to personal property taxes; active-duty personnel are generally exempt from payment of personal property taxes, so adding your spouse's name to an automobile title can cost you a lot of money.

INCOME TAXES

Military pay in general is subject to income tax. You do not pay tax on subsistence, quarters, and uniform allowances. Dislocation allowance, special duty pays, and hardship pay, however, are taxable.

Any nonmilitary earnings, including the pay received while employed during off-duty hours and the income of any of your dependents, are taxable. Military pay is excluded from federal income tax for service in any area that the president of the United States designates by executive order to be a combat zone. This exclusion is unlimited for enlisted members. If you spend a single qualifying day in the combat zone, your pay for the entire month is excluded from taxable income. Bonuses and special pays are also excluded from taxable income if within the previously stated limitations and earned in the same month in which you served in a combat zone.

The Servicemembers Civil Relief Act ensures that a state in which a soldier is stationed but that is not the servicemember's legal residence cannot tax service pay. Legal residence is established at enlistment or thereafter when a soldier executes DD Form 2058, *State of Legal Residence Certificate.*

The following states do not withhold income tax from the pay of military personnel: Alaska, Florida, Nevada, New Hampshire, South Dakota, Tennessee, Texas, Washington, and Wyoming. Pay exemptions for some categories of military pay are allowed for legal residents in Kentucky, Minnesota, New Mexico, and Oklahoma. Soldiers claiming legal residence in foreign countries or U.S. territories are also exempt from paying state income taxes.

WHERE TO FIND HELP

In addition to what follows, you can refer to the Guide for Obtaining Information or the "My Benefits" tab under "Self Service" at Army Knowledge Online (*www.us .army.mil*) for more information.

Army Community Services (ACS)

The ACS is an official Department of the Army organization established to provide information, aid, guidance, and referral services to military personnel and their families. ACS activities are monitored by the Army adjutant general. The ACS web page is at *www .myarmyonesource.com.*

The ACS provides a wide variety of services, including the following:

- Referrals for handicapped dependents.
- Family counseling services.
- Financial planning services.
- Lending services to provide bedding, linens, and housewares to military families until they can get settled at a new post.
- Volunteer services providing transportation to dependents when required.
- Child abuse information and referral.
- An emergency food locker from which needy families may draw supplies.

Army Emergency Relief (AER)

The Army Emergency Relief (AER) operates as a part of the Army Community Services. AER provides needed financial assistance to soldiers and their dependents. A local AER officer can authorize interest-free cash loans. Large loans must be approved by Headquarters, AER. The AER website is at *www.aerhq.org.*

AER loans may be approved for the following purposes:

- Defray living expenses because of nonreceipt of military pay.
- Provide money to help defray emergency travel expenses.
- Help pay rents, security deposits, and utilities.
- Help pay "essential POV [privately owned vehicle] expenses."
- Pay funeral expenses above and beyond those allowed by the government.
- Pay grants to the widows and orphans of deceased soldiers, in some cases.
- Provide cash to buy food when it is not available from the Army Community Services (ACS) food locker.
- Provide money to replace lost funds.

Soldiers must apply for AER loans through their unit commanders by filling out DA Form 700, *Application for AER Financial Assistance.* The soldier must document his or her expenses or financial situation, and an allotment must be executed before the AER will disburse any money.

Each year, AER disburses millions of dollars to help soldiers and their families. The only source for these funds is cash donations by Army members solicited annually during Army-wide fund-raising drives.

Army Family Action Plan (AFAP)

Today, more than half the active Army force is married. The Army pays considerable attention to soldiers' families.

A partnership exists between the Army and Army families and is strengthened by the Army Family Covenant, the Army's commitment to provide soldiers and their families the quality of life that they deserve for their service and sacrifice. The Army's unique missions, concept of service, and lifestyle of its members all affect the nature of this partnership. Toward the goal of building a strong partnership, the Army remains committed to ensuring adequate support to families in order to promote wellness, to develop a sense of community, and to strengthen the mutually reinforcing bonds between the Army and its families.

The Army Family Action Plan includes an opportunity for soldiers, family members, DA civilians, retirees, and survivors to voice how they rate Army quality of life and services. From the Installation Community Services Office, unit AFAP liaison personnel, and online submissions of concerns or feedback, the Army Family Action Plan allows the leadership to gain an understanding of program needs and modifications. The prioritization of needs and discussions are heard all the way to the top of the Army leadership chain, where policy decisions and funding support can be allocated as determined by a General Officer Steering Committee. Family members who are interested in becoming involved with AFAP can contact the local Army Community Services Office or go to *https://www.myarmyonesource.com/familyprogramsandservices/familyprograms/army-familyactionplan/default.aspx* for more information.

Since the first AFAP conference was held in 1983, many laws have been passed or amended to resolve more than 115 quality-of-life issues affecting the Army family.

Better Opportunities for Single Soldiers (BOSS)

BOSS is a program designed to improve unit morale and provide single soldiers a voice to the chain of command about their concerns on quality of life and other issues. By focusing on three key areas—community service, recreation and leisure, and quality of life—BOSS is a powerful tool not only for single soldiers to better enjoy and have an enhanced experience in the military, but it also provides commanders and other leaders with a valuable measurement tool of morale within their organizations. Soldiers who are members of BOSS can be a part of organizing recreation and leisure activities or simply sign up for them and take part. They can become active members of community projects, learning important skills and meeting new people along the way. They also have the opportunity to attend or take roles in meetings and help provide important information to the leadership of their organizations on quality of life issues. The BOSS program includes a national annual meeting attended by organization delegates, which is widely attended by senior Army leaders, usually including the Sergeant Major of the Army. When you are new to an organization and single, this is a tremendous opportunity to get to know soldiers in your unit and start meeting other like-minded soldiers who are looking to make the most of their time in uniform. More information about BOSS is available at *http://www.armymwr.com/recleisure/single/boss.aspx.*

Legal Assistance

A legal assistance officer will advise you on such matters as a will, power of attorney, divorce and separation actions, estates, tax problems, and other civil matters. The legal assistance officer can also provide you with a very useful "legal checkup," which is designed to identify any potential legal problems that you may have.

This officer is not normally permitted to represent you in civil court or to give you advice in matters of a criminal nature. Neither may he or she advise you about court-martial investigations or charges (a military counsel appointed by the judge advocate will assist you in such cases). If your problem requires the services of a civilian lawyer, the legal assistance officer can refer you, through cooperating bar associations, to civilian legal advisors or legal aid bureaus.

The *Servicemember's Legal Guide*, 5th edition, published by Stackpole Books, provides comprehensive information on what soldiers and their families need to know about the law.

Chaplains

Chaplains are available to help soldiers, family members, and civilians with any type of concern they may have, be it spiritual, work related, or otherwise. Chaplains can help in areas ranging from marriage and family counseling to stress management and suicide prevention. Soldiers seeking counseling don't necessarily have to be churchgoers to use the chaplains to help them through rough times. Importantly, Army chaplain regulations state that any communications to a chaplain acting as a spiritual advisor must be kept in confidence and cannot be told to anyone else without permission.

Defense Health Agency (DHA)

The Defense Health Agency is the agency that oversees the management of the military health system. Metropolitan Life Insurance Company (MetLife) handles enrollments, customer service, and claims processing. They also support the TRICARE Dental Program (discussed in detail below). Your TRICARE Service Center at the local military treatment facility can provide details. More information is also available at the Tricare website at *http://www.tricare.mil/coveredservices/,* or by calling them at (855) 638-8371 in the continental United States or (855) 638-8372 overseas.

MEDICAL INSURANCE—TRICARE

Army health-care beneficiaries—you and your family—should take a long-term view toward medical and dental health. Eat foods that contribute to a longer life. Exercise regularly for the same reason. Rest properly. Brush and floss after meals. Get periodic physical and dental examinations. Follow the advice of doctors, dentists, and other Army health- and medical-care providers. Stay healthy to limit the effects of illness or disease. Beware of unsafe acts and unsafe conditions to avoid injury. When a person is ill or injured, nothing matters more than recovery.

When an active-duty soldier becomes sick or gets hurt, the Army direct-care medical system provides care at no cost. In fact, AR 40-3, *Medical, Dental, and Veterinary Care*, prohibits active-duty soldiers, including active-duty reserve component soldiers, from seeking and obtaining medical and dental care from civilian sources without prior authorization from the local Army medical treatment facility commander. So, while soldiers are on active duty, they do not need medical and dental insurance. But Army family members do—and they have it provided by TRICARE and the accompanying dental plan, which is also offered through TRICARE.

Eligibility for TRICARE is determined by the Defense Enrollment Eligibility Reporting System (DEERS), a database of uniformed services members (sponsors), family members, and others worldwide who are entitled under the law to TRICARE benefits. Active-duty and retired servicemembers are automatically registered in DEERS, but it's the sponsor's responsibility to ensure that his or her eligible family members are registered correctly in the system. All sponsors should ensure that their family members' status (marriage, divorce, new child, etc.), residential address, telephone numbers, and e-mail address are current in DEERS so that TRICARE can send out information and have claims processed quickly and accurately.

Tricare

TRICARE is a health-care program for members of the uniformed services and their families, and survivors and retired members and their families. TRICARE brings together the health-care resources of each of the military services and supplements them with networks of civilian health-care professionals to provide better access and high-quality service while maintaining the capability to support military operations. There are three TRICARE regions in the United States, each with an assigned lead agent who is responsible for the military health services system in that region.

Under TRICARE, family members have two basic choices for seeking medical care: (1) the Enrolled Choice (TRICARE Prime) and (2) the Nonenrolled Choice (TRICARE Extra/TRICARE Standard). Active-duty members must enroll in TRICARE Prime, and thus are not eligible for the Nonenrolled Choice.

Choice 1. Enrolled Choice (TRICARE Prime) provides the most comprehensive health-care benefits to the patient at the lowest cost. TRICARE Prime guarantees priority access to care at a military treatment facility or, where available, an off-post, civilian, contracted doctor's office.

All active-duty military members must enroll in this choice and must use military facilities. Family members must also enroll to use this option. Those who select the Enrolled Choice will be assigned to a primary care manager (PCM). This is a health-care provider who you will see first for all of your medical needs. If necessary, your PCM will refer you to specialty medical care when needed. There are no enrollment fees for active-duty families in TRICARE Prime.

Choice 2. The Nonenrolled Choice (TRICARE Extra/TRICARE Standard) allows family members to seek medical care from any physician of their choice in the civilian community. The Nonenrolled Choice is a more costly option than the Enrolled Choice. This choice incorporates two programs: TRICARE Extra and TRICARE Standard. Medical expenses are covered under these programs when family members are not enrolled in TRICARE Prime. A single deductible covers the use of either program.

Active enrollment and preauthorization are not required for your family to use the Nonenrolled Choice, but a nonavailability statement must be obtained for civilian inpatient care. See your local health benefits advisor for more information.

TRICARE Standard is the basic TRICARE health-care program, offering comprehensive health-care coverage, for people not enrolled in TRICARE Prime. (Active-duty servicemembers are automatically enrolled in Prime, and many other beneficiaries choose to enroll.) Standard does not require enrollment.

Fee-for-service flexibility: Standard is a fee-for-service plan that gives beneficiaries the option to see any TRICARE-certified/authorized provider—doctor, nurse-practitioner, lab, clinic, and so on. Standard offers the greatest flexibility in choosing a provider, but it will also involve greater out-of-pocket expenses for you, the patient. You also may be required to file your own claims.

Costs: Standard requires that you satisfy a yearly deductible before TRICARE cost sharing begins, and you will be required to pay co-payments or cost shares for outpatient care, medications, and inpatient care. A nonavailability statement for civilian inpatient care may be required for areas surrounding military treatment facilities.

TRICARE Extra is an option that allows Standard beneficiaries to save money by making appointments with civilian doctors, nurse practitioners, labs, clinics, and so on, that are "participating" providers. Providers who participate in TRICARE agree to accept the TRICARE maximum allowable charge (TMAC) as payment in full for services they render.

Nonparticipating providers may, by law, charge up to 15 percent above the TMAC for their services, and the TRICARE Standard beneficiary is responsible for the amount above the TMAC.

Participating providers will file claims forms for the TRICARE beneficiary. (Certified providers may or may not file claims on behalf of the Standard patient; the doctor may choose to do so, or not, on a case-by-case basis.)

Using the Nonenrolled Choice allows family members the freedom to choose any civilian physician. Some physicians' services will be less costly than others. Your family members may continue to use military facilities on a space-available basis, but obtaining appointments may become very difficult.

TRICARE Pharmacy

Prescriptions may be filled (up to a ninety-day supply for most medications) at a military treatment facility (MTF) pharmacy free of charge, although not all medications are available at MTF pharmacies. The TRICARE Mail Order Pharmacy (TMOP) is available for prescriptions you take on a regular basis. You can receive up to a ninety-day supply (for most medications) of your prescription through the mail by using TMOP. Finally, prescription medications that your doctor requires you to start taking immediately can be obtained through a retail network pharmacy as part of the TRICARE Retail Pharmacy (TRRx) program.

What Will TRICARE Cost?

The charts below provide examples of cost shares for families using TRICARE. Health benefits advisors at the military treatment facilities or representatives at the TRICARE Service Centers can assist you and your family in obtaining the medical care and services you and your family may need.

Active-Duty Family Members

If you have questions about your military health-care benefits under TRICARE, there are many places to get answers. A member handbook may be obtained by visiting or calling your local TRICARE Service Center; by calling the health benefits advisor at your nearest military hospital or clinic; or by visiting the website at *www.tricare.mil*. Each medical facility has a health benefits advisor, Managed Care Office, or TRICARE Service Center. This should be your first contact for information. Additionally, below are telephone numbers for each region, where you can call and get information about TRICARE and your health-care benefits.

ACTIVE-DUTY FAMILY MEMBERS

	TRICARE Prime E-1 through E-4	TRICARE Prime E-5 and above	TRICARE Extra/Standard Families of E4 and Above	TRICARE Extra/Standard Families of E5 and Below
Annual Deductible (Individual/Family)	None	None	$50/$100	$150/$300
Civilian Outpatient Visit	$0	$0	Extra: 15 percent; Standard: 20 percent	Extra: 15 percent; Standard: 20 percent;
Civilian Inpatient Admission	$0	$0	Greater of $25 or $13.90/day	Greater of $25 or $13.90/day
Civilian Inpatient Mental Health	$0	$0	$20 per day	$20 per day

TRICARE REGIONS

TRICARE   *www.triwest.com*
WEST   (888) TRIWEST; (888) 874-9378
Alaska, Arizona, California, Colorado, Hawaii, Idaho, Iowa (except
for the Rock Island Arsenal area), Kansas, Minnesota, Missouri
(except for the St. Louis area), Montana, Nebraska, Nevada, New
Mexico, North Dakota, Oregon, South Dakota, the extreme western
portion of Texas, Utah, Washington, and Wyoming.

TRICARE   *www.healthnetfederalservices.com*
North   (877) TRICARE; (877) 874-2273
Connecticut, Delaware, the District of Columbia, Illinois, Indiana,
the Rock Island Arsenal area of Iowa, Kentucky, Maine, Maryland,
Massachusetts, Michigan, the St. Louis area of Missouri, New
Hampshire, New Jersey, New York, North Carolina, Ohio, Penn-
sylvania, Rhode Island, Fort Campbell area of Tennessee, Vermont,
Virginia, West Virginia, and Wisconsin.

TRICARE   *www.humana-military.com*
South   (800) 444-5445
Alabama, Arkansas, Florida, Georgia, Louisiana, Mississippi,
Oklahoma, South Carolina, most of Tennessee, and the eastern por-
tion of Texas.

TRICARE
Overseas   1-888-777-8343
TRICARE Prime and TRICARE Standard for active duty and their
families. Only TRICARE Standard is for Military retirees; their
families who live overseas cannot enroll in TRICARE Prime, but
they can use TRICARE Standard.

TRICARE REGIONS
TRICARE Prime and TRICARE Standard are for active-duty servicemembers and their
families. Only TRICARE Standard is allowed for military retirees; their families cannot
enroll in TRICARE Prime, but they can use TRICARE Standard. For servicemembers
and their families residing overseas and for assistance for those on temporary duty (TDY)
or on leave outside the United States, the TRICARE Overseas Program (TOP) has three
regions of support that include Asia and the Pacific; Latin America; and Europe, the Middle East, and Africa. By going to *www.tricare-overseas.com*, you can quickly find the
region and country and then contact the TOP call center for that area for information
needed to receive care and benefits. If you are planning a trip overseas on TDY or leave,

this is an especially important website to know and investigate first, so if an emergency happens, you have the important information at hand.

TRICARE Reserve Select (TRS)

TRICARE Reserve Select (TRS) is a premium-based TRICARE health plan offered for purchase by certain members and former members of the reserve component (RC) and their families, if specific eligibility requirements are met. TRS coverage must be purchased. TRS members pay a monthly premium for health-care coverage (for self only or for self and family). Adjusted effective January 1 each year, the premiums for calendar year 2015 were $50.75 for TRS member-only coverage and $295.62 for TRS member and family coverage. Those select reserve who are covered by or qualify for the Federal Employee's Health Benefits program do not qualify for this package.

TRICARE FOR LIFE (TFL) is a Medicare wraparound coverage available to:

- Medicare-entitled uniformed service retirees, including retired guard members and reservists.
- Medicare-entitled family members and widows/widowers (dependent parents and parents-in-law are excluded).
- Medicare-entitled Medal of Honor recipients and their family members.
- Certain Medicare-entitled unremarried former spouses.

TRICARE pays the balance on the Medicare claim—everything Medicare did not pay—for everything that is a TRICARE benefit. Note that Veterans Administration providers and some other providers who opt out of Medicare will cause you more out-of-pocket money, since they are prohibited from billing Medicare. Be sure to check with your provider before signing up for this plan.

TRICARE Supplements

TRICARE supplements are not part of the TRICARE program. The different commercial plans are designed to be secondary coverage to TRICARE. Dependent upon the level of coverage, TRICARE supplements pay the cost share, deductible, and eligible excess charges under the TRICARE Standard and Extra options so that on a combined basis, eligible participants have 100 percent coverage in most cases. For more detailed information, check with any of the various associations representing the different members of the armed forces.

TRICARE DENTAL PROGRAM

Active-duty soldiers receive all dental care, at no cost, from military dental treatment facilities and are therefore ineligible for the TRICARE Dental Program (TDP). The TDP is a voluntary dental plan open to families of all active-duty, selected Reserve, and individual Ready Reserve soldiers ordered to active duty for more than thirty consecutive days.

Sponsors must have at least twelve months remaining on their service commitments at the time of enrollment. After completing the initial twelve-month enrollment period, they may continue in the TDP on a month-by-month basis.

Soldiers failing to pay premiums or disenrolling before completing the twenty-four-month lock-in time are responsible for payment of all remaining premiums. Unless disenrolling for a valid reason, soldiers are prohibited from reentering the program for twelve months.

Soldiers may disenroll from the TDP before completion of the mandatory twenty-four-month enrollment for the following reasons: when a sponsor or family member loses Defense Enrollment Eligibility Reporting System (DEERS) eligibility, when TDP enrolled members relocate outside the CONUS service area, or when an active-duty member transfers with enrolled family members to a duty station where space-available dental care for the enrolled members is readily available at the local uniformed services dental treatment facility.

LONG-TERM CARE

TRICARE or Medicare do not cover long-term care. The Federal Long-Term Care Insurance Program is an important benefit for members of the Army family, including retiree members and qualified relatives. It is insurance that helps you pay for care to help you perform daily activities if you have an ongoing illness or disability. It also includes the kind of care you would need if you had a severe cognitive problem such as Alzheimer's disease. It is help with eating, bathing, dressing, transferring from a bed to a chair, toileting, continence, and so forth. This type of care isn't received in a hospital and isn't intended to cure you. It is not acute care. It is chronic care that you might need for the rest of your life. It can be received in your own home, at a nursing home, or at another long-term care facility.

If you are younger than forty and healthy when you retire, the Federal Long-Term Care Insurance Program may not be the best deal. You may obtain comparable coverage at a lower monthly premium from one of the large companies that handle long-term care. Check the premiums calculator offered by the Office of Personnel Management on the Internet at *www.ltcfeds.com/ltcWeb/do/assessing_your_needs/ratecalcOut* for more information. To qualify, you must answer more questions about your health and habits than regular military personnel. Retirees can also call (800) 582-3337, Monday through Friday, from 8 a.m. to 8 p.m. EST.

WOUNDED SOLDIER AND FAMILY MEMBER HOTLINE

The wounded soldier and family member hotline was established to ensure that personalized assistance can be received at any time, any place, with just a phone call. While it does not replace the chain of command and was not intended to do so, it does provide soldiers and families a way to voice concerns about patient care and services, and provides senior Army officials a way to gather general information to see how they can best move forward in continuing excellent standards of treatment. The hotline even offers an Anonymous Concerns Form for those who desire to use it. The phone is answered night and day at (800) 984-8523.

ARMY WOUNDED WARRIOR PROGRAM (AW2)

The Army Wounded Warrior Program serves as the Army's official program to help those soldiers with the most severe wounds, injury, or illness. Eligible soldiers with 30 percent disability or more are cared for regardless of status. The program is designed to help soldiers and their families through transition back to military life or to civilian life as needed. Those enrolled may remain in the program for as long as needed, including after transition into veteran status. For more information, check with your local military medical treatment facility or Veterans Administration medical center. You can also get more details at *http://www.wtc.army.mil/modules/veterans/v2-aw2EligibilityEnrollment.html*

WARRIOR TRANSITION UNITS (WTU)

As a part of the Warrior Transition Command, Warrior Transition Units provide a "unit"-type atmosphere for those who require at least six months of treatment and complex medical care. They are located on major installations around the world, based on need. The WTU provides assistance with three supporting roles: primary care provider, squad leader, and nurse case manager. The intent and mission of the WTU is to help soldiers through recovery and healing in an atmosphere that is motivating and cohesive, in an effort to speed transition back into the mainstream Army or on to civilian life. A part of the WTU program are the Community Care Units (CCU). These units are designed to allow eligible soldiers to heal at their home community instead of at the physical WTU. Only those without complex care and who meet other case-by-case criteria are allowed to use this program. More information about the CCU may be read at *www.wtc.army.mil/documents/factsheets/CCU_Factsheet.pdf*.

Closely aligned with the WTU are the Soldier and Family Assistance Centers (SFACs). SFACs serve much like the administrative and logistical staffs in a standard unit. However, the staff members at an SFAC are centralized professionals and volunteers who focus specifically on the needs of those soldiers and families assigned to a WTU. They offer a wide variety of support services, including financial, personnel, and transition services and family assistance and support programs.

Appendix 1

Chain of Command

It is to your benefit to know your chain of command. Listed here are the personnel normally found in the formal chain of command. Check with your supervisor and NCO Support Channel to fill in the names. The number of personnel and the terminology for the positions within the chain vary in some Army units.

CHAIN OF COMMAND

Commander in Chief	<u>President of the United States</u>
Secretary of Defense	_____
Secretary of the Army	_____
Chairman of the Joint Chiefs of Staff	_____
Chief of Staff, Army	_____
MACOM Commander	_____
Corps Commander	_____
Post/Division/Command Commander	_____
Brigade/Group Commander	_____
Battalion Commander	_____
Company Commander	_____
Platoon Leader	_____
Squad/Section Leader	_____

The NCO support channel complements and parallels the chain of command and provides a structure for the day-to-day activities of the Army.

NCO SUPPORT CHANNEL

Sergeant Major of the Army   _____

MACOM Command Sergeant Major   _____

Corps Command Sergeant Major   _____

Post/Division/Command Sergeant Major   _____

Brigade/Group Command Sergeant Major   _____

Battalion Command Sergeant Major   _____

First Sergeant   _____

Platoon Sergeant   _____

Squad Leader   _____

Appendix 2

Acronyms

1SG	first sergeant
AAFES	Army and Air Force Exchange Service
AAM	Army Achievement Medal
AAR	after-action review
ABCMR	Army Board for the Correction of Military Records
AC	active component
ACAP	Army Career and Alumni Program
ACE	American Council on Education
ACES	Army Continuing Education System
ACS	Army Community Services
ACT	American College Testing Program Assessment; also, Army Career Tracker
ACTPEP	American College Testing Proficiency Examination Program
ACU	Army Combat Uniform
ADA	air defense artillery
ADAPCP	Alcohol and Drug Abuse Prevention and Control Program
ADP	Army Doctrine Publication
ADRP	Army Doctrine Reference Publication
AEA	assignment eligibility and availability
AEC	Army Education Center
AEN	Army Employment Network
AEPS	Army electronic product support
AER	Army Emergency Relief
AFAP	Army Family Action Plan
AFQT	Armed Forces Qualification Test
AG	Adjutant General
AGR	Active Guard and Reserve
AI	assignment instruction
AIDS	acquired immunodeficiency syndrome
AIP	Assignment Incentive Pay
AIPD	Army Institute for Professional Development
AIT	advanced individual training

AKO	Army Knowledge Online
ALC	Advanced Leader Course
AM	Air Medal
AMD	Army Medical Department
AMOS	additional military occupational specialty
AMTP	Army Mission Training Plan
ANC	Army Nurse Corps
AOL	Army Online
AP/CPB	Annenberg Project and Center for Public Broadcasting
APFT	Army Physical Fitness Test
APOD	aerial port of debarkation
APOE	aerial port of embarkation
AR	Army Regulation
ARC	American Red Cross
ARCAM	Army Reserve Components Achievement Medal
ARCOM	Army Commendation Medal
ARNG	Army National Guard
ARTEP	Army Training and Evaluation Program
ASAP	Army Substance Abuse Program
ASEP	Advanced Skills Education Program
ASI	additional skill identifier
ASK	Assignment Satisfaction Key
ASVAB	Armed Services Vocational Aptitude Battery
ATACMS	Army Tactical Missile System
ATIMP	Army Training Information Management Program
ATN	Army Training Network
ATRRS	Army Training Requirements and Resources System
ATSC	Army Training Support Center
AUSA	Association of the U.S. Army
AUTODIN	Automated Digital Network
AW2	Army Wounded Warrior Program
AWOL	absent without leave
BAH	basic allowance for housing
BAQ	basic allowance for quarters
BAS	basic allowance for subsistence
BASD	basic active service date
BCT	basic combat training; also, brigade combat team
BDE	brigade
BEQ	bachelor enlisted quarters
BESD	basic enlisted service date
BLC	Basic Leader Course
BSM	Bronze Star Medal
BT	basic training
CAP III	Centralized Assignment Procedure III System

CE	Commander's Evaluation
CFC	Combined Federal Campaign
CFP	contingency force pool
CHAMPUS	Civilian Health and Medical Program of the Uniformed Services
CIB	Combat Infantryman Badge
CID(C)	Criminal Investigation Division (Command)
CLEP	College Level Examination Program
CLI	Command List Integration
CMF	career management field
CMH	Center for Military History
COHORT	Cohesion, Operational Readiness, and Training
COLA	cost-of-living allowance
CONAP	Continental United States Area of Preference
CONUS	continental United States
COOL	Credentialing Opportunities Online
COT	consecutive overseas tour
CPL/SPC	corporal/specialist
CPMOS	career progression military occupational specialty
CQ	charge of quarters
CSM	command sergeant major
CTT	common task training
CVC	combat vehicle crewman
DA	Department of the Army
DANTES	Defense Activity for Nontraditional Education Support
DCPC	Direct Combat Probability Coding
DCSPER	Deputy Chief of Staff for Personnel
DDSM	Defense Distinguished Service Medal
DEERS	Defense Enrollment Eligibility Reporting System
DEROS	date of estimated return from overseas
DFAS	Defense Finance and Accounting Service
DFC	Distinguished Flying Cross
DIEMS	date initially entered military service
DMOS	duty military occupational specialty
DMPO	defense military pay office
DMSM	Defense Meritorious Service Medal
DOD	Department of Defense
DODDS	Department of Defense Dependents Schools
DOE	Department of Education
DOR	date of rank
DRF	Deployment Ready Force
DROS	date returned from overseas
DSC	Distinguished Service Cross
DSM	Distinguished Service Medal

DSN	Defense Switched Network
DSSM	Defense Superior Service Medal
DSST	Defense Subject Standardized Tests
DUI	distinctive unit insignia
DVA	Department of Veterans Affairs
EAD	entry on active duty
EANGUS	Enlisted Association of the National Guard of the United States
eArmyU	Electronic Army University
EDAS	Enlisted Distribution and Assignment System
EDSAV	Educational Savings Allotment
EFMP	Exceptional Family Member Program
EFT	electronic funds transfer
EHWBDU	enhanced hot weather battle dress uniform
EMF	enlisted master file
EML	environmental and morale leave
E/MSS	Employee/Member Self Service
ENTNAC	Entrance National Agency Check
EO	equal opportunity
EOD	explosive ordnance disposal
EOM	end of month
EPMD	Enlisted Personnel Management Directorate
EPMS	Enlisted Personnel Management System
EPW	enemy prisoner of war
ESGR	Employer Support of the Guard and Reserve
ETS	expiration of term of service; also, enlisted training system
FAO	Finance and Accounting Office
FAST	Functional Academic Skills Training
FININ	payment to a financial institution for credit to a member's account
FIST	fire support team
FM	field manual
FORSCOM	U.S. Army Forces Command
FS	Force Sustainment
FSA	family separation allowance
FSA-T	family separation allowance for temporary duty
FTX	field training exercise
GCM	general court-martial; also, Good Conduct Medal
GCMCA	General Court-Martial Convening Authority
GED	General Educational Development
GRE	Graduate Record Examination
GWOT	Global War on Terror
GWOTEM	Global War on Terrorism Expeditionary Medal
GWOTSM	Global War on Terrorism Service Medal
HAAP	Homebase and Advance Assignment Program

HALO	high-altitude, low-opening (parachute jumps)
HBA	health benefits adviser
HDP-L	hardship duty pay for location assignment
HDP-M	hardship duty pay for mission assignment
HIV	human immunodeficiency virus
HMMWV	high-mobility multipurposed wheeled vehicle
HOR	home of record
HQDA	Headquarters, Department of the Army
HRC	Human Resources Command
HSCP	High School Completion Program
HW	hot weather
IET	initial entry training
IFV	infantry fighting vehicle
IG	Inspector General
IHA	interim housing allowance
ISR	Individual Soldier's Report
ITEP	Individual Training Program
ITT	intertheater transfer
IVRS	Interactive Voice Response Telephone System
JAG	Judge Advocate General
JFTR	Joint Federal Travel Regulations
JSAM	Joint Service Achievement Medal
JSCM	Joint Service Commendation Medal
JSEP	Job Skills Education Program
JTR	Joint Travel Regulations
JUMPS	Joint Uniform Military Pay Schedule
JUSMAG	Joint U.S. Military Advisory Group
KDSM	Korea Defense Service Medal
KFOR	Kosovo Force
LDRSHIP	loyalty, duty, respect, selfless service, honor, integrity, and personal courage
LES	Leave and Earnings Statement
LI	leader's identification
LOD	line of duty
LTC	lieutenant colonel
MAAG	Military Assistance Advisory Group
MAC	Military Airlift Command
MACOM	Major Army Command
MACP	Married Army Couples Program
MCM	Manual for Courts-Martial
MEDDAC	Medical Department Activity
METL	Mission Essential Task List
MFE	Maneuver, Fires and Effects
MFT	master fitness trainer

MGIB/ACF	Montgomery GI Bill/Army College Fund
MI	military intelligence
MILES	Multiple Integrated Laser Identification System
MILPER	military personnel
MLC	Master Leader Course
MLRS	Multiple Launched Rocket System
MOH	Medal of Honor
MOOTW	military operations other than war
MOS	military occupational specialty
MOVSM	Military Outstanding Volunteer Service Medal
MP	military police
MRBM	medium-range ballistic missiles
MSC	Medical Service Corps
MSM	Meritorious Service Medal
MTOE	modified table of organization and equipment
NAC	National Agency Check
NATO	North Atlantic Treaty Organization
NBC	nuclear, biological, and chemical
NCO	noncommissioned officer
NCOA	Noncommissioned Officer Academy; also, Noncommissioned Officers Association
NCOER	Noncommissioned Officer Evaluation Report
NCOES	Noncommissioned Officer Education System
NMS	New Manning System
OCAR	Office of the Chief, Army Reserve
OCONUS	outside continental United States
OCS	Officer Candidate School
OEF	Operation Enduring Freedom
OIF	Operation Iraqi Freedom
OJE	on-the-job experience
OJT	on-the-job training
OMPF	Official Military Personnel File
OP	operating procedures
OPM	Office of Personnel Management
OS	Operational Support
OSR	overseas service ribbon
OSUT	one-station unit training
PCM	primary care manager
PCS	permanent change of station
PDS	permanent duty station
PERSCOM	Total Army Personnel Command
PH	Purple Heart
PLDC	Primary Leadership Development Course
PMCS	preventive maintenance checks and services

PMOS	primary military occupational specialty
POR	preparation of replacements for overseas movement
POV	privately owned vehicle
POWM	Prisoner of War Medal
PPG	Priority Placement Group
PSB	personnel support battalion; also, personnel service branch
PSB/MPD	personnel services battalion/military personnel division
PSC	Personnel Service Center
PSNCO	personnel staff noncommissioned officer
PT	physical training
PX	Post Exchange
QM	Quartermaster
QMP	Qualitative Management Program
RA	Regular Army
RC	reserve component
RC-PLC	Reserve Component Primary Leadership Course
RC-PLDC	Reserve Component Primary Leadership Development Course
RC-PNCOC	Reserve Component Primary Noncommissioned Officer Course
RE Code	Reenlistment Code
ROE	Rules of Engagement
ROTC	Reserve Officers' Training Corps; also, Reserve Officers' Training Course
R&R	rest and recuperation
S-1	Battalion- and brigade-level staff, personnel section
SAM	Soldier Assignment Module
SAT	Scholastic Assessment Test
SB	special branches
SCRA	Servicemembers Civil Relief Act
SD	special duty
SDNCO	staff duty noncommissioned officer
SF	Special Forces
SFAC	Soldier and Family Assistance Center
SFC	sergeant first class
SFL	Soldier for Life
SFOR	Stabilization Force
SGLI	Servicemen's Group Life Insurance
SGM	sergeant major
SGT	sergeant
SHARP	Sexual Harassment/Assault Response and Prevention
SIDPERS	Standard Installation/Division Personnel Reporting System
SKB	skills, knowledge, and behavior
SL	skill level
SLC	Senior Leader Course

SM	Soldier's Medal
SMOS	secondary military occupational specialty
SMP	Simultaneous Membership Program
SOC	Servicemembers Opportunity Colleges
SOFA	status of forces agreement
SOP	standard operating procedures
SPC	specialist
SPT-V	payment to a dependent
SQI	special qualification identifier
SRB	selective reenlistment bonus
SS	Silver Star
SSB	special separation bonus
SSG	staff sergeant
SSN	Social Security Number
STP	Soldier Training Publication
SWASM	Southwest Asia Service Medal
TA	tuition assistance
TAO	tuition assistance officer; also, transition assistance office
TAPDB	Total Army Personnel Database
TASS	Total Army Schools System
TBD	to be determined
TC	Transportation Corps; also, training circular
TCO	test control officer
TDA	table of distribution and allowances
TDP	TRICARE Dental Program
TDY	temporary duty
TE	technical escort
TEC	training extension course
TFL	TRICARE for Life
TIG	time in grade
TIS	time in service
TLA	temporary lodging allowance
TLE	temporary lodging expense
TMA	TRICARE Management Activity
TOE	table of organization and equipment
TOS	time on station
TRADOC	U.S. Army Training and Doctrine Command
TRS	TRICARE Reserve Select
TSO	test scoring officer
TSP	Thrift Savings Plan; also, Training Support Package
UA	Unit of Action
UCMJ	Uniform Code of Military Justice
USAEREC	U.S. Army Enlisted Records and Evaluation Center
USAR	U.S. Army Reserve

USASMA	U.S. Army Sergeants Major Academy
USASMC	U.S. Army Sergeants Major Course
USASSI	U.S. Army Soldier Support Institute
USATC	U.S. Army Training Center
USCENTCOM AOR	U.S. Central Command's Area of Responsibility
USERRA	Uniformed Services Employment and Reemployment Rights Act
USMA	U.S. Military Academy
USMAPS	U.S. Military Academy Preparatory School
USMC	U.S. Marine Corps
VA	Veterans Administration
VEAP	Veterans Educational Assistance Program
VGLI	Veterans Group Life Insurance
VHA	variable housing allowance
VSI	Voluntary Separation Incentive
VTC	Video Teleconferencing
WTU	Warrior Transition Unit
YTD	year to date

Index

About the Author

SGM Tom Gills (USA, Ret.) took off his boots for the last time after thirty years of active duty service and capping his military career as the Human Resources SGM for the U.S. Army, the top position in his career field. He simultaneously served as an adjunct faculty member, teaching college foundation courses with a focus on English and college-level writing for over seven years. He holds a master's degree in Public Administration from Troy University in Dothan, Alabama, suma cum laude, and membership in Pi Alpha Alpha. He also holds a bachelor's degree in Business from Excelsior College, magna cum laude. He currently works with SMA Jack Tilley (Retired) at JTilley, Inc., and in supporting Kaplan University in the development of tailored mappings for enlisted military members to increase college credit for their military schooling and experience, as well as scholarships for their family members in partnership with the American Freedom Foundation.

He has taught seminars and attended as a keynote speaker for numerous audiences in subjects ranging from leadership training, Army policies and programs, to international tripartite (U.S./Afghanistan/Pakistan) meetings on cooperation and development. He has also served as guest speaker at Troy University's commencement ceremony.

During his military career, he served in numerous locations across the globe including Germany, Hawaii, Alaska, Afghanistan, and six continental U.S. locations. He has served in virtually every leadership position within his career field of human resources management, and additionally has served as a basic training drill sergeant, drill instructor at the U.S. Army Drill Sergeant School and as an infantry first sergeant. He also served as chief of enlisted promotions for Human Resources Command, on the Army staff as the key HR adviser to the Sergeant Major of the Army, as well as the command sergeant major of the Combined Security Transition Command-Afghanistan, a Multinational Joint NATO Headquarters, overseeing 5,700 personnel in the training and education of the Afghanistan National Army and Police. His numerous awards and honors include the Bronze Star Medal, Audie Murphy Medal, Distinguished Member of the Adjutant General's Corps Regiment and was inducted in 2016 into the Adjutant General's Corps Regimental Hall of Fame, with select military artifacts on display in the Post Museum at Fort Jackson, South Carolina. Additionally, he serves as president, SGM Larry Strickland Educational Leadership Award Foundation. He resides in Virginia with his wife and has two married children and one grandchild.